# E-LEARNING
## Uncovered℠

# Adobe©
# Captivate© 7

Diane Elkins
Desirée Pinder

E-Learning Uncovered: Adobe Captivate 7

By Diane Elkins and Desirée Pinder

Alcorn, Ward, & Partners, Inc. dba Artisan E-Learning

2771-29 Monument Road #329

Jacksonville, FL 32225

www.artisanelearning.com

Trademarks

Adobe Captivate is a registered trademarks of Adobe Systems Incorporated.  Microsoft is a registered trademark of Microsoft Corporation.  iPad and iPhone are trademarks of Apple Inc., registered in the U.S. and other countries.

Other product and company names mentioned herein may be trademarks of their respective owners.  Use of trademarks or product names is not intended to convey endorsement or affiliation in this book.

Warning and Disclaimer

The information provided is on an "as is" basis.  Every effort has been made to make this book as complete and as accurate as possible, but no warranty or fitness is implied.  The authors and the publisher shall have neither liability nor responsibility to any person or entity with respect to any loss or damages arising from the information contained in this book.

# Chapter Table of Contents

1. Getting to Know Captivate ........................................................... 1

2. Creating New Projects................................................................ 13

3. Adding and Managing Slides ..................................................... 31

4. Adding Content Objects ............................................................ 49

5. Audio and Video ....................................................................... 69

6. Managing Objects..................................................................... 91

7. Actions & Interactions.............................................................. 113

8. Editing Software Simulations.................................................... 135

9. Variables & Advanced Actions ................................................. 153

10. Questions & Quizzes ............................................................... 167

11. Special Tools & Wizards .......................................................... 201

12. Publishing............................................................................... 223

Appendix ....................................................................................... 243

Index ............................................................................................. 259

# Detailed Table of Contents

## 1. Getting to Know Captivate ........................................ 1

The Captivate Interface....................................................................................................3

   Primary Menus & Toolbars...........................................................................................4

   Customize the Interface.................................................................................................5

   Saving Customized Workspaces....................................................................................7

Opening and Closing Files ................................................................................................8

   Open an Existing Project...............................................................................................8

   Moving Around a Project...............................................................................................8

   Save a Project...............................................................................................................9

   Close a Project..............................................................................................................9

The Properties Panel.......................................................................................................10

Objects and the Timeline.................................................................................................11

   Select Objects.............................................................................................................11

   Preview a Project ........................................................................................................12

## 2. Creating New Projects................................................ 13

Create a New, Blank Project ...........................................................................................15

Adding PowerPoint Content ............................................................................................16

Image Slideshow and Images .........................................................................................18

Software Simulations ......................................................................................................19

   Preparing for a Screen Recording Session...................................................................19

   Record a Software Simulation......................................................................................20

   Recording Settings .....................................................................................................21

   Change Recording Preferences....................................................................................23

Video Demos...................................................................................................................27

## 3. Adding and Managing Slides ...................................... 31

Inserting New Slides........................................................................................................33

   Insert a New or Blank Slide.........................................................................................33

   Insert a PowerPoint Slide ............................................................................................33

      Edit a PowerPoint Slide in Captivate.......................................................................34

      Update an Imported Slide........................................................................................35

   Add an Image Slide.....................................................................................................36

Slide Properties 7 ..........................................................................................................37

Slide Notes.....................................................................................................................39

Master Slides...................................................................................................................40

   Modify a Main Master Slide.........................................................................................40

   Create a Content Master Slide .....................................................................................41

   Apply a Master Slide...................................................................................................41

Themes ...........................................................................................................................42

   Apply a Theme to a Project..........................................................................................42

# Detailed Table of Contents

Apply a Content Master From a Theme ...................................................................................43

Create a New Slide With A Theme .........................................................................................43

Managing Slides .......................................................................................................................44

Hide Slides..............................................................................................................................44

Delete Slides ..........................................................................................................................44

Move Slides............................................................................................................................45

Copy, Paste, and Duplicate Slides ........................................................................................45

Lock Slides..............................................................................................................................46

Group Slides ...........................................................................................................................47

## 4. Adding Content Objects ........................................................ 49

Working With Captions.............................................................................................................51

Add a New Caption .................................................................................................................51

Edit Caption Text ...................................................................................................................52

Formatting Caption Text........................................................................................................52

Apply Text Effects...................................................................................................................53

Change Caption and Callout Type .........................................................................................54

Exporting and Importing Captions..........................................................................................55

Export Captions......................................................................................................................55

Import Captions ......................................................................................................................55

Working With Images................................................................................................................57

Add an Image to a Slide ........................................................................................................57

Image Properties....................................................................................................................58

Using Photoshop Files ...........................................................................................................60

Characters ................................................................................................................................61

Drawing Smart Shapes.............................................................................................................62

Draw a Smart Shape ..............................................................................................................62

Add a Highlight Box ...............................................................................................................63

Adding Animations....................................................................................................................64

Add an Animation Slide..........................................................................................................64

Add an Animation ...................................................................................................................65

Add a Text Animation.............................................................................................................66

Zoom Areas..............................................................................................................................67

Insert a Zoom Area ................................................................................................................67

Equations 🔲 ............................................................................................................................68

## 5. Audio and Video ................................................................... 69

Working With Audio ..................................................................................................................71

Import Audio to the Background..............................................................................................71

Import Audio to an Object ......................................................................................................72

Import Audio to One or More Slides........................................................................................73

## Detailed Table of Contents

Distribute Audio Across Slides....................................................................................74
Configure Audio Compression....................................................................................75
Calibrate Audio Input................................................................................................76
Record Audio to a Slide or Object.............................................................................77
Record Audio Across Slides .......................................................................................77
Record Audio While Capturing...................................................................................78
Edit Audio................................................................................................................79
Export Audio ............................................................................................................81
Other Audio Management Options .............................................................................81
Remove Audio...........................................................................................................82
Change Settings in the Audio Pane ............................................................................82
Create Audio With Text-to-Speech .............................................................................83
Closed Captioning .........................................................................................................84
Create Closed Captions..............................................................................................84
Change Closed Caption Settings .................................................................................85
Adding Video.................................................................................................................86
Insert a Multi-Slide Synchronized Video......................................................................86
Change Slide Distribution ..........................................................................................87
Insert an Event Video ...............................................................................................88
Event Video Properties...............................................................................................89
Video Management....................................................................................................90
Update Project Video ................................................................................................90

## 6. Managing Objects..................................................................... 91

Object Properties...........................................................................................................93
Object Information ....................................................................................................93
Fill & Stroke Pane.....................................................................................................94
Colors......................................................................................................................94
Color Gradients ........................................................................................................95
Fill Texture...............................................................................................................96
Shadow & Reflection Pane..........................................................................................97
Transition Pane ........................................................................................................98
Transform Pane ........................................................................................................98
Managing Objects..........................................................................................................99
Cut/Copy/Paste/Duplicate Objects .............................................................................99
Delete Objects .........................................................................................................99
Group/Ungroup Objects.............................................................................................100
Show/Hide Objects in Edit Mode................................................................................101
Lock Objects in Edit Mode.........................................................................................101
Aligning Objects [7].................................................................................................102
Layering ..................................................................................................................103

# Detailed Table of Contents

Styles ................................................................................................................ 104

    Modify an Existing Style ................................................................................ 104

    Create a New Style ...................................................................................... 105

    Set the Default Style .................................................................................... 105

    Apply Styles to an Object ............................................................................. 106

    Additional Style Options ............................................................................... 106

    Import and Export Styles .............................................................................. 107

    Delete Styles ............................................................................................... 107

Object Effects **7** .............................................................................................. 108

    Add a Time-Based Effect ............................................................................. 108

    Add an Action-Based Effect .......................................................................... 109

    Managing Effects ......................................................................................... 110

Timing Slide Objects .......................................................................................... 111

## 7. Actions & Interactions ................................................ 113

Smart Interactions **7** ........................................................................................ 115

    Add a Smart Interaction ............................................................................... 115

    Configure Interaction Content ....................................................................... 116

    Interaction Gallery ....................................................................................... 117

Rollover Objects ................................................................................................ 119

    Insert a Rollover Caption .............................................................................. 119

    Insert a Rollover Image ................................................................................ 120

    Insert a Rollover Smart Shape ...................................................................... 120

    Insert a Rollover Slidelet .............................................................................. 121

Actions ............................................................................................................. 122

    Action Types **7** ........................................................................................... 122

Adding Actions .................................................................................................. 127

    Add Actions to a Slide .................................................................................. 127

    Add a Hyperlink to Text ................................................................................ 127

    Add a Click Box ........................................................................................... 128

      Click Box Properties .................................................................................. 128

    Add a Button ............................................................................................... 130

      Button Properties ...................................................................................... 130

      Button Widgets ......................................................................................... 131

    Add a Text Entry Box ................................................................................... 132

      Text Entry Box Properties **7** ...................................................................... 132

## 8. Editing Software Simulations ....................................... 135

The Editing Process ........................................................................................... 137

Editing Typing ................................................................................................... 138

## Detailed Table of Contents

Mouse Movements ....................................................................................................................... 139
    Move the Mouse Click Position ............................................................................................. 139
    Change Initial Mouse Position ............................................................................................... 140
    Align Mouse Paths ................................................................................................................. 140
    Hide/Show Mouse Movement ............................................................................................... 141
    Change Mouse Properties ...................................................................................................... 142
Editing Full-Motion Recording .................................................................................................. 143
Editing Slide Backgrounds ......................................................................................................... 144
    Copy and Paste Backgrounds ................................................................................................ 144
    Merge With Background ......................................................................................................... 145
Recording Additional Slides ....................................................................................................... 146
Managing Practice Slides ........................................................................................................... 147
    Elements of a Click Box Slide ................................................................................................ 147
    Elements of a Text Entry Box Slide ▨ .................................................................................... 148
Managing Video Demo Projects ................................................................................................. 149
    Trim and Split the Recording ................................................................................................ 149
    Add Transitions ..................................................................................................................... 149
    Add Pan & Zoom Effects ....................................................................................................... 150
    Create Picture-in-Picture (PIP) Effects .................................................................................. 151
    Add a Video Demo Slide to a Project ▨ ................................................................................ 152

## 9. Variables & Advanced Actions ................................................ 153

Working With Variables .............................................................................................................. 155
    Manage Variables .................................................................................................................. 155
    Add a User Variable ............................................................................................................... 156
    Add a Text-Entry Variable ..................................................................................................... 156
    Modify Variables With the Actions Pane ............................................................................... 157
    Display a Variable .................................................................................................................. 158
Advanced Actions ...................................................................................................................... 159
    Add a Standard Advanced Action ▨ ..................................................................................... 159
    Advanced Action Commands ................................................................................................ 160
Conditional Actions .................................................................................................................... 161
    Add a Conditional Advanced Action ..................................................................................... 161
    Creating IF Conditions .......................................................................................................... 162
    Creating Actions and Else Actions ........................................................................................ 163
    Creating Multiple Decisions .................................................................................................. 163
Shared Actions ▨ ....................................................................................................................... 164
    Save as a Shared Action ........................................................................................................ 164
    Create a New Action Based on a Shared Action .................................................................... 164
    Import and Export Shared Actions ........................................................................................ 165
    Execute a Shared Action ....................................................................................................... 165

# Detailed Table of Contents

Managing Actions ............................................................................. 166
  Managing Advanced Actions ...................................................... 166
  Advanced Interaction Panel ........................................................ 166

## 10. Questions & Quizzes ........................................... 167

Creating Questions ......................................................................... 169
  Add a Question ........................................................................... 169
  Question Types ........................................................................... 170
Configuring Questions .................................................................... 172
  Add Question Content................................................................. 172
  Add Standard Feedback .............................................................. 173
    Set Number of Attempts ........................................................ 173
  Add Progressive Feedback.......................................................... 174
  Set Success and Failure Actions ................................................. 174
  Add Advanced Feedback ............................................................ 175
    Branching Quizzes ................................................................. 175
    Option-Specific Feedback ...................................................... 175
    Remediation Back to Content Slides ....................................... 175
  Assign Points to Questions ......................................................... 176
  The Review Area ......................................................................... 176
  Additional Quiz Properties .......................................................... 177
Individual Question Options............................................................. 178
  Multiple-Choice Question Options .............................................. 178
  True/False Question Options ....................................................... 178
  Fill-in-the-Blank Question Options.............................................. 179
  Short Answer Question Options .................................................. 180
  Matching Question Options ........................................................ 181
  Hot Spot Question Options......................................................... 182
  Sequence Question Options ....................................................... 183
  Rating Scale (Likert) Question Options ....................................... 184
Importing Questions 🔲 ................................................................... 185
  Import GIFT-Format Questions ................................................... 185
Drag-and-Drop Interaction Wizard 🔲 ............................................. 186
  Create a Drag-and-Drop Interaction........................................... 186
  Drag-and-Drop Interaction Properties ........................................ 187
Creating Pretests ........................................................................... 191
  Add a Pretest Question .............................................................. 191
  Configure Pretest Logic .............................................................. 191
Quiz Master Slides ......................................................................... 192

## Detailed Table of Contents

Question Pools ....................................................................................................... 193

    Create a Question Pool ..................................................................................... 193

    Add Questions to a Question Pool ................................................................... 194

    Manage Questions in the Question Pool ......................................................... 194

    Pull a Question From a Pool to Your Project .................................................. 195

Quiz Results Slides ............................................................................................... 196

Quiz Preferences .................................................................................................. 197

# 11. Special Tools & Wizards ................................................. 201

Aggregator Projects ............................................................................................. 203

    Create an Aggregator Project ......................................................................... 203

    Publish an Aggregator Project ........................................................................ 204

    Aggregator Preferences .................................................................................. 205

    Manage Aggregator Files ................................................................................ 205

Templates ............................................................................................................. 206

    Create a Project Template ............................................................................... 206

    Create a New Project From a Template .......................................................... 207

Text-Editing Tools ................................................................................................ 208

    Check Spelling ................................................................................................ 208

    Find and Replace ............................................................................................ 209

The Library ........................................................................................................... 210

    Manage Assets in the Library ......................................................................... 211

Widgets ................................................................................................................ 212

    Add a Widget From the Properties Panel ....................................................... 212

    Add a Widget From the Insert Menu .............................................................. 213

    Add the Twitter Widget 7 ............................................................................... 214

Sharing and Reviewing ........................................................................................ 216

    Upload Files to Acrobat.com .......................................................................... 216

    Share Files on Acrobat.com ........................................................................... 217

    Adobe Captivate Reviewer ............................................................................. 218

Preferences .......................................................................................................... 220

    General Settings 7 .......................................................................................... 220

    Default Settings .............................................................................................. 221

Exporting and Importing XML .............................................................................. 222

    Export to XML ................................................................................................. 222

    Import From XML ............................................................................................ 222

# 12. Publishing ................................................................. 223

Output-Related Options ........................................................................................ 225

    Rescale a Project ............................................................................................ 225

    Configure Project Skin: Playback Controls ..................................................... 226

## Detailed Table of Contents

Configure Project Skin: Border Options ............................................................. 227
Configure Project Skin: Table of Contents......................................................... 228
Change Project Preferences............................................................................. 230
Project Information Settings............................................................................. 230
SWF Size and Quality Settings......................................................................... 231
Publish Settings [NEW]................................................................................... 232
Start and End Settings .................................................................................... 233
Reporting and Tracking ......................................................................................... 234
Quiz Reporting Preferences [NEW] ................................................................. 234
Publishing ............................................................................................................. 236
Publish Your Project......................................................................................... 236
Sample Output Files ........................................................................................ 236
SWF/HTML5 Publishing Options [NEW]........................................................... 237
Best Practices for HTML5 Output [NEW] ................................................. 238
Other Publishing Options ................................................................................ 239
Adobe Connect [NEW] ............................................................................ 239
Media .................................................................................................... 239
E-Mail..................................................................................................... 239
FTP ........................................................................................................ 239
Publishing to Print/Microsoft Word ................................................................ 240
Publish to YouTube.......................................................................................... 241
Adobe App Packager [NEW] ........................................................................... 242

# Appendix ............................................................................... 243

Accessibility [NEW] ......................................................................................... 245
Mac and PC Interface Tools ................................................................................. 249
Tips for Using Captivate for Macintosh ........................................................... 249
Captivate for Mac Menus................................................................................. 250
Captivate for PC Menus.................................................................................... 252
Useful Keyboard Shortcuts .............................................................................. 254
System Variables .................................................................................................. 255
Movie Control Variables................................................................................... 255
Movie Information Variables............................................................................. 256
Movie Metadata Variables................................................................................ 257
System Information Variables ........................................................................... 257
Quizzing Variables ........................................................................................... 258

# Index .................................................................................... 259

# Getting the Most Out of This Book

This book assumes you are a functional user of Windows software. If you are familiar with how to use dialog boxes, drop-down menus, and other standard Windows conventions, then you'll be fine. The book is written for the PC version of Captivate. If you are using Captivate for Mac, you'll still get a lot out of this book, but you may find some differences in some of the procedures. The Appendix has a few quick tips for Mac users.

Use the detailed table of contents and comprehensive index to help you find what you are looking for. In addition to procedures, look for all the hints, tips, and cautions that can help you save time, avoid problems, and make your courses more engaging.

## DESIGN TIP

Design Tips give you insight on how to implement the different features and include everything from graphic design to instructional design to usability.

## BRIGHT IDEA

Bright Ideas are special explanations and ideas for getting more out of the software.

## TIME SAVER

Time Savers...well...save you time. These tips include software shortcuts and ways to streamline your production efforts.

## CAUTION

Pay special attention to the Cautions (which are full of "lessons learned the hard way") so you can avoid some common problems.

## POWER TIP

Power Tips are advanced tips and secrets that can help you take your production to the next level.

This symbol indicates a cross-reference to another part of the book.

This symbol indicates a feature that is new or significantly enhanced since Captivate 6.0 (including interim releases).

Find practice files and useful resources at
**www.elearninguncovered.com**

# Getting to Know Captivate

## Introduction

Adobe Captivate is an e-learning development tool with two main purposes: simulating computer procedures and creating non-simulation content.

For example, you might be creating a course on how to use a new time and attendance software program. You can use Captivate to:

- Record your desktop while you are performing the steps so that your students can sit back and watch the procedure being performed.

- Record your desktop while you are performing the steps, and convert it to an interactive practice where the students get to perform the steps and get feedback.

- Create several screens of content with text, images, and media that cover business rules such as leave-request policies, approval workflow, and important deadlines.

- Build a quiz that tests the students on key business rules.

Adobe Captivate can be used alone or in conjunction with other software packages. For example, you might:

- Create a single simulation or quiz in Captivate, and publish it as a course.

- Create a series of simulations, and publish them all together as a single course.

- Create a series of simulations, and embed each one into a web page, a help file, or a course created in a different authoring tool.

- Export your simulations to Adobe Flash to add custom programming.

Captivate can be purchased alone or as part of the Adobe eLearning Suite. Some features in the software are only available if you have the full eLearning Suite.

### In This Chapter

- The Captivate Interface
- Customizing the Interface
- File Management
- Objects and the Timeline
- Previewing Projects

# Notes

# The Captivate Interface

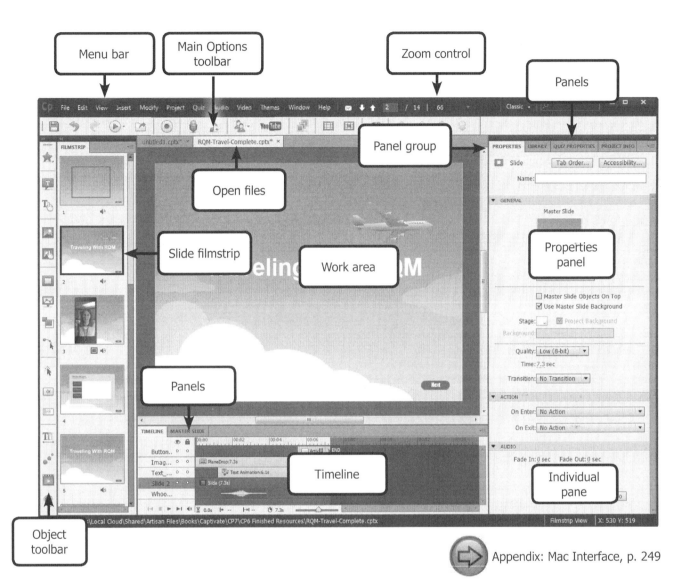

Menu bar

Main Options toolbar

Zoom control

Panels

Open files

Panel group

Properties panel

Slide filmstrip

Work area

Panels

Timeline

Individual pane

Object toolbar

Appendix: Mac Interface, p. 249

# Primary Menus & Toolbars

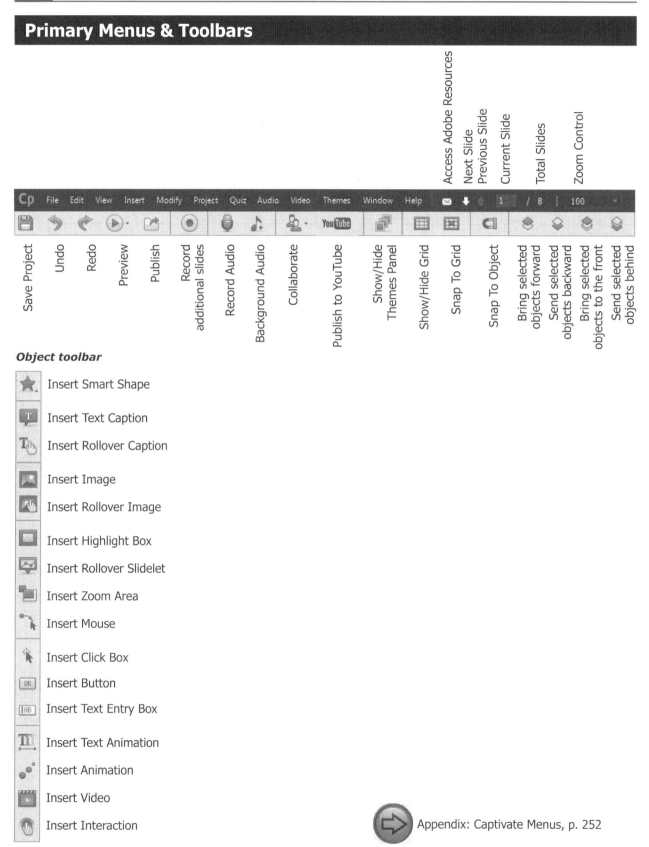

Access Adobe Resources
Next Slide
Previous Slide
Current Slide
Total Slides
Zoom Control

Save Project
Undo
Redo
Preview
Publish
Record additional slides
Record Audio
Background Audio
Collaborate
Publish to YouTube
Show/Hide Themes Panel
Show/Hide Grid
Snap To Grid
Snap To Object
Bring selected objects forward
Send selected objects backward
Bring selected objects to the front
Send selected objects behind

*Object toolbar*

Insert Smart Shape

Insert Text Caption

Insert Rollover Caption

Insert Image

Insert Rollover Image

Insert Highlight Box

Insert Rollover Slidelet

Insert Zoom Area

Insert Mouse

Insert Click Box

Insert Button

Insert Text Entry Box

Insert Text Animation

Insert Animation

Insert Video

Insert Interaction

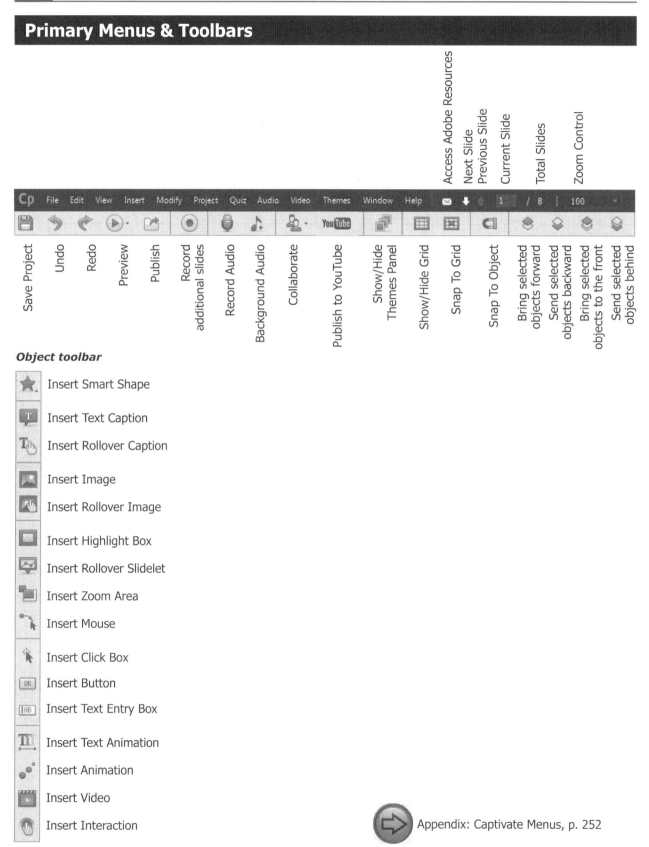 Appendix: Captivate Menus, p. 252

# Customize the Interface

You can customize the Captivate interface to best fit your needs and working styles.

**To show or hide a toolbar or panel:**
1. Go to the **Window** menu. **(A)**
2. Select or de-select the element you want to show or hide.

**To expand or collapse a whole panel group:**
- Click the double-arrows in the top corner of the group. **(B)**

**To close a panel:**
1. Click the icon in the upper-right corner of the panel. **(C)**
2. Select **Close** to close just that panel, or select **Close Group** to close all panels in that group.

**To move a panel:**
- Click and drag the tab with the panel name to where you want it. **(D)**

**To move a whole panel group:**
- Click and drag the dark gray bar for the group. **(E)**

**To change the order of panels in a given group:**
- Click and drag the tab left or right to where you want it. **(D)**

**To expand or collapse panes within a panel:**
- Click the arrow on the left side of the pane heading. **(F)**

**To move a toolbar:**
- Click and drag the double-dotted line to the place where you want it. **(G)**

## BRIGHT IDEA

When moving panels and toolbars, look for a subtle blue highlight as you approach other panes or the edge of the interface. If you release the toolbar or panel when there is a blue highlight showing, that item will be "docked" in place. If there is no highlight showing, the panel or toolbar will be free floating.

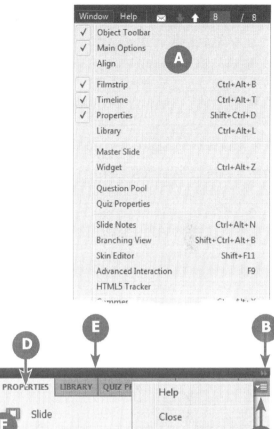

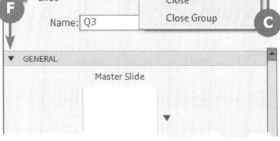

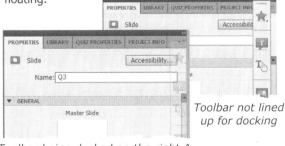

*Toolbar not lined up for docking*

*Toolbar being docked on the right ^*

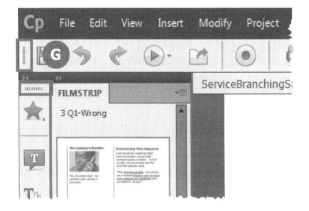

# Customize the Interface (cont'd)

**To change the height of a panel:**

1. Hover your mouse over the panel border until you see the double-headed arrow. **(A)**
2. Click and drag the border to the size you want.

**To change the size of the thumbnails in the Filmstrip:**

1. Right-click a thumbnail.
2. Select **Filmstrip**.
3. Select the size you want. **(B)**

**To change the magnification of the slide in the work area:**

1. Click the zoom drop-down menu. **(C)**
2. Select the magnification option you want.

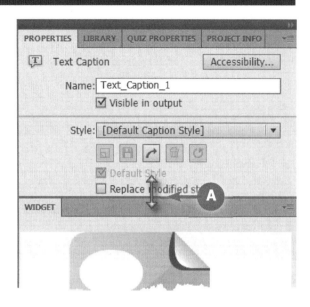

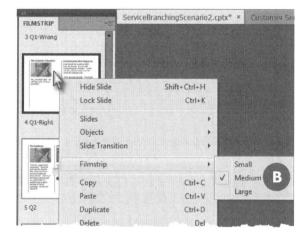

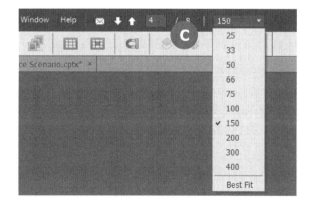

# Saving Customized Workspaces

Workspaces are saved interface configurations. Captivate comes with several pre-made workspaces that are optimized for different functions. Each workspace has different panels showing or hidden based on what is needed for a given task. In addition, you can save your own custom workspaces to fit your needs. For example, you can create a workspace with the **Slide Notes** panel showing if you plan to use closed captioning.

**To apply an existing workspace:**

1. Click the **Workspace** drop-down menu.
2. Select the workspace you want.

**To create your own workspace:**

1. Configure the toolbars and panels the way you want them.
2. Click the **Workspace** drop-down menu.
3. Select **New Workspace**.
4. Enter a name for the workspace.
5. Click **OK**.

**Additional Workspace Options**

Select **Manage Workspace** from the drop-down menu if you want to rename or delete any workspaces that you have created.

If you made changes to a workspace and want to go back to the original state, select the **Reset** option on the drop-down menu.

# Opening and Closing Files

## Open an Existing Project

**To open Captivate:**

1. Click the **Start** menu.
2. Select **All Programs**.
3. Select **Adobe Captivate 7**.

When you open Captivate, the **Welcome** screen appears, which has many of the same options as the **File** menu.

**To open a project from the Welcome screen:**

1. Select the file under **Open Recent Item**. **(A)**

———— or ————

1. Click the **Open** link. **(B)**
2. Find and select the file you want.
3. Click **Open**.

**To open a project from the File menu:**

1. Click the **File** menu. **(C)**
2. Select **Open**.
3. Find and select the file you want.
4. Click **Open**.

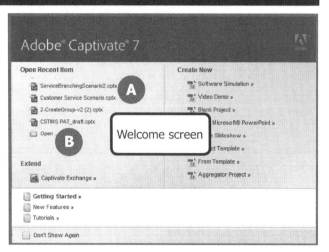

 **CAUTION**

When you launch Captivate, you may receive a warning about features not being available unless you have administrator privileges. If you encounter problems, such as the inability to record audio, check with your I.T. department to get administrator privileges on the computer. Then run Captivate as an administrator: right-click **Adobe Captivate 7** on the **Start** menu, and select **Run as Administrator**. **(D)**

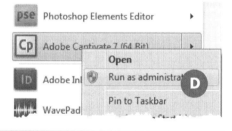

## Moving Around a Project

Use any of the following methods to move around a project.

- Select a thumbnail in the **Filmstrip** to go to that slide. **(A)**
- Use your **Page Up** and **Page Down** keys to move up or down one slide.
- Use the **Next Slide** and **Previous Slide** buttons to move up or down one slide. **(B)**
- Type a slide number in the field next to the arrows to jump to that slide. **(C)**

If you have more than one project open, move from project to project by clicking the tabs. **(D)**

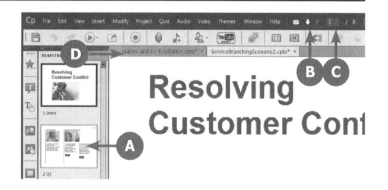

# Save a Project

**Options for saving a project:**

- Click the **Save** button on the **Main Options** toolbar.
- Go to the **File** menu, and select **Save**.
- Press **Ctrl + S**.

**Other saving options:**

- Go to the **File** menu, and select **Save As** to save the file under a different name or in a different location.
- Click **Save All** on the **File** menu to save all open projects.

 **CAUTION**

It is best to save your project on a local drive (such as your C drive) instead of a network drive or removable storage (such as a USB drive). Saving to something other than your local drive can cause problems with performance, saving, etc.

Projects created in version 7 can be opened in version 6. If you do this, be sure to check your file carefully to make sure everything still works properly. Files from previous versions can be opened in 7; however, once they are saved in version 7, they can no longer be opened in versions earlier than version 6.

# Close a Project

**Options for closing a project:**

- Go to the **File** menu, and select **Close** to close the current project.
- Go to the **File** menu, and select **Close All** to close all open projects.
- Click the **X** in the tab to close a project but leave Captivate open. **(A)**
- Click the **X** in the top right corner of the window to close Captivate completely. **(B)**

# The Properties Panel

Your slides and every object on your slides have properties: images, captions, audio, etc.  These properties are displayed and modified in the **Properties** panel.  You will learn more about specific properties for each type of object in their respective chapters.  Here are a few guidelines that apply to the **Properties** panel for any object type.

- If the **Properties** panel isn't showing, go to the **Window** menu, and select **Properties**.

- Select an object in the work area or **Timeline** to view and change its properties in the panel.

- Select more than one object to view and change certain shared properties.

- Click the arrow next to the name of a pane to expand or collapse that pane. **(A)**

- Click the **Collapse to Icons** button to minimize the whole panel group. **(B)**

- Click the drop-down menu in the top corner to close the individual panel. **(C)**

The options in the **Properties** panel will vary based on the item or object you have selected.

## TIME SAVER

In blue, underlined number fields (known as hot text), either click and type a new number, or click and drag right to increase or left to decrease the number. **(D)**

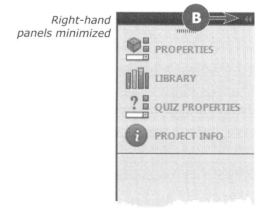

*Right-hand panels minimized*

# Objects and the Timeline

When you place an object on a slide, a corresponding line item is added to the **Timeline**. Among other things, you can adjust:

- **Layering**: Objects at the top of the **Timeline** appear in front of objects at the bottom of the **Timeline**.

- **Visibility**: Click the dot next to an object under the "eyeball" icon to hide it from view while working. (This does not affect your published movie, just what shows in the work area.)

- **Start Time and Length**: When the slide plays, objects appear when the bar for that object starts, and they disappear when the bar ends.

**TIME SAVER**

Objects in the **Timeline** are color-coded:
- Green: Interactive objects
- Blue: Standard content objects
- Beige: Placeholder objects

 Object Properties, ch. 6
Timing Objects, p. 111

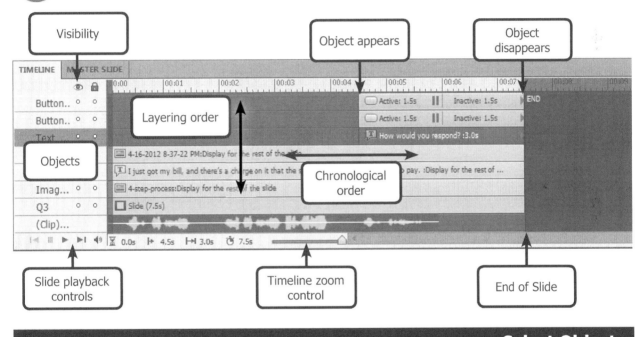

**Select Objects**

You can select objects in the work area or in the **Timeline**.

**Work Area**

- Select a single object by clicking on it.
- Select multiple objects by holding the **Ctrl** or **Shift** key down while clicking on them. Or drag your mouse around the objects.

**Timeline**

- Select a single object by clicking it in the **Timeline**.
- Select multiple objects by holding the **Ctrl** key down while clicking on them individually.
- Select consecutive items on the **Timeline** by clicking the first object, holding down the **Shift** key, and then clicking the last object.

**TIME SAVER**

Click anywhere in the work area and press **Ctrl** + **A** to select all objects on a slide.

# Preview a Project

**To preview an individual slide:**

1. Click the **Play** button in the **Timeline**. **(A)**

——— or ———

1. Click the **Preview** button. **(B)**
2. Select **Play Slide**.

**To preview more than one slide:**

1. Click the **Preview** button.
2. Select the option you want.

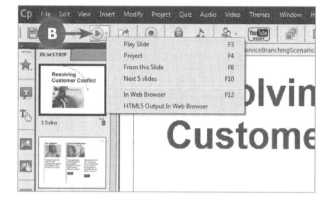

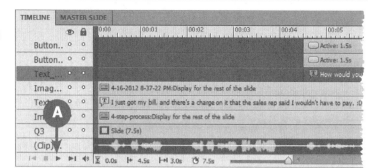

## CAUTION

When you preview a single slide, certain elements may not play properly, such as full-motion recording or certain highlight boxes. Previewing more than one slide at a time gives you a more representative view of what your project will look like when published.

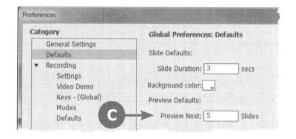

## BRIGHT IDEAS

- You can change the **Next 5 slides** option to a different number, such as the next 3 slides. Go to the **Edit** menu, select **Preferences**, and click the **Defaults** category to change this option. **(C)**

- Previewing in a browser has two advantages. It more closely simulates what your published course will look like if you are publishing to a browser. Since the preview appears in a browser window instead of a Captivate window, you can make changes to the Captivate file while you preview the project.

- If you will be publishing to HTML5, be sure to preview in that mode to make sure you are getting the results you want.

- Be sure to learn the keyboard shortcuts for previewing. They are big time savers!

 Useful Keyboard Shortcuts, p. 254

# Creating New Projects

## Introduction

Because Captivate is such a versatile tool, you can create many different types of projects, pulling from many different types of content. In this chapter, you will learn how to create the primary project types. In the Special Tools and Wizards chapter (chapter 11), you will learn about some of the more specialized project types.

**Primary Project Types**

**Blank Project**: Create a blank project when you want to build a lesson from scratch and add slides and elements individually. (You can also add blank slides to any project.)

**Project From MS PowerPoint**: Create a new project from an existing PowerPoint presentation, where each slide in PowerPoint becomes a slide in your Captivate project. (You can also add individual PowerPoint slides to any project.)

**Image Slideshow**: Create a new project from a series of images, where each image becomes a slide in your project. (You can also add individual image slides to any project.)

**Software Simulation**: Create a project by recording what you do on your computer, creating either a sit-back-and-watch demonstration or an interactive, try-it-yourself practice. (You can also add software simulations to any project.)

**Video Demo**: Create a full-motion video of what you do on your computer.

**Special Project Types (covered in chapter 11)**

**Project Template**: Create a template that includes slides, objects and object placeholders, settings, etc. to be used over and over again.

**Project From Template**: Create a new project based on a saved template.

**Aggregator Project**: Create a new project that combines existing movies. For example, if you have five simulations and five practices to teach a new time reporting system, you can combine and publish them all as a single course.

**Multi-SCORM Packager**: Create a course from multiple projects that integrates with a learning management system (LMS).

### In This Chapter

- Blank Projects
- PowerPoint Projects
- Image Slideshows
- Software Simulations
- Recording Settings & Preferences
- Video Demos

# Notes

# Create a New, Blank Project

**To create a new, blank project:**

1. Select **Blank Project** on the **Welcome** screen.

—— or ——

1. Go to the **File** menu.
2. Select **New Project**.
3. Select **Blank Project**.
4. Enter the dimensions for your project from the drop-down menu or by manually entering the dimensions.
5. Click **OK**.

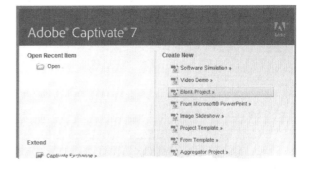

 **DESIGN TIPS**

- The drop-down menu with preset sizes includes resolutions that are optimized for iPad, iPhone, and YouTube.

- If you will be importing any PowerPoint slides, your resolution will be better if your Captivate project has the same dimensions as your PowerPoint file. The default size for a PowerPoint file is 960 x 720.

# Adding PowerPoint Content

Rather than building your slides in Captivate, you can import existing content from PowerPoint. Slide notes, audio, and some animations carry over to the Captivate slide. Slide notes go into the **Slide Notes** panel in Captivate, audio is added as an audio object in the **Timeline**, and certain types of animations (both automatic and on-click) will work in Captivate as well. You can edit the PowerPoint slides directly from Captivate (assuming you have PowerPoint installed on your computer) and even link your project to the PowerPoint document to make sure you are working with the latest information.

You can either create a new project from PowerPoint or add individual slides to an existing project. In either case, one slide is created in Captivate for each imported slide from PowerPoint.

## Create a New Project From PowerPoint

**To create a new project from PowerPoint:**

1. Select **From Microsoft® PowerPoint** on the **Welcome** screen.

——— or ———

1. Go to the **File** menu.
2. Select **New Project**.
3. Select **Project From MS PowerPoint**.

——— then ———

4. Find and select the file you want.
5. Click **Open**.
6. Enter the properties you want. (See below.)
7. Click **OK**.

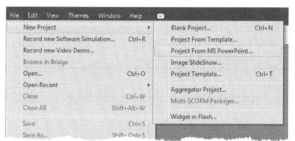

### Project Properties

This section is only available when creating a new project from PowerPoint. If you are importing slides into an existing project, then the project's properties will be used.

**Name**: The name of the PowerPoint file is used as the default name for the project. You can change the name here if you want to.

**Width, Height, and Preset Sizes**: Either select a preset size from the menu, or enter your own values for the size of the project. The default size is the size of your PowerPoint presentation.

**Maintain Aspect Ratio**: Check this box if you want the project to have the same proportions as the PowerPoint slides. This prevents the images from being stretched in one direction or the other.

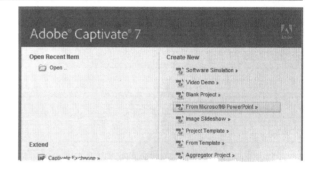

### Slide Thumbnails

Check or uncheck the box **(A)** for each slide to indicate which slides you want to import. To save time, use the **Select All** and **Clear All** buttons to change them all at once.

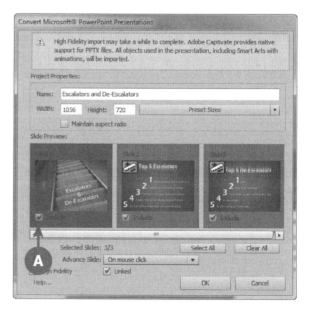

# Create a New Project From PowerPoint (cont'd)

## Project Properties (cont'd)

### Advance Slide

Indicate if you want the slides to advance automatically on the **Timeline** (like any other slide in your project) or advance on mouse click. If you select the mouse-click option, Captivate inserts a click box that covers each slide. When the student clicks anywhere on the slide, the slide advances, just like it would in PowerPoint.

### High Fidelity (A)

The **High Fidelity** option proves better support for PowerPoint features found in .pptx files, such as SmartArt, hierarchical animations, certain text and object effects, etc. (In versions 5.5 and earlier, Captivate converted .pptx to .ppt as part of the import, removing some of these features.) If you have a .pptx file with any of these features, check the **High Fidelity** box to have them included in the import.

If you check **High Fidelity**, a **Slide Duration** check box appears. **(C)** Check this box if you want to retain any special timings you added in PowerPoint via **Rehearse Timings** or **Advance Slide** > **After**.

### Linked (B)

When this box is checked, Captivate links to the PowerPoint file instead of embedding it into the presentation. This makes your project size smaller, but it also means you have to have access to the PowerPoint file to edit the project. In addition, if you link the file, any edits you make to the slide in Captivate are made to the original PowerPoint file as well—which you may or may not want.

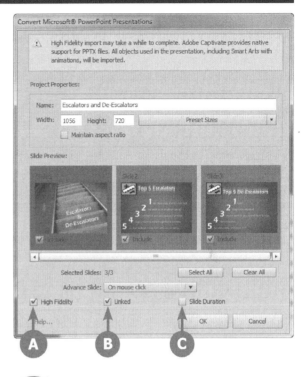

Import Individual PowerPoint Slides, p. 33
Edit a PowerPoint Slide, p. 34
Update an Imported Slide, p. 35

| **Link** when you want to... | **Embed** when you want to... |
|---|---|
| • Keep the file size small.<br>• Update the PPT file when you update the Captivate slide. | • Work with the project even if you don't have access to the PowerPoint file.<br>• Import a PPT file that is likely to change locations.<br>• Make changes to the Captivate slide without changing the original PPT file. |

## CAUTION

- Students may not know that they are supposed to click on the slide to trigger an animation or advance to the next slide. Make sure you include clear instructions.

- With a linked file, make sure the PPT file stays in the same location with the same file name. Otherwise, the link between the two will be broken.

- Avoid editing both versions of a slide at the same time (the PPT slide and the linked Captivate slide) as your edits might not be saved properly.

- During a high-fidelity import, make sure PowerPoint is closed, and do not do any copying or pasting until the importing is done.

# Image Slideshow and Images

There are three ways to add images to your projects:

Adding Image Slides, p. 36
Adding Images to a Slide, p. 57

- **New image slideshow**: Select a folder of images and create a new project with each selected image on its own slide. Use this to create a quick and easy slideshow.

- **Image slide**: Add a new slide with the image as the background.

- **Image on slide**: Place an image on any existing slide and either keep it as a slide object that can be moved, resized, and manipulated, or merge it to become part of the background.

## Create a New Image Slideshow

**To create a new image slideshow:**

1. Select **Image Slideshow** on the **Welcome** screen.

—— or ——

1. Go to the **File** menu.

2. Select **New Project**.

3. Select **Image SlideShow**.

—— then ——

4. Select a preset size from the menu or enter in your own values for the size of the project. **(A)**

5. Click the **OK** button.

6. Find and select the images you want to add.

7. Click the **OK** button.

If your images are larger than the dimensions for the project, you get a dialog box after step 5 that gives you options for resizing the image as well as image editing tools.

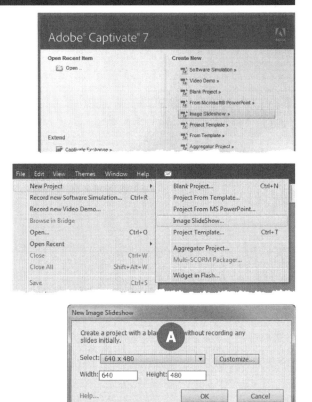

### Resizing Options

**Fit to Stage**: This option shrinks the image to the largest size that will fit fully on the page. Since the image and the slide may have different aspect ratios (height/width proportions), you may end up with empty space either above and below or to the left and right of the image.

**Crop**: This option lets you crop the picture for a better fit. Drag the crop frame handles, and move the crop frame to select the part of the image you want to keep. The portion of the image selected will then appear as large as possible on the slide.

**Constraint Proportion**: If you are cropping the image, check this box to make the crop frame maintain the same aspect ratio as the slide. Uncheck it if you want to use a different aspect ratio.

**Apply to All**: Click this button if you want to use the same sizing specifications for all pictures being imported. If you do not want to treat them all the same, click the arrows at the bottom of the screen to move from picture to picture, adjusting each one individually.

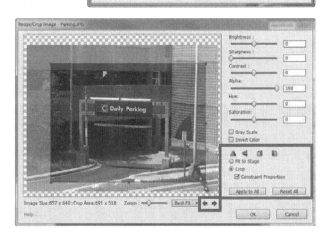

# Software Simulations

Software simulations, also known as screen recordings, let you capture whatever you are doing on your computer. You can create two different types of simulations: sit-back-and-watch demonstrations and interactive, try-it-yourself practices where the student gets to perform the steps and get feedback.

The standard Captivate software simulation is a series of static screen captures (one for every click, typing, etc. you perform) with an animated mouse movement on top. When published, it plays like a movie, even though it is more of a filmstrip behind the scene. In addition, you can also create a video demo, which is a full-motion recording of your actions (on a single slide), which plays back as a video.

## Preparing for a Screen Recording Session

There are many things you'll need to plan and do before you even open up Captivate, both in your computer settings and in the software you plan to capture. To help ensure you get a good, clean capture, use this checklist before you click the **Record** button.

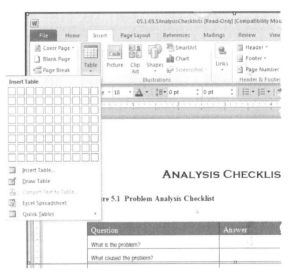

*A drop-down menu like this one that extends beyond your recording window can cause havoc during a recording session.*

❑ Create sample files, scenarios, etc. to demonstrate during the capture. For example, to demonstrate how to approve a timesheet, you might first need to set up a supervisor, set up an employee, and create the timesheet to be submitted.

❑ Walk through all the steps you plan to demonstrate. You'd be surprised at how many times this helps you realize you weren't sure about a step or that you need to do some more prep work.

❑ Undo anything you did during the walk-through. For example, if you walked through the steps for authorizing a timesheet, you might need to go back and unauthorize it or create a new one for the actual capture.

❑ Decide how big you want the application to be. Just because you have a monitor with a 1330 x 960 resolution doesn't mean you should record the application window that big. It is usually best to make the application window as small as possible without hiding features or having to scroll back and forth a lot.

❑ Position your application window so any drop-down menus stay within the recording area (designated by a red frame). Usually, moving the window to the edge of your monitor helps with this. It may force the drop-down menu to reposition itself.

❑ A camera shutter sound plays every time Captivate takes a capture. Turn up your volume so you can hear this sound.

❑ Turn off email, instant messenger, and any other application that might generate an unwanted pop-up window while you are in the middle of a capture.

# Record a Software Simulation

**To record a software simulation:**

1. On the **Welcome** screen, click **Software Simulation**.

—— or ——

1. Go to the **File** menu.

2. Select **Record new Software Simulation**.

—— then ——

3. Configure the recording settings (covered in the remainder of this chapter). **(A)**

4. Adjust the red recording frame around the part of your screen you want to record.

5. Click the **Record** button. **(B)**

6. Perform the steps of the procedure you are demonstrating.

7. Press the **End** button on your keyboard, or click the **Captivate** icon in your system tray.

## Recording Size Settings

When you set up your recording size, select **Screen Area** if you want to lock the pixel size of the red recording frame, and then manually size your application window. Select **Application** to have Captivate make adjustments to the red recording frame and the application together for a precise fit.

If you select **Screen Area**, you get the following options:

**Window Selection menu:** This menu is only active if you select **Application** instead of **Screen Area** as the recording type.

**Custom Size**: Enter the pixel dimensions you want your recording to be, or select from one of the presets in the drop-down menu. Use the **Customize** button to add your own presets if there is a certain dimension you use regularly.

**Full Screen**:  This option records everything on your entire monitor.  If you have more than one monitor, you can pick which one you want to record.

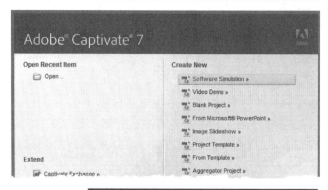

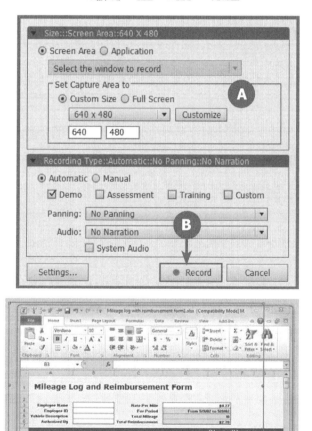

*Red recording frame, not yet positioned properly*

## Recording Size Settings (cont'd)

If you select **Application**, you get the following options:

**Application Drop-Down Menu (A)**: Select the application you want to record.  This menu shows all open applications.

**Snap to: Application window**: The recording frame snaps to the application at its current size.

**Snap to: Application Region**: The recording frame snaps to a specific region of the application, such as the toolbars across the top.  Move your mouse around the application until the recording frame "finds" the region you want to record, and then click the mouse to set it there.

**Snap to: Custom Size**: You can enter a custom pixel dimension, and have the application snap to fit those dimensions.

## 💡 BRIGHT IDEA

What's the difference between **Screen Area: Custom Size** and **Snap to: Custom Size**?   Both let you enter the specific dimensions you want.  The difference is that with **Screen Area**, you need to manually size your application to fit within the red recording frame.  With **Snap to**, Captivate resizes the application for you.

If you want to record the entire application (instead of just part of it), then **Snap To** is usually a better choice.  Captivate is likely to resize the window more precisely than you can manually, so you aren't likely to be off by a pixel or two.  This is especially helpful if you have to go back later and take more captures, because both captures will be consistent.

*Red recording frame trying to "find" the application region you want, based on the location of your mouse*

## Recording Settings (cont'd)

### Recording Type Settings

**Automatic**: Captivate automatically takes captures when you perform certain steps (such as mouse clicks and keystrokes) and when the system performs certain functions (such as displaying a warning).

You can record in up to four modes at once, based on which boxes are checked at the time of recording. You can customize each by clicking the **Settings** button, which is covered on the next page.

> **Demo**: Use this for a sit-back-and-watch lesson of the procedure—good for introducing the procedure and explaining all of the variations, hints, tips, etc.
>
> **Assessment**: Use this to test the students' knowledge as they perform every step themselves, with scoring for every step and the option to limit the number of attempts.
>
> **Training**: Use this to help students practice the procedure themselves, providing feedback but not grading their attempts.
>
> **Custom**: Use this method for completely custom recording settings.
>
> For this book, any simulation in which the student performs the steps (assessment, training, and some custom settings) will be called a practice.

**Manual**: All captures are done manually by you when you press the **Print Screen** key. You might use this if you just want an overview of the main screens, rather than showing every single step. (In **Automatic** mode, you can manually add a screen capture at any time with the **Print Screen** key on your keyboard.)

**Panning**: By default, panning is turned off, meaning the red recording frame is fixed in one place during the recording. You can also choose **Automatic Panning**, which moves the red recording frame around automatically if your mouse goes outside of the frame. **Manual Panning** lets you move the recording frame around manually during recording.

**Audio**: By default, audio is not recorded during capture. If you want to record audio while you capture, select a microphone from the menu.

**System Audio**: In addition to recording audio from a microphone, you can capture audio from your system. For example, the software you are demonstrating might make alert noises. Check this box if you'd like to record the system audio.

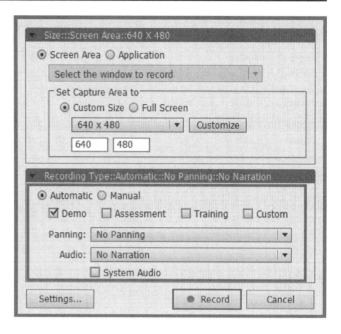

### DESIGN TIP

You can save time by recording in several modes at once. However, it is less challenging to the student if the practice exercise is exactly the same as the demonstration. Consider having a separate practice that has variations of the procedure. For example, if the demo is of someone entering a day of vacation on Tuesday, you may want a practice of someone entering a sick day on Wednesday.

*With a wide application like this, it might be useful to use panning to move back and forth between the left and the right, rather than reduce the size to fit in the red recording frame.*

# Change Recording Preferences

**To change recording preferences:**

1. Click the **Settings** button in the recording window.

2. In the **Category** pane, select the category for the settings you want to work with.

3. Make the changes you want.

4. Click the **OK** button.

## Recording Settings Category

**Generate Captions In**: If you are having Captivate automatically add captions, use this menu if you want to select a language other than English for those captions.

### Audio Options

**Narration**: Check this if you want to record narration into a microphone during the capture.

**System Audio**: Check this to record any sounds generated by your computer during the capture.

**Actions in Real Time**: By default, each captured slide is the same length. Check this box if you want to base the slide length on how long it takes you to perform that step.  This does not affect the path of the mouse.

**Camera Sounds**: During recording, a camera shutter sound plays every time a capture is taken, letting you know if you are getting the captures you need. Uncheck this box if you don't want those sounds. (The sounds are not included in the finished movie.)

**Keystrokes**: When you type during a capture, Captivate captures each keystroke.  Uncheck this box if you don't want individual keystrokes captured, but just want the whole typed passage to appear at once.

**Hear Keyboard Tap Sounds**:  During recording, a tap sound plays for each key you type.  Uncheck this box if you don't want to hear these sounds.  (There is a separate option in **Publish Settings** for including keystroke sounds in the published movie.)

### Hide

**Recording Window:** Check this box if you don't want to see the red recording frame.

**Task Icon and System Tray Icon**: If you are recording your full screen, check these boxes to hide the Captivate icons.  The task icon is what you use to move from program to program.  The system tray icon is in the bottom-right corner of your screen.

**Move New Windows Inside Recording Area**: If another window opens during a capture, such as a dialog box, the pop-up window will be moved into the red recording area, unless you uncheck this box.

**Smoothen movements for:** During automatic recording, full-motion recording is triggered every time you use a dragging action or the mouse wheel. Uncheck these boxes if you don't want that.

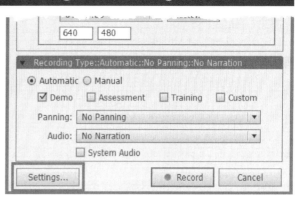

 Working with Audio, ch. 5

## CAUTION

If you are recording audio while you are capturing, be sure to turn off the options for camera sounds and keyboard tap sounds. Otherwise, they'll get recorded with your voiceover!

## BRIGHT IDEAS

If you are recording narration and system audio, they are added as separate tracks in the **Timeline**.

If you turn on the **System Audio** feature, other preferences, such as **Camera Sounds** are turned off to avoid conflicts.

# Change Recording Preferences (cont'd)

## Video Demo Category

**Show Mouse in Video Demo Mode**: By default, the mouse is included in any full-motion recording. Uncheck this box if you don't want the mouse recorded. For example, you might want a recording of some sort of animation and wouldn't want the mouse in the way.

**Working Folder**: This folder stores the temporary file of your full-motion recording after you save your project. Captivate decodes the files and stores them in this location to make it quicker to open and save files. This location can be changed by clicking the **Browse** button.

**Video Color Mode**: You can select the color setting for any full-motion video. **16 bit** creates a smaller file size, but the fewer number of available colors may affect your quality. **32 bit** gives you more colors, but will create a larger file.

## Keys Category

This category displays the various keyboard shortcuts that can be used during recording. If you want to change any of them, just click in a field and type the shortcut you want to use instead. For example, you may be taking a capture of an application that uses some of these function keys. In this case, you'd want to change the shortcut in Captivate so it doesn't create a conflict.

 Recording Shortcuts, p. 29

## CAUTION

The **Print Screen** key is the default for manually capturing a screen in both Captivate and Snagit. If you have Snagit installed on your computer and press **Print Screen** during a capture, it may launch Snagit. You'll want to change the hotkey for manual captures in either Captivate or in Snagit to avoid a conflict during your capture session.

# Change Recording Preferences (cont'd)

## Modes Category

In the **Modes** category, you can configure settings for each of the automatic recording modes. First, select the mode you want to configure from the drop-down menu **(A)**, and then make any changes for that mode.

### Captions

**Add Text Captions**: Captivate automatically adds captions to your steps (e.g., "Click the **OK** button.").

**Convert Tooltips to Rollover Captions**: If your software has tooltips (small captions that give the name of the tool when you hover over it), Captivate creates a similar rollover caption for you.

**Use Smart Shapes**: If you are including captions or rollovers, you can choose to use Smart Shapes instead of traditional captions. To do this, check the box, and then select the type of Smart Shape you want: **Rectangle**, **Rounded Rectangle**, **Oval**, or **Cloud**.

### Mouse

**Show Mouse Location and Movement**: Captivate includes the mouse along a streamlined path from one click to the next.

**Add Highlight Boxes on Click**: Captivate adds a highlight box around the item that you click. This provides visual emphasis and makes it easy to create job aids with the **Publish to Print** publishing option.

The default settings for **Demonstration** mode (shown below) include captions, mouse movement, and highlight boxes. The default settings for the two practice modes (**Assessment** and **Training**) do not include these objects, but instead, include the interactive elements covered on the next page.

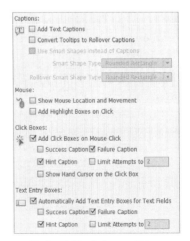

## CAUTION

This category in the **Preferences** dialog box only changes the *settings* for each mode, NOT which mode you will actually be recording in. That is determined by the recording window.

 Recording Type Settings, p. 22

 Smart Shapes, p. 62

*Default **Demonstration** settings*  *Default **Assessment** settings*  *Default **Training** settings*

## Change Recording Preferences (cont'd)

### Modes Category (cont'd)

#### Click Boxes

When this option is checked, Captivate converts every click you make while recording into a click box that the student must click during the practice playback.

#### Text Entry Boxes

When this box is checked, Captivate converts your typing during recording into a text entry box that the student must fill in during the practice playback.

#### Options

**Success Caption**: Check this box if you want to add a caption after each successful click or text entry to let the students know they were correct.

**Failure Caption**: By default, Captivate adds captions after each unsuccessful click or text entry to let students know they were incorrect. Uncheck this box if you don't want them.

**Hint Caption**: Check this box if you want to add a roll-over caption with a hint the students see when they roll over the click box or the text entry box.

**Limit Attempts to X**: By default, students cannot move forward in the practice until they complete the click or typing step correctly. You can check this box and indicate a specific number of attempts.

**Show Hand Cursor on the Click Box**: Check this box if you want the student's cursor to change to a hand cursor when it is over the click box area. Your students may recognize that this means they are over a hot spot.

### Defaults Category

Before you record, you can set the styles to be used for captions, highlight boxes, and other elements added to your project.

To change the style, select an option from any of the drop-down menus. Each item has a number of preset styles already available. When you select one, you can see a preview in the **Styles Preview** pane in the bottom corner.

To add your own style, click the **Create New Style** button. New styles are then added to the appropriate drop-down lists. If you have a project open, the style changes apply only to that project. If you don't have a project open, the style changes apply to all future projects.

Styles, p. 104

# Video Demos

A video demo is a type of software simulation where you create a high-definition, full-motion recording of the steps you are performing. A new project is created with the recording as a single movie.

## Record a Video Demo

**To record in video demo mode:**

1. On the **Welcome** screen, click **Video Demo**.

——— or ———

1. Go to the **File** menu.

2. Select **Record new Video Demo**.

——– then ———

3. Configure the recording settings (covered on the previous pages).

4. Adjust the red recording frame that appears around the application being recorded, if needed.

5. Click the **Record** button.

6. Perform the steps of the procedure you are demonstrating.

7. Press the **End** button on your keyboard, or click the **Captivate** icon in your system tray.

 **BRIGHT IDEAS**

- Video demos are saved as a Captivate Video Composition file (.cpvc).

- Once you finish your recording, you can add captions and other objects, create zoom and pan effects, trim off portions of the beginning and end, etc.

  Managing Video Demos, p. 149

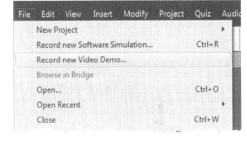

# DESIGN TIPS

Here are some important instructional design and usability decisions to make when designing a practice.

- ❑ How will you communicate the task your students need to accomplish? Will an audio introduction tell them they are supposed to request a day of vacation in the system?

- ❑ Do you want to give them step-by-step instructions or just the general task? Will you tell them the first step is to click the **Request Leave** button, or do they need to remember that on their own?

- ❑ If you do include step-by-step instructions, where will they appear? In audio? In timed captions? In a text box down the side of the slide?

- ❑ Do you want to show a success caption for each step, or does the fact that the practice continues serve as adequate feedback?

- ❑ How many attempts should the student get? For a graded assessment, perhaps they should only get one. If the practice is for the student's benefit, perhaps they should have two. Will unlimited attempts cause the user to get frustrated and not be able to finish?

- ❑ Do you want to provide hints with hint captions and the hand cursor? For a graded assessment, you might not want to. Determine if they add value or not, as the student has to be on the trigger area to see the hints.

- ❑ How much help do you want to give them in a failure caption? Tell them simply to try again? Remind them what they are supposed to accomplish in general terms? Tell them the specific step? Point to the step?

# BRIGHT IDEAS

## Things to Do DURING Your Capture

### Typing

Type carefully. If you fix a typo as you type, the mistake and your correction both show up in the final output. Yes, you can edit it later, but it is quicker to type carefully the first time.

If you are typing a longer passage, such as a sentence or two in a field about why the employee is requesting time off, consider just pasting it in rather than typing it. It can be cumbersome for a student to watch the typing of a long passage, and you are more likely to have a typo in a long passage. Pasting text already typed and ready in another document can be cleaner and easier for everyone.

If you do make a mistake with your typing, press the **Pause** key. Delete all of what you have typed. Press the **Pause** button again, and start typing from the beginning. This separates the incorrect typing on one slide and starts the new typing on another slide. During editing, delete the slide with the incorrect typing.

### Scrolling and Dragging

Anytime you scroll or drag your mouse, full-motion recording is triggered, unless you have changed the defaults. The video increases your file size and is hard to edit, so it is often simpler if you reserve video for tasks that really need the moving video. Plan your steps carefully to avoid video when it is not needed. For example, if you need to scroll down to the bottom of the screen, click in the bottom of the scroll bar instead of dragging the slider down. If you need to select a word, double-click it instead of dragging across it with the cursor.

### Tooltips

As you are capturing your steps, your mouse may be resting on a feature in your software long enough to trigger the tooltip to appear. If it does, it can appear in your capture. Pay attention to these tooltips when they appear, and, if needed, move your mouse and take another screen capture manually to get a clean shot.

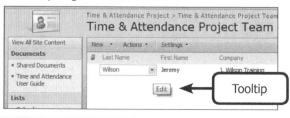

## BRIGHT IDEAS

### Useful Keyboard Shortcuts

**Pause**

Press the **Pause** key on your keyboard if you need to do anything during the capture that you don't want to record. For example:

- A window pops up, and you need to resize it or move it into the recording area.
- You get to a step and realize something isn't set up properly and needs to be fixed.
- You make a mistake and need to undo it.

While you are paused, the **Captivate** icon in your system tray has a very small orange dot, letting you know you are paused.

When you are done and ready to resume the capture, simply press the **Pause** key again.

**Print Screen**

During automatic recording, you can manually add an extra screen capture at any time by pressing the **Print Screen** key on your keyboard. For example, perhaps it took an extra second for a dialog box to load, and you aren't sure if the capture was taken before it fully appeared. It's easier to delete unneeded manual captures than to later recreate something you missed.

**End**

Press the **End** key to finish your capture.

**Undo Marker**

If you perform a step you don't want and will probably delete the slide, press **Ctrl** + **Shift** + **Z**.

The screen is still captured, but it shows up as a hidden slide with a caption across it saying "Marked for Undo." You can unhide the slide and delete the caption later if you want to keep the slide after all.

**Other Recording Shortcuts**

There are many other keyboard shortcuts available, many of which can be customized. You can find them in **Preferences** on the **Keys** tab.

Keys Category, p. 24
Useful Keyboard Shortcuts, p. 254

### After Your Capture

You will most likely do a fair amount of editing to your project once you've captured it. For example, you may add or delete slides and captions, adjust mouse movements, etc. However, it doesn't make sense to spend time fine-tuning your capture if there is something wrong with it, and it needs to be re-captured.

When you are finished with your capture, save it, and then walk through each of the slides to check for the following before you start editing:

- ❏ Are there any screens that were still loading when the screen shot was taken?

- ❏ Are there any typos in the on-screen typing?

- ❏ Is there anything showing that the student should not be seeing? A tooltip? An Outlook message indicator? Sensitive data?

- ❏ Are there any steps missing?

These are the big problems that are hard to resolve during editing. It is often quicker to just start the capture over again, rather than trying to fix these problems. Otherwise, you could spend 30-60 minutes trying to fix a problem that could have been eliminated if you took 5 minutes to take the capture over again.

Smaller problems, such as the mouse in the wrong place, are easier to fix during editing. As you become more familiar with taking captures, you'll learn what to look out for and which problems are best resolved with a re-capture.

### Editing and Refining Your Captures

In the next several chapters, you'll learn ways to take your raw capture and turn it into a polished lesson or practice.

- Chapters 4 and 6 show you how to add and modify on-screen elements, such as text captions and highlight boxes.

- Chapter 5 shows you how to add audio narration.

- Chapter 7 shows you how to add or modify the interactive elements, such as an explanatory rollover caption or the click boxes and text entry boxes, for a practice.

- Chapter 8 covers a few features specific to simulations, such as editing mouse movements.

# Notes

# Adding and Managing Slides

## Introduction

Your slides are the backbone of your project.  In some cases, when you first create your project, the slides are set up at that point.  For example, if you are creating a software simulation, each individual screen capture is added as a slide.  In the finished output, all of the slides are played together like a movie.  If you are importing a PowerPoint presentation, then you'll have one Captivate slide for each of your PowerPoint slides.  In other cases, you will want to add individual slides with any number of content types to a blank or existing project.

In this chapter, you'll learn how to add several slide types that correspond to the project types: blank slides, PowerPoint slides, and image slides.  You'll also learn how to manage your slides effectively, whether changing the slide properties, creating master slides to maintain a consistent look, or rearranging and grouping slides to keep them organized.

In future chapters, you'll learn about additional slide types, such as text animation slides.

| Slide Type | Chapter |
|---|---|
| **New slide** | **3** |
| **Blank slide** | **3** |
| Question slide | 10 |
| **PowerPoint slide** | **3** |
| Recording slide | 8 |
| **Image slide** | **3** |
| CPVC slide | 8 |
| Animation slide | 4 |
| **Master slide** | **3** |
| Placeholder slide | 11 |

## In This Chapter

- New & Blank Slides
- PowerPoint Slides
- Image Slides
- Slide Properties
- Slide Notes
- Master Slides
- Slide Themes
- Managing Slides

# Notes

# Inserting New Slides

## Insert a New or Blank Slide

**To insert a new or blank slide:**

1. Go to the **Insert** menu.
2. Select **New Slide** or **Blank Slide**.

With **New Slide**, the added slide uses the master slide and theme of the slide before it.  With **Blank Slide**, the added slide is truly blank with no master or theme applied.

Themes, p. 42
Master Slides, p. 40

## Insert a PowerPoint Slide

**To insert individual PowerPoint slides:**

1. Go to the **Insert** menu.
2. Select **PowerPoint Slide**.
3. Indicate where you want the slides to appear in your project. **(A)**
4. Click **OK**.
5. Find and select the file you want.
6. Click **Open**.
7. Enter the properties you want. **(B)**
8. Click **OK**.

PowerPoint Import Properties, p. 16

 **CAUTION**

How many slides is too many?  Captivate recommends a length of 50 to 60 slides, with a maximum of 150 slides.

# Edit a PowerPoint Slide in Captivate

You can edit a PowerPoint slide from within Captivate. When you initiate editing, PowerPoint opens up within the Captivate interface, letting you access the capabilities of PowerPoint without having to leave Captivate.

**To edit an imported PowerPoint slide from within Captivate:**

1. Right-click the slide.
2. Select **Edit with Microsoft® PowerPoint**.
3. Select the editing option you want. (See below.)
4. Make your changes to the slide, using the PowerPoint interface.
5. Click the **Save** button. **(A)**

## Editing Options

**Edit Slide**: Just the selected slide will be opened for editing.

**Edit Presentation**:  The entire presentation will be opened for editing.

**Find Presentation in the Library**: This highlights the presentation in the **Library**. You can access more editing options from the **Library**. (See next page.)

**Export Animation**: This option converts the selected slide to a .swf file.  You can then save the .swf file and use it in other places, such as on a web page or even another Captivate project.

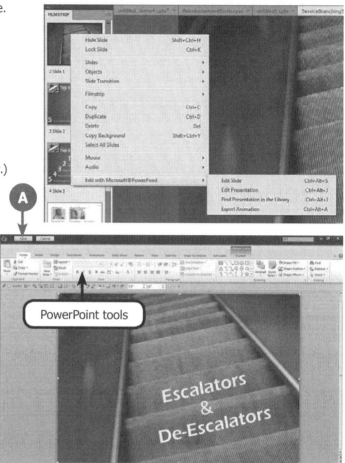

*Imported PowerPoint slide being edited in Captivate*

# Update an Imported Slide

When you have a linked PowerPoint slide, changes made to the PowerPoint source file can be updated in the Captivate file, but it doesn't happen automatically. You need to initiate the update.

**To update an imported PowerPoint slide:**

1. Go to the **Library** panel.
2. Right-click the presentation in the **Library**.
3. Select **Update**.
4. Select which linked presentations you want to update.
5. Click the **Update** button.
6. Click **OK**.

If any new slides have been added to the PowerPoint file, you will be asked to select which ones you want to add.

 Linking PowerPoint slides, p. 17
Library, p. 210

 **BRIGHT IDEAS**

- Notice that there are other options on the **Library**'s right-click menu. For example, you can switch between linking and embedding the file.

- An embedded file also has a **Compact** option. This permanently deletes any slides from the original PowerPoint file that are not currently being used in the Captivate file.

- A green dot next to a linked presentation in the **Library (A)** tells you that the file is current. The dot becomes orange if it is not current. It becomes a question mark if the link is broken because the file is renamed, moved, or unavailable from a network. Click the question mark to re-establish the link.

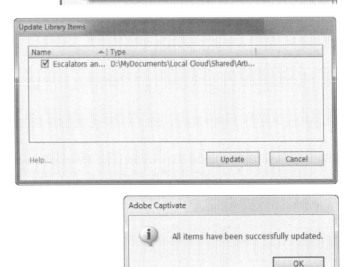

## Add an Image Slide

When you add an image slide, the image is merged to the background of the slide.

Captivate accepts the following image types: .jpg, .gif, .png, .bmp, .ico, .emf, .wmf, .pot, .potx, and .pict.

**To add an image slide:**

1. Go to the **Insert** menu.
2. Select **Image Slide**.
3. Find and select the image you want to use.
4. Click **Open**.

The image is now the background of a slide. As such, it can not be repositioned, resized, or edited on the slide.

| Insert | Modify | Project | Quiz | Audio | Video |
|---|---|---|---|---|---|
| New Slide | | | | | Shift+Ctrl+V |
| New Slide from | | | | | ▶ |
| Blank Slide | | | | | Shift+Ctrl+J |
| Question Slide... | | | | | Shift+Ctrl+Q |
| PowerPoint Slide... | | | | | Shift+Ctrl+P |
| Recording Slide... | | | | | Ctrl+Alt+O |
| Image Slide... | | | | | Shift+Ctrl+Alt+S |
| CPVC Slide... | | | | | |
| Animation Slide... | | | | | Shift+Ctrl+N |

## BRIGHT IDEA

If you want an image to "float" on the slide so that you can time, move, or resize it, then add it as an image instead of as an image slide.

If you want to have the image as part of the background but want to make some changes first (move, resize, rotate, crop, etc.), add it as an image instead of an image slide. Then, once you have it how you want it, simply right-click it and merge it to the background.

Merge With Background, p. 145
Add an Image to a Slide, p. 57

You can swap out the image in a background in the **Background** section of the slide properties.

Slide Properties, p. 37

# Slide Properties

**Tab Order:** When you click this button, a dialog box appears **(B)** that lets you set the tab order of any interactive objects on the page. For students using keyboards instead of the mouse for navigation (including those using a screen reader), it is helpful if you put your objects in a logical order.

 Accessibility/Section 508, p. 245

**Accessibility**: Click the **Accessibility** button to get a dialog box **(A)** that lets you enter a text description for the slide. This text will be read to students using screen readers who cannot see the content of the slide. Either type your text in the space provided, or click the **Import Slide Notes** button to use your slide notes for the accessibility text.

 Accessibility/Section 508, p. 246
Slide Notes, p. 39

**Name**: You can give a unique name to each slide. It shows up in the Filmstrip and in any drop-down menus where you need to select a slide. Naming the slides makes it easier to identify the right slide quickly. In addition, the slide label is read to students using a screen reader if the accessibility features are turned on for a project.

## General Pane

**Master Slide**: Master slides in Captivate are very much like master slides in PowerPoint. You are able to create slide backgrounds that you can use over and over again. Select the master you want from the drop-down menu.

 Master Slides, p. 40

**Stage**: If you want to change the background color of the slide, uncheck the **Project Background** box, and then click the **Stage** color swatch to pick a new color or gradient.

 Colors and Color Gradients, p. 94

**Background:** This field shows you what background image is being used. Use the **Browse**, **Delete**, and **Edit** buttons below the field to make changes to the background image. These options are disabled for certain slide types, such as master slides or imported PowerPoint slides.

Library, p. 210

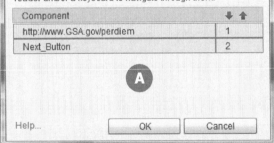

# Slide Properties Panel (cont'd)

## General Pane (cont'd)

**Quality**: This drop-down menu lets you select the image quality of the slide. You can increase the quality to **Optimized**, **JPEG**, or **High (24-bit)** if your published quality is not what you want.

**Time**: By default, each slide displays for three seconds. Adjust the time here or in the **Timeline** panel.

 Timing Objects, p. 111

**Transitions**: Transitions are effects that play when a project goes from one slide to the next. A slide transition plays at the beginning of a slide. For example, if a transition is applied to slide 3, it appears when the project goes from slide 2 to slide 3.

 **BRIGHT IDEA**

You can also apply transitions and effects to individual objects. Apply simple fade in/out transitions in the **Transition** pane for that object or apply special effects, such as motion paths or flying in/out, from the **Effects** tab.

 Object Transitions, p. 98
Object Effects, p. 108

## Action Pane

The **Action** pane lets you designate certain actions when the slide first begins (**On Enter**) or when the movie reaches the very last frame of the slide (**On Exit**). For example, you might want to disable a button when the student first comes to a slide.

 Actions, ch. 7 & 9

## Audio Pane

The **Audio** pane lets you add and manage audio attached to the slide. The options vary slightly based on whether or not there is already audio on the slide.

 Audio, ch. 5

# Slide Notes

Slide notes let you put text notes on individual slides. These might be development notes for your team or the transcript of your audio for your students. By default, slide notes are not included in your published project. Once you add your text to the **Slides Notes** panel, you can then:

- View the notes while recording audio.
- Convert the text to computerized audio using the text-to-speech converter.
- Create closed captions for accessibility purposes that *do* appear in the published movie.

Text-to-Speech, p. 83
Closed Captioning, p. 84
Accessibility/Section 508, p. 246

## TIME SAVER

When you import slides from PowerPoint, the slide notes from that file are automatically imported into your Captivate slide notes.

---

## Add Slide Notes

**To view the Slide Notes panel:**

1. Go to the **Window** menu.
2. Select **Slide Notes**.

**To add slide notes:**

1. Select the slide you want.
2. Click the **Plus** button in the **Slide Notes** pane. **(A)**
3. Type or paste your text.
4. Repeat the steps for additional notes for that slide.

**To remove slide notes:**

1. Select the heading row **(B)** for the note you want to delete.
2. Click the **Minus** button.

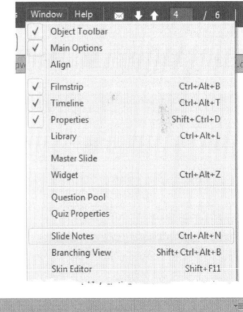

# Master Slides

Master slides can help you create a consistent look quickly. Just as with Microsoft PowerPoint, you can add design elements to a master slide that can then be used as a template for one or more of your slides.

Master slides are managed in the **Master Slide** tab. Go to the **Window** menu, and select **Master Slide** to view the tab. Masters are applied to individual slides on the **Properties** panel.

There are three types of master slides: main, content, and question. The main master slide appears in the shaded area on the left side of the **Master Slide** panel **(A)**. Content master slides are individual layouts based on the main master **(B)**. Changes made to the main master appear on all the content master slides, unless you choose to exclude those objects **(C)**. A question master is like a content master, but is for quiz questions **(D)**.

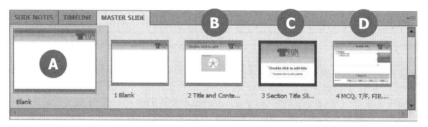

Master slides (both main and content) can have regular objects and placeholder objects. Regular objects include text, images, and animations. However, some objects (mainly interactive objects) are grayed out in **Master Slide** view, and cannot be used on a master slide. Placeholder objects are formatted content frames, with the specific content being added in edit mode to each individual slide using that master.

## Modify a Main Master Slide

Any changes you make to the main master slide will appear on any of its content master slides, unless you choose to exclude them.

**To modify a main master slide:**

1. Select the main master on the left side of the **Master Slide** panel.

2. Add standard content objects from the **Insert** menu or the **Object** toolbar.

3. Add placeholder objects from the **Insert** menu.

4. Configure the properties of the objects.

 Placeholder Objects, p. 206

## ⓘ CAUTION

It can be confusing when you move back and forth between the regular slide view and master slide view. If you aren't careful, you might make changes to the wrong one. Click a slide in the **Filmstrip** to change an individual slide. Click a slide in the **Master Slide** panel to change the underlying master. The slide you are working on will be outlined in black. **(C)**

# Create a Content Master Slide

**To create a content master slide:**

1. Go to the **Insert** menu.
2. Select **Content Master Slide**.
3. Configure properties in the **Properties** pane.
4. Add objects to the slide in the work area.

## Content Master Slide Properties

**Name**: Names are very important for master slides, making it easier to later select the one you want.

**Show Main Master Slide Objects** and **Use Master Slide Background**: Leave these checked if you want your content master to inherit the objects and background of the main master. Uncheck them if you want to exclude individual objects and/or the background of the main master.

The following options become available if you uncheck **Use Master Slide Background**:

**Stage**: Click the color swatch to select a color for the content master slide background, if needed.

**Project Background**: If you are not using the master slide background, the project background is used. If you don't want that either, uncheck this box. You can then either leave the background blank or click the **Browse** button that appears to find and select a different background.

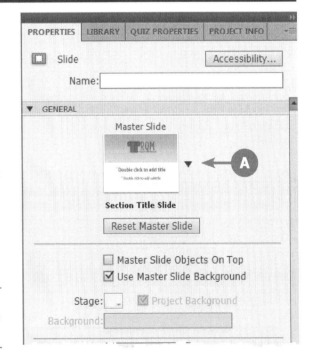

# Apply a Master Slide

**To apply a master to a project slide:**

1. Select the slide(s) you want to apply the master to.
2. Click the **Master Slide** drop-down arrow. **(A)**
3. Select the master you want.
4. Configure the master slide options.

**Master Slide Objects on Top**: By default, the master slide objects appear behind anything you add to the individual slide. Check this box if you want the master slide elements to appear on top of the individual slide elements. You cannot reorder the individual master objects, but they can be moved all to the front or all to the back.

The rest of the options are the same as for a content master slide, as described above.

 **TIME SAVER**

Remember that you can insert a *blank* slide when you don't want a master slide, and a *new* slide when you want the master of the slide before it.

# Themes

Slide themes in Captivate work very much like they do in PowerPoint. A theme is a family of pre-designed elements including master slides (main and content), object styles, skin settings, and recording defaults.

*Some of the available theme options*

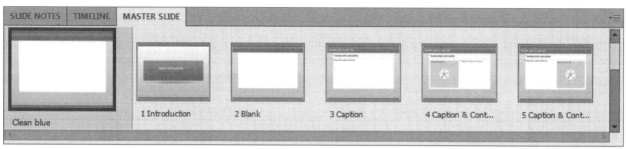

*Some of the content master slides based on the chosen theme*

## Apply a Theme to a Project

**To apply a theme to a project:**

1. Click the **Show/Hide Themes Panel** button **(A)**, if the panel is not showing.

2. Select the theme you want.

### ! CAUTION

When you apply a theme, all overrides to object styles and properties will be lost.

### ⏱ TIME SAVER

If you right-click a theme thumbnail, you can set it as the default, meaning all new projects will start with that theme. You can also remove thumbnails from the panel from that right-click menu.

### 📐 DESIGN TIP

Click the drop-down arrow in the top-right corner of the panel for more theme choices, including browsing or downloading additional themes. Themes have a .cptm file extension.

# Apply a Content Master From a Theme

Once you have applied a theme to your project, you can select one of many different content master slides. They are applied the same way that any master slide is applied.

**To apply a slide master from a theme:**

1. In the **Properties** panel, click the **Master Slide** drop-down menu.

2. Select the layout you want.

## POWER TIP

If you make changes to any of the elements of a theme (such as a style or a master slide layout), you can save it from the **Themes** menu. To apply a saved theme (.cptm extension), go to the **Themes** menu, and select **Apply a New Theme**.

# Create a New Slide With A Theme

When you have a theme applied to your project, you can insert a new slide with one of the master layouts from that theme.

**To create a new slide with a theme:**

1. Go to the **Insert** menu.

2. Select **New Slide from**.

3. Select the layout you want.

# Managing Slides

## Hide Slides

Just as in PowerPoint, hidden slides do not show up in preview mode or in your published movie, but they remain in the **Filmstrip** and work area.

**To hide a slide:**

1. Right-click the slide thumbnail in the **Filmstrip**.
2. Select **Hide Slide**.

**To unhide a slide:**

1. Right-click the slide thumbnail.
2. Select **Show Slide**.

——— or ———

1. Click the "eyeball" icon under the thumbnail. **(A)**

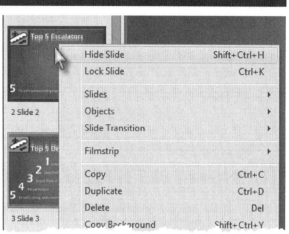

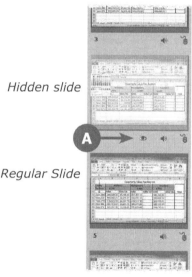

Hidden slide

Regular Slide

### 💡 BRIGHT IDEA

When capturing a software simulation, it is not uncommon to end up with extra captures. If you delete these slides and then later realize you need them, you may have a problem. Instead, you can hide the unwanted slides and delete them later once you are sure you don't need them.

## Delete Slides

**To delete a slide:**

1. Right-click the slide thumbnail in the **Filmstrip**.
2. Select **Delete**.

——— or ———

1. Select the slide in the **Filmstrip**.
2. Press the **Delete** key on your keyboard.

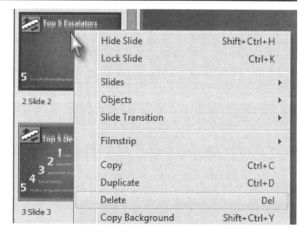

## Move Slides

**To move a slide to another position:**

1. Click the slide's thumbnail, and drag it to the location you want.

## Copy, Paste, and Duplicate Slides

Slides cannot be cut, but they can be copied and pasted. Once you select a slide in the **Filmstrip**, you can copy, paste, and duplicate it in three different ways:

- The **Edit** menu **(A)**
- Keyboard shortcuts **(B)**
- The **Filmstrip** or work area right-click menu **(C)**

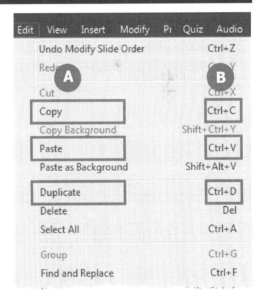

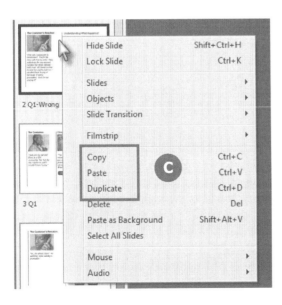

### TIME SAVERS

You can select more than one slide when you use these functions. For consecutive slides, press **Shift** while clicking the first and last slide in a range. If they aren't consecutive, press **Ctrl** while clicking each individual slide.

The **Duplicate** function combines the copy and paste actions into one step. The duplicated slide is pasted directly after the selected slide.

## Lock Slides

If you want to ensure that certain slides don't get deleted, you can lock them. Locking a slide also keeps you from adding or editing objects on the slide.

**To lock a slide:**

1. Right-click the slide thumbnail in the **Filmstrip**.
2. Select **Lock Slide**.

**To unlock a slide:**

1. Right-click the slide thumbnail.
2. Select **Unlock Slide**.

——— or ———

1. Click the **Lock** icon in the top corner of the thumbnail.

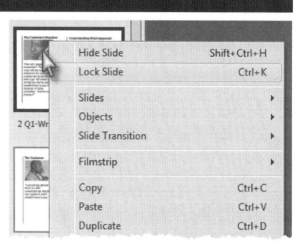

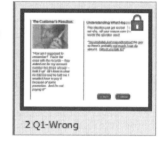

*Locked Slide*

### BRIGHT IDEA

You can make the thumbnails in the **Filmstrip** larger or smaller from the thumbnail right-click menu.

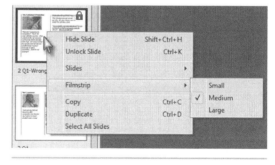

# Group Slides

Grouping slides can help you manage a large project. When slides are grouped, you can identify them quickly and move, hide, or delete them as a group. Only consecutive slides can be grouped.

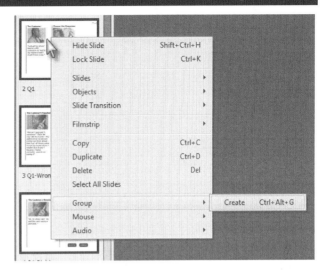

### To group slides:

1. Select all the slides you want to group together.
2. Right-click any one of the selected slides.
3. Select **Group**.
4. Select **Create**.

Once you create a group, the slides are collapsed in the **Filmstrip** with a placeholder slide. **(A)** When the placeholder is selected, the **Slide Group Properties** pane appears. **(B)**

## Slide Group Properties

**Title**: When you enter a title in the **Properties** panel, it appears on the placeholder slide and under the thumbnail.

**Master Slide**: You can change the standard options for master slides for every slide in the group.

Master Slides, p. 40

**Color**: Use the color swatch to set the outline color used in the **Filmstrip**. Using different colors can make it easy to find the slides you are looking for. These colors only appear in the developing environment, not in the published course.

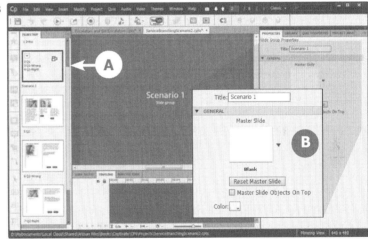

## Managing Groups

### To expand a group:

1. Click the down arrow icon on the group placeholder thumbnail. **(C)**

### To collapse a group:

1. Click the up arrow icon on the thumbnail of the first slide in the group. **(D)**

### To ungroup slides:

1. Right-click any one of the slides in the group.
2. Select **Group**.
3. Select **Remove**.

Collapsed Group

Expanded Group

# Notes

# Adding Content Objects

## Introduction

The next several chapters deal with how to add content to your slides.

- In this chapter, you'll learn about adding content objects, including captions, images, shapes, highlight boxes, animations, and equations.
- Chapter 5 covers how to add audio and video to your projects.
- Chapter 6 covers object properties that relate to most object types, such as how to select colors, how to apply styles, and how to adjust timing.
- In chapter 7, you'll learn how to add interactive objects, such as rollover objects, text entry boxes, and buttons.
- In chapter 10, you'll learn how to add questions and quizzes.

## In This Chapter

- Captions
- Images
- Smart Shapes and Highlight Boxes
- Animations
- Text Animations
- Zoom Areas
- Equations

# Notes

# Working With Captions

Captions are one way to add text to your slides, whether you want to point out a step in a computer procedure, provide feedback on a practice activity, provide instructions on what to do, or add text in a branching scenario.

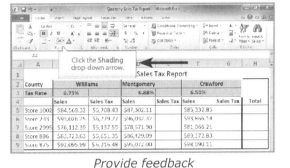

*Reinforce teaching points*

*Provide feedback*

*Give instructions*

*Add "non-caption" text*

---

 **DESIGN TIP**

You can also add text to shapes. Shapes don't have all of the behind-the-scenes logic that captions have (like automatic recording or exporting), but you have more formatting options, such as custom colors and gradients.

Smart Shapes, p. 62

---

## Add a New Caption

**To add a new caption:**

1. Click the **Insert Caption** button on the **Object** toolbar.

2. Type your caption text.

3. Configure any settings in the caption **Properties** panel. (See following pages.)

4. Click off the caption.

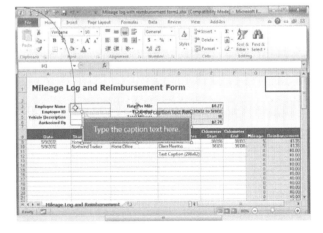

# Edit Caption Text

**To make text edits to your captions:**

1. Double-click the caption to get a cursor.
2. Make your edits.
3. Click off the caption.

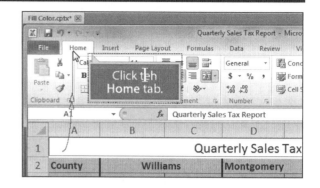

# Formatting Caption Text

Formatting is done in the **Properties** panel. Select the caption to format all text in the caption, or select just the part of the text you want to format.

## Character Pane

**Family**: Select the font type you want, such as **Myriad Pro**.

**Style**: Select the font style you want, such as **Condensed**.

**Size**: Type or drag your mouse for the point size you want.

**Format**: Click the buttons for bold, italics, underlining, superscript, or subscript, as needed.

**Color**: Click the swatch to select the font color.

**Highlight**: Click the swatch to select the color for highlighting the text.

 Colors, p. 94

## Format Pane

**Align**: Select the buttons you want for horizontal and vertical alignment of text within the caption.

**Indentation**: Click the **Decrease Indent** or **Increase Indent** buttons to change the left margin on the caption.

**Bullets**: Select a bullet/numbering option from the drop-down menu, as needed.

**Spacing**: Type or drag your mouse to change the vertical spacing between lines.

**Margins**: Enter a number to put a margin on the inside of the caption, leaving more room between your text and the edge of the caption.

**Insert**: Click the **Insert Symbol** button to insert symbols, such as a copyright symbol or a foreign currency symbol.

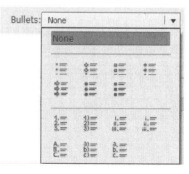

# Apply Text Effects

When you select a caption or shape instead of the text within the object, there is an extra option in the **Character** pane: text effects. **(A)** Text effects are special font formatting options that can be applied to the entire object.

**To apply a text effect:**

1. Select a caption or a shape with text.
2. In the **Character** pane, click the **Text Effects** button.
3. Select the effect you want.

**To create your own effect:**

1. Select a caption or a shape with text.
2. In the **Character** pane, click the **Text Effects** button.
3. Click a button with a plus sign.
4. In the pane on the left, check the box for the attribute you want to modify.
5. In the pane on the right, make the changes to the properties for that attribute.
6. Repeat steps 4 and 5 to modify additional attributes.
7. Click **OK** to apply the effects to the selected object only, or click **Save** to add the effects to the options on the **Text Effects** drop-down menu.

## POWER TIPS

You can insert variables into a caption. For example, you might want a caption that displays the current date, the score of a test, the answer to a question, etc.

Variables, p. 155

You can also insert hyperlinks into text captions.

Add a Hyperlink to Text, p. 127

# Change Caption and Callout Type

The *caption* type determines the color, shape, and outline of the captions. The *callout* type determines if and where the caption is pointing.

**To change the caption type:**

1. Select the caption you want to change.
2. In the **General** pane, click the **Caption** drop-down menu.
3. Select the caption type you want.

**To change the callout type:**

1. Select the caption you want to change.
2. In the **Callout** field, click the type you want.

## BRIGHT IDEA

You can also insert caption widgets, giving you more choices for your caption type. In the **General** pane of the caption's properties, click the **Caption Widgets** link.

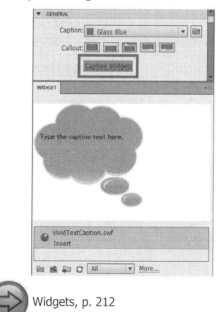

Widgets, p. 212

## DESIGN TIPS

- Use different caption types for different purposes. For example, you could use **Adobe Blue** when the student should read and **Glass Blue** when the student should act.

- Use a transparent caption when you want to put plain text on a slide. For example, you might want to fill in a blank on a form or add a title to the top of a slide.

- You can use styles to save and apply formatting attributes.

Styles, p. 104

## POWER TIP

If none of the existing caption types fit your needs perfectly, you can create your own using photo-editing software. Search Captivate help for **custom text caption files** to get the details.

# Exporting and Importing Captions

Exporting caption text into a Microsoft Word document can be useful for creating print materials, such as a job aid. You can also export captions, make changes to them, and import them back into your project—a huge time saver when you have lots of edits or if you need to translate/localize the captions.

When you use this option, caption text, smart shape text, and placeholder text boxes are all exported.

| Adobe Captivate | | | | Wednesday, October 20, 2010 | |
|---|---|---|---|---|---|
| Slide Id | Item Id | Original Text Caption Data | Updated Text Caption Data | | Slide |
| 961 | 975 | Select **Quarterly Sales Tax Report** | Select the cell(s) you want to format. | | 3 |
| 997 | 1011 | Select **Shading** | Click the **Shading** drop-down arrow. | | 6 |
| 1017 | 1031 | Select the **No Fill** menu item | Select the fill color you want. | | 7 |

Caption as exported    Edited caption to import

## Export Captions

### To export captions

1. Go to the **File** menu.
2. Select **Export**.
3. Select **Project Captions and Closed Captions**.
4. Find and select the folder where you want to save the Word document.
5. Click the **Save** button.

## TIME SAVER

If you plan to use the exported captions in other documents, such as a help manual, set up a macro in Word to delete the unneeded columns and rows and take the text out of the table. Then, with one stroke, you have a ready-to-use list of steps.

## Import Captions

### To import captions

1. Go to the **File** menu.
2. Select **Import**.
3. Select **Project Captions and Closed Captions**.
4. Find and select the document previously exported.
5. Click the **Open** button.

## CAUTION

For the import to work properly, make sure you import back into the same Captivate file. Be sure to only change the caption text in the Word document and not add/delete rows, change Item Id numbers, etc.

# DESIGN TIPS

- For systems training, create a style guide for terminology so that your language is consistent.  For example:

  Do you refer to a "drop-down" or a "drop-down arrow"?

  Do you bold the name of the feature or put it in quotations?

  Do you always capitalize the name of a feature, never capitalize it, or match what is in the system?

- You may end up resizing your finished movie down to a smaller size to fit on a web page or in a course interface.  If you are likely to do this, make your captions a larger font size than you think you need.  That way they are still legible when you shrink the movie.

- Never sacrifice legibility for creativity! Consider the color scheme of the software being captured, the color and size of the caption, and the color and size of the text to make sure the captions stand out and are easy to read.

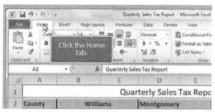

*Legible*

*Not legible*

# POWER TIP

You may use different terminology and punctuation than the automatic captions use. Rather than edit each caption, you can change the template used for the captions.

*Original format*      *Your preference*

First, you need to find the text template document for the language you want, which is in your program files. Make a backup copy of it in case you want to return to the original template.  Then open the file in Notepad or Wordpad to edit it.

As you scroll through the document, it may seem overwhelming, but it is really quite simple.  If you look at the end of every line, you'll see there is one group for each type of software feature (button, tab, etc.).  Within each group, you can see the language to be used in the caption, shown in quotation marks.  **%s** indicates the name of the software feature, such as **Home**, as in the example above.

Make whatever changes you want to the text INSIDE the quotation marks at the end of each line, being very careful not to change anything else or delete the **%s**.

*Original format*

```
</Object>
<Object Name="PageTab" DefaultTemplate="Select the %s tab">
  <Event Name="LeftDBClick" Template="Double-click the %s tab"/>
  <Event Name="RightClick" Template="Right click the %s tab"/>
  <Event Name="RightDBClick" Template="Double-click the %s tab"/>
  <Event Name="MiddleDBClick" Template="Double-click the %s tab"/>
  <Event Name="KeyPress" Template="Press %s key"/>
```

*Your preference*

```
</Object>
<Object Name="PageTab" DefaultTemplate="click the %s tab.">
  <Event Name="LeftDBClick" Template="Double-click the %s tab."/>
  <Event Name="RightClick" Template="Right-click the %s tab."/>
  <Event Name="RightDBClick" Template="Double-click the %s tab."/>
  <Event Name="MiddleDBClick" Template="Double-click the %s tab."/>
  <Event Name="KeyPress" Template="Press the %s key."/>
```

Next, save the file.  You can then share this file with anyone else on your development team. They just need to copy the file over the one currently in their program files.

# Working With Images

## Add an Image to a Slide

**To add an image to a slide:**

1. Click the **Insert Image** button.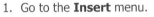

  —— or ——

1. Go to the **Insert** menu.
2. Select **Image**.

  —·— then ——

3. Find and select the image you want to use.
4. Click **Open**.

The image is now an object on the slide, which can be moved, resized, deleted, timed to audio, etc.

### TIME SAVER

You can also add an image by:

- Pasting it. For example, you can copy an image from a PowerPoint document or a Photoshop file and paste it onto a slide.

- Dragging and dropping it. Open up the folder with the image, and drag the image onto the slide.

| Insert | Modify | Project | Quiz | Audio | Video |
|---|---|---|---|---|---|
| New Slide | | | | Shift+Ctrl+V | |
| New Slide from | | | | ▸ | |
| Blank Slide | | | | Shift+Ctrl+J | |
| Question Slide... | | | | Shift+Ctrl+Q | |
| PowerPoint Slide... | | | | Shift+Ctrl+P | |
| Recording Slide... | | | | Ctrl+Alt+O | |
| Image Slide... | | | | Shift+Ctrl+Alt+S | |
| Animation Slide... | | | | Shift+Ctrl+N | |
| Quiz Master Slide | | | | ▸ | |
| Content Master Slide | | | | Ctrl+Alt+M | |
| Standard Objects | | | | ▸ | |
| Placeholder Objects | | | | ▸ | |
| Placeholder Slides | | | | ▸ | |
| Image... | | | | Shift+Ctrl+M | |
| Animation... | | | | Shift+Ctrl+A | |
| Text Animation | | | | Shift+Ctrl+X | |

# Image Properties

Many of the properties and options for an image, such as moving, resizing, and timing, are the same as for any other object type. Learn more about these settings in chapter 6. In this section, you will learn about some of the properties and options unique to an image.

## Image Pane

**Make the Selected Color Transparent**: You can select a single color and make it transparent in your image. This is useful for removing the white background in a photo or clipart.

### To make a color transparent:

1. Click the color swatch. **(A)**

2. Click the eyedropper icon in the pop-up menu that appears.

3. Click the color in the image that you want to make transparent.

**Reset to Original Size**: If you have resized the image, click this button to return it to its original size. This option does not undo cropping.

## Image Edit Pane

**Brightness**: Move the slider right or enter a positive number to brighten the image. Move the slider to the left or enter a negative number to darken the image.

**Sharpness**: Move the slider right or enter a positive number to better define the edges in the image. Move the slider left or enter a negative number to soften the edges.

**Contrast**: Move the slider right or enter a positive number to increase the contrast (make darks darker, lights lighter, and colors brighter). Move the slider left or enter a negative number to decrease the contrast.

**Alpha**: Alpha refers to the opacity of an image. 100% means fully opaque. Use a lower number if you want to make the image partially or fully transparent.

**Hue**: Move the slider left or right to change the colors of the image. For example, sliding it one way might make an image more blue and sliding it the other way might make it more red.

**Saturation**: Move the slider right or enter a positive number to increase the saturation (richness) of the colors. Move the slider left or enter a negative number to make them less saturated.

Original image          Image with the white
                        set as transparent

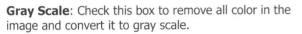

# Image Properties (cont'd)

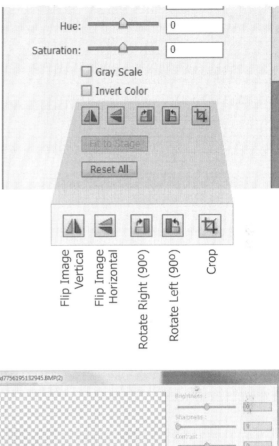

**Gray Scale**: Check this box to remove all color in the image and convert it to gray scale.

**Invert Color**: Check this box to change darks to lights, lights to darks, and all colors to their opposite on the color wheel. This gives the appearance of a film negative.

**Rotation Icons**: Click any of the four rotation options to flip or rotate the image.

 Transform Pane, p. 98

**Crop**: Click the **Crop** button to bring up the **Resize/Crop Image** dialog box.

Drag the crop frame handles and move the crop frame to indicate the part of the image you want to keep. That portion of the image will then be enlarged to fit the slide.

**Constrain Proportions**: If you are cropping the image, check this box to make the crop frame the same aspect ratio as the slide. Uncheck it if you want to be able to change the aspect ratio.

**Fit to Stage**: This option enlarges or shrinks the image to the largest size that will fit completely on the slide. Since the image and the slide may have different aspect ratios (height/width proportions), you may end up with empty space either above and below or to the left and right of the image.

**Reset All**: Click this button to return the image to its original settings. However, this does not undo any cropping.

Flip Image Vertical    Flip Image Horizontal    Rotate Right (90°)    Rotate Left (90°)    Crop

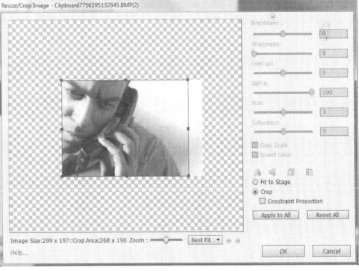

 **CAUTION**

If you crop out areas of your image, you cannot come back later and bring those areas back. If you want those parts of the image back, you either need to re-add the image or find the uncropped version in the **Library** and add it back.

 Library, p. 210

# Using Photoshop Files

In addition to using image types such as .gif and .png, you can import Photoshop .psd files. When you do, you can bring in each layer individually for more control, edit the file in Photoshop without leaving Captivate, and update the image when the source file changes.

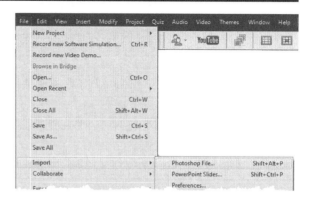

**To import a Photoshop file:**

1. Go to the **File** menu.
2. Select **Import**.
3. Select **Photoshop File**.
4. Find and select the file you want
5. Click the **Open** button.
6. Select the options you want.
7. Click **OK**.

## Photoshop Import Options

**Photoshop Layer Comps**: In Photoshop, you can create several versions of a design in the same file. These versions are called layer comps. If you have more than one comp in your file, select **Multiple**, and then select the comp you want from the drop-down menu.

**Scale According to Stage Size**: If you check this box, Captivate will resize the image to be as large as possible and still fit on the slide.

**Select Photoshop Layers to Import**: If your Photoshop file has layers, check or uncheck the box for each layer to indicate which ones you want to import. Each layer will appear as its own image in Captivate.

**Import As**: If your file has layers, but you want to import it all as a single image, select **Flattened Image**. This will bring it in as a single image without changing the layers of the underlying Photoshop file.

**Merge Layers**: If you don't want the image flattened but do want some of the layers combined, select the layers you want to merge (shift-click the layer names), and then click the **Merge Layers** button.

**To edit a Photoshop file from Captivate:**

1. Right-click the image in the **Library**.
2. Select **Edit with**.
3. Find and select Photoshop in your program files.
4. Click the **Open** button.
5. Make your changes in Photoshop.
6. Save your changes.

After you've done this once, **Edit with Adobe Photoshop** will appear on the right-click menu.

 **POWER TIP**

If you have the Adobe eLearning Suite installed, your imported .psd is linked to the underlying source file. A green dot next to the file in the **Library** means you are working with the most updated version. A red dot means there has been a change to the source file. A question mark means the link has been broken. Click the red dot or question mark to update or relink the file.

# Characters

Captivate offers photographic and illustrated characters, each in a variety of poses, that you can add to your projects. Characters are available in the following categories: business, casual, illustrated, and medicine.

## Insert a Character

**To insert a character:**

1. Go to the **Insert** menu.
2. Select **Characters**.
3. Select the category you want from the drop-down menu.
4. Select the character you want.
5. Select the pose you want.
6. Click **OK**.

 **DESIGN TIPS**

- The first time you use the characters, you will have to download the files using the link provided in a pop-up window.

- Use the links at the bottom of the **Characters** dialog box to browse for more characters, either for purchase or free.

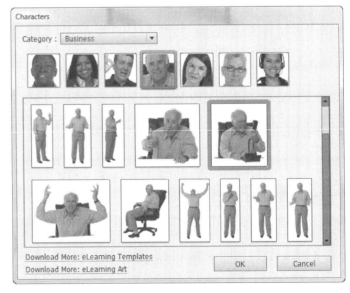

# Drawing Smart Shapes

The drawing tools in Captivate let you create basic shapes, such as rectangles, ovals, and lines, as well as special shapes, such as thought bubbles and flowchart elements.

Refer to chapter 6 for information on shape properties, such as fill and stroke colors.

## Draw a Smart Shape

**To draw a Smart Shape:**

1. Click the **Insert Smart Shape** button on the **Object** toolbar.
2. Select the shape type you want.
3. Drag your mouse to create the shape you want.

 **DESIGN TIPS**

- When drawing a polygon, do not click and drag as with the other shapes. Instead, click wherever you want to add a point.

- To use the same shape several times, hold the **Ctrl** key when you click the shape, which lets you use that shape until you press **Esc** or select another tool.

- For a perfect square or circle, press and hold the **Shift** key while drawing a rectangle or oval.

- When drawing a line or polygon, press and hold the **Shift** key while drawing to keep the lines at 45° increments.

- To change the points on a polygon, right-click the shape, and select **Edit Points**.

- To edit the points of a different shape type, first right-click and select **Convert to Freeform**. Then you can right-click and edit the points.

- To add text to a shape, double-click the shape, or right-click the shape, and select **Add Text**.

 **TIME SAVER**

If you need to make changes to your shape, you don't need to start from scratch. Right-click the shape, and select **Replace Smart Shape** to draw a different shape. For polygons, right-click the shape and select **Redraw Smart Shape** to draw it over. With both of these options, the timing, formatting, and other properties remain, which wouldn't be true if you deleted the shape and started over.

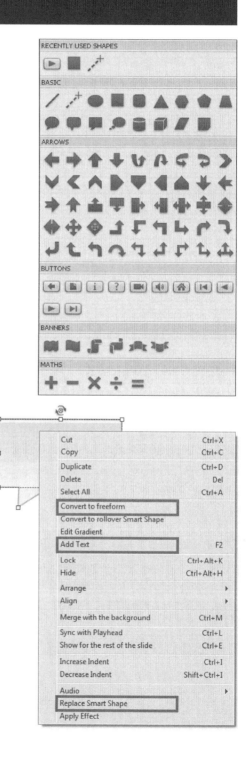

# Add a Highlight Box

A highlight box is a different way to add a rectangle. It is commonly used to add visual emphasis to parts of the screen being discussed.

**To add a highlight box:**

1. Click the **Insert Highlight Box** button on the **Object** toolbar.

2. Move and resize the highlight box over the area you want to highlight.

3. Format the highlight box in the **Properties** panel.

## Options: Fill Outer Area

By default, the inside of a highlight box is filled with your fill color. If you check this option, the *inside* of the box remains clear, and the *outside* of the box is filled, creating a more noticeable spotlight effect.

*Default inner fill*          *Fill Outer Area selected*

---

# DESIGN TIP

How do you decide if you want a rectangle or a highlight box?

**Rectangles:**

- Have more formatting options, such as gradients.
- Can contain text.
- Can have accessibility text.
- Can have the points edited.

**Highlight boxes:**

- Can have an inner fill or an outer fill.
- Can be added automatically to highlight the object you are clicking during a screen capture session.
- Can be used to create a quick job aid using the **Publish to Print** option, where just the part of the capture under the highlight box is exported to the print document.

 Recording Settings, p. 26
Publish to Print, p. 240

# CAUTION

Don't worry if your fill area is missing. Highlight boxes with an outer area fill do not show the fill color in edit mode. You can only see the fill when previewing or viewing the published movie.

# Adding Animations

Animations might come from: Adobe Flash or other software that outputs to Flash, an animated .gif that you create in Photoshop or purchase from stock clipart sources, or a published Captivate project. Animations are a great way to add specialized interactions, functionality, or visual effects.

When you add an animation *slide*, the animation becomes part of the background of the slide. This means that the animation cannot be resized, repositioned, or adjusted in the **Timeline**. However, when you add an animation to an existing slide, it becomes an object on that slide that can be edited, moved, etc.

 **DESIGN TIP**

Captivate comes with a gallery of Flash animations you can use in your projects. Look for the **Gallery** folder in your Adobe Captivate system files.

## Add an Animation Slide

**To add an animation slide:**

1. Go to the **Insert** menu.
2. Select **Animation Slide**.
3. Find and select the animation you want.
4. Click the **Open** button.

 **CAUTION**

- Make sure the frame rate of any inserted animations is the same frame rate as your project. Otherwise, you may get some unpredictable results. The default setting for Captivate projects is 30 frames per second, which can be changed in **Preferences** on the **Edit** menu.

- If you are creating a Flash file for use in Captivate, use embedded fonts instead of system fonts. Otherwise, your text may not appear properly.

- Flash files added to your project will not convert to HTML5 when you publish.

 **BRIGHT IDEA**

Even though the animation on an animation slide does not appear as its own object, you can still change or delete it. In the **Properties** panel for the slide, click the **Browse** button **(A)** to select a different animation or the **Delete** button **(B)** to delete the animation from the slide.

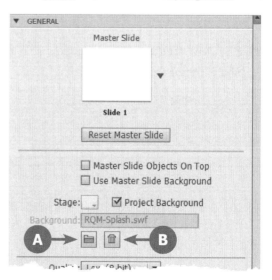

# Add an Animation

**To add an animation to a slide:**

1. Click the **Insert Animation** button on the **Object** toolbar.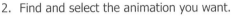

2. Find and select the animation you want.

3. Click the **Open** button.

## Animation Properties Pane

Animations placed as objects on slides have an extra section in the **Properties** panel for animation properties.

**Information**: Click the information icon **(A)** to see the Flash version, size, duration, and other information about the animation. (Information provided varies based on the type of animation being used.)

If you are using Captivate as part of the Adobe eLearning Suite, you have the following options available:

**Linkage**: This shows the link to the file.

**Update**: Click this button to update the animation if the linked file has changed.

**Source**: If your animation was created in Flash, you can link to the corresponding .fla file, making it quicker to edit the animation in Flash.

**Edit**: If the .fla file is shown in the **Source** field, you can click the **Edit** button to edit the .fla file.

**Alpha**: Reduce the percentage if you want the animation to become partially or fully transparent.

**Swap**: Click this button to replace the animation with another animation, either from the **Library** or via import.

## Timing Properties Pane

In addition to the standard options of **Display For** and **Appear After**, there are two additional options available for animations.

**Synchronize with Project**: Check this box to help synchronize your animation with the **Timeline** speed. It is helpful to try checking this box if your animation is not playing smoothly.

**Loop**: Check this box if you want the animation to continue from the beginning when it is finished, continuing to do so until the slide itself is finished.

 Timing Slide Objects, p. 111

## Add a Text Animation

Captivate comes with a wizard that lets you quickly create your own text-based animations.

**To create a text animation:**

1. Click the **Insert Text Animation**  button on the **Object** toolbar.

2. In the **Text Animation Properties** dialog box, enter your text in the **Text** field.

3. Format your text.

4. Click the **OK** button.

5. In the **Properties** panel, select the animation effect you want from the **Effect** drop-down list. **(A)**

**To make text and font formatting changes later:**

1. Click the **Properties** button in the **Properties** panel. **(B)**

2. Make your changes in the dialog box.

3. Click **OK**.

## DESIGN TIPS

- Make each individual letter appear faster or slower by changing the value in the **Delay** field.  This is the number of seconds between each letter.

- Check the **Loop** box if you want the animation to play over and over until the end of the object's time in the **Timeline**.

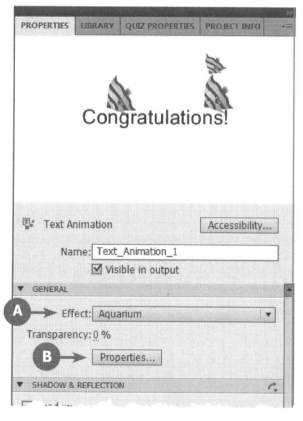

# Zoom Areas

Zoom areas take a portion of your slide and magnify it for the student. For example, if you are doing a screen recording and want to emphasize a certain set of tools on screen, you can use a zoom area to magnify that section of the screen.

## Insert a Zoom Area

**To add a zoom area:**

1. Click the **Insert Zoom Area** button on the **Object** toolbar.

2. Move and resize the **Zoom Source** box over the area you want to magnify.

3. Move and resize the **Zoom Destination** box to the position and magnification you want.

*Objects as they first appear on the slide*

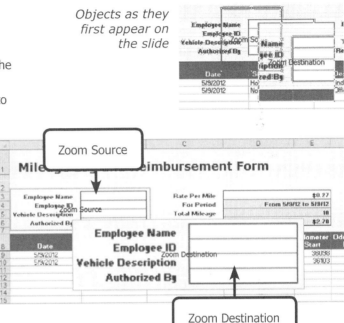

## BRIGHT IDEA

Use the **Timeline** to adjust when the zoom area appears and disappears. In addition, you can control how fast or slow it zooms in by clicking and dragging the divider line in the object placeholder. Drag it to the left for a faster zoom or to the right for a slower zoom.

Timing Slide Objects, p. 111

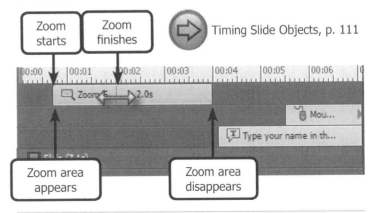

# Equations

If you are teaching scientific or mathematical content, you can now build custom equations right from within Captivate. The equation utility is made by MathMagic. From the **Help** menu in the equation editor, you can go to the MathMagic website, which provides some tips on how to use their software.

## Build an Equation

**To build an equation:**

1. Go to the **Insert** menu.
2. Select **Equation**.
3. In the MathMagic editor, use the buttons along the top to build your equation.
4. Go to the **File** menu.
5. Select **Save**.
6. Go to the **File** menu.
7. Select **Exit**.

 **BRIGHT IDEAS**

- Use the buttons in the first row to create structure placeholders, such as brackets or superscripts.

- In the placeholders, either type your values or use the bottom row of buttons for special symbols, such as sigma.

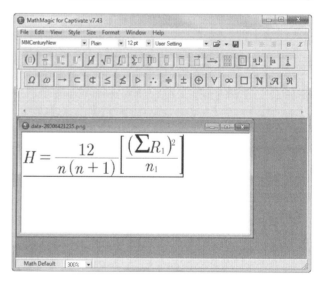

$$H = \frac{12}{n(n+1)} \left[ \frac{(\sum R_1)^2}{n_1} \right]$$

# Audio and Video

## Introduction

Audio can be used to add voice-over narration, add fun or dramatic effects with sounds, or set a certain tone or mood with music.  In Captivate, you can add audio files to individual objects, individual slides, or the project as a whole.

Audio can be either imported or recorded directly in Captivate.  If you are recording screen captures, you can either record in Captivate while you capture or add it after the capture is finished.  You can import .mp3 and .wav files into Captivate.

Captivate also provides useful audio tools, such as text-to-speech, which adds automated narration based on the text you enter, as well as closed captions for those who are unable to hear your audio (for technical, environmental, or physical reasons).

In chapter 6, you'll learn how to time individual elements to audio, so that the right text, image, or other object appears exactly when it should.

In addition to audio, you can add video files to your projects.  For example, you might want to introduce a course on a new policy with a video introduction from the CEO.

### In This Chapter

- Working With Audio
- Closed Captioning
- Adding Video

# Notes

# Working With Audio

## Import Audio to the Background

Background audio plays across slides—in the background. Even if you have background audio, you can still have slide-level audio, such as narration. For example, this is how you would add background music to your project.

**To import audio to the background:**

1. Click the **Audio** menu.
2. Select **Import to**.
3. Click **Background**.
4. Navigate to and select the file you want.
5. Click **Open**.
6. Set the background audio options you want. **(A)**
7. Click the **Save** button.
8. Click the **Close** button.

### Background Audio Options

**Fade In/Fade Out:** If you want the background audio to fade in or out, enter the duration of each fade, in seconds.

**Loop Audio:** By default, this box is checked, meaning the audio will play over and over until the movie ends. Uncheck it if you want the audio to play only once.

**Stop Audio at End of Project:** By default, this box is checked, meaning that when the movie is over, the audio will stop. Uncheck it if you want the audio to continue playing until the window is closed.

**Adjust Background Audio Volume on Slides With Audio:** By default, background audio will lower to 50% volume on any slide with its own audio (such as voice-over narration). Uncheck this box if you don't want the audio automatically reduced, or use the slider to change how much to reduce the volume.

## DESIGN TIP

Just because you can doesn't mean you should! Use background audio with care as it can easily overpower or distract from your instructional goals.

## TIME SAVER

Captivate comes with music and sound effects in the Gallery!

OS (C:) ▸ Program Files ▸ Adobe ▸ Adobe Captivate 7 x64 ▸ Gallery ▸ Sound ▸

## Import Audio to an Object

You can add audio to individual objects such as a specific caption. For example, you can add a cheering sound effect to the correct feedback caption in a practice activity.

**To import audio to an object:**

1. Select the object you want to import the audio to.
2. Click the **Audio** menu.
3. Select **Import to**.
4. Click **Object**.
5. Find and select the file you want.
6. Click **Open**.
7. Click **Yes** to extend the object length, if needed.
8. Click **Close**.

## CAUTION

You can still adjust the length of the object in the **Timeline**. However, if you make the object shorter than the audio, the audio will get cut off.

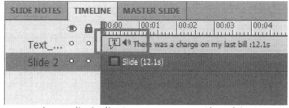

*An audio indicator appears on the object in the **Timeline**.*

# Import Audio to One or More Slides

## To import audio to one or more slides:

1. Select the slide you want to import audio to, or select the first slide if the audio is for the whole movie.

2. Click the **Audio** menu.

3. Select **Import to**.

4. Click **Slide**.

5. Navigate to and select the file you want.

6. Click **Open**.

7. Choose how to import the audio. **(A)**

8. Click **OK**.

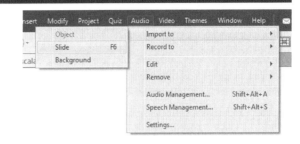

## Audio Import Options

The dialog box in step 7 only appears if the imported audio is longer than the slide you are importing it into.  These three options determine how that audio is distributed.

### Show the slide for the same amount of time as the length of the audio file

Use this option if you are importing audio for a single slide and you want to make the slide as long as the audio.

### Distribute the audio file over several slides

Use this option if you are importing audio for more than one slide, such as the whole movie.  This brings up a dialog box that lets you split up the audio across the slides.

The waveform for the audio appears in the **Timeline**.

### Retain current slide duration and distribute the audio files over several slides

Use this option if you are importing audio for more than one slide, but you want Captivate to split up the audio based on the current slide lengths.

## DESIGN TIP

Which option is best? Generally, when you record voice-over for computer simulations, it is best to record the entire script in one file. This tends to take less time and create a more natural tone and flow than trying to record each slide's audio as a separate file.  Then, all you need to do is add the one audio file to the first slide and select the second import option, which lets you chop up the audio across the slides.

# Distribute Audio Across Slides

If you import audio for several slides as a single file, you then need to distribute it across the slides. If you select the **Distribute the audio...** option when importing, the distribution dialog box appears automatically. Otherwise, you can go to the **Audio** menu to bring up the dialog box.

**To distribute audio across multiple slides:**

1. Click the **Audio** menu.
2. Select **Edit**.
3. Select **Project**.
4. Click **Yes** in the warning dialog box (if appropriate).
6. Position the playhead in the waveform where you want the next slide to start (play the audio or click in the waveform).
7. Click the **Start Next Slide** button.
8. Click and drag slide dividers to adjust the position.
9. Click the **Save** button.
10. Click the **Close** button.

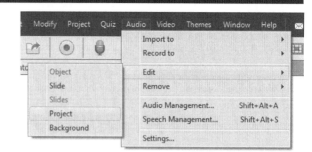

 **CAUTION**

Pay attention to the warning in step 4. If you have closed captions timed to audio, continuing with this process will remove the timing. It is best to time your closed captions at the end of production. After that, use only the slide-level audio editing.

> If you edit the project audio, all closed captions in the project will be disabled and the timing information of the captions will be lost. However, after editing the audio, you can:
>
> \* Enable the closed captions by selecting the Audio CC check boxes in the Slide Notes panel.
>
> \* Adjust the timing of the captions by clicking the Closed Captioning tab in the Slide Audio dialog box (Audio > Edit > Slide).
>
> Do you want to continue?

 Closed Captions, p. 84

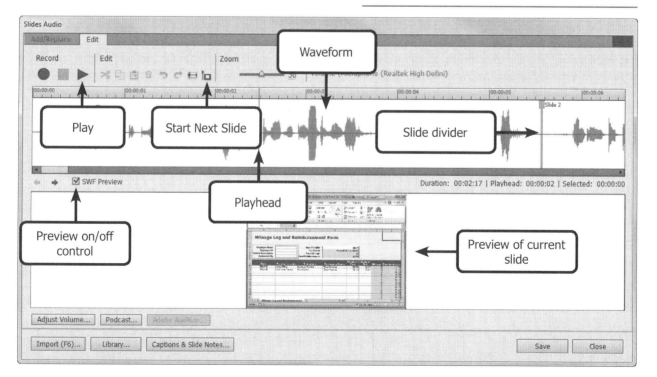

# Configure Audio Compression

The audio settings apply to the entire published file, whether you import the audio or record it in Captivate.

**To configure audio compression:**

1. Click the **Audio** menu.
2. Select **Settings**.
3. Select the compression level you want in the **Bitrate** section.
4. Click **OK**.

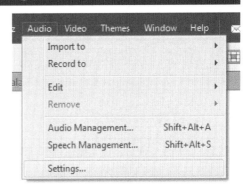

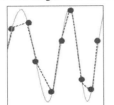

## BRIGHT IDEA

What is bitrate?

The bitrate determines how many points along the sound wave curve are captured in a digital file. It is measured in kbps (kilobits per second).

The more points captured, the higher the quality and the larger the file size.

| Lower bitrate | Higher bitrate |

**Constant Bitrate** captures the same number of points for the entire project. **Variable Bitrate** adjusts the number of points based on what is happening in the audio. For example, variable bitrate uses fewer points during pauses than during spoken words. For voice-over, variable bitrate is likely to give you the same quality as constant bitrate, but at a lower file size.

For constant bitrate, the 48 to 96 range offers a good balance between compression and quality.

When you record audio in Captivate, it records at a high quality. The settings you choose here determine how it is compressed when you publish. The original high-quality recording is not affected, meaning you can come back and change your mind about these settings later.

## CAUTION

Make sure you test the audio settings by publishing your file and testing it on a target computer. A small change in bitrate can significantly affect quality and file size, so make sure you have the right balance.

# Calibrate Audio Input

Before recording audio in Captivate, you will want to calibrate your microphone for the best volume levels. You will be prompted to do this the first time you record audio per session (once for every time you launch Captivate), or you can calibrate it yourself at any time.

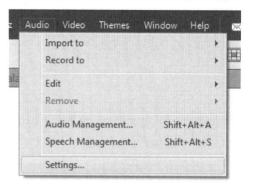

**To calibrate audio input:**

1. Click the **Audio** menu.

2. Select **Settings**.

3. Select the microphone you want to use (if you have more than one available). **(A)**

4. Click the **Calibrate Input** button. **(B)**

5. Click the **Auto calibrate** button. **(C)**

6. Speak into the microphone until you see the **Input Level OK** message. **(D)**

7. Click **OK**.

## POWER TIP

You can manually control the calibration. Instead of clicking **Auto calibrate**, click the **Record** button, and record some audio. Click the **Stop** button, and then the **Play** button to listen to it.

From there, you can adjust the **Pre-amplifier value** to get the volume you want during recording.

- **1** means no change in audio.

- Less than **1** means the recording volume will be reduced.

- Higher than **1** (up to **10**) means the recording volume will be increased.

## BRIGHT IDEA

You will want to calibrate your audio every time you sit down to record audio. However, if you are recording more than one project in a sitting, you don't need to calibrate for each file you work on.

# Record Audio to a Slide or Object

**To record audio to a slide or project:**

1. Select the slide or object you want to record audio to.
2. Click the **Audio** menu.
3. Select **Record to.**
4. Select **Slide** or **Object**.
5. Click the **Record** button.
6. Speak into your microphone.
7. Click the **Stop** button.
8. Click the **Save** button.
9. Click the **Close** button.

## BRIGHT IDEAS

- If you added your script in the **Slide Notes** panel, click the **Captions & Slide Notes** button **(A)** to see them while you record.
- If you are recording to a slide, you can click the **Record Audio** button on the **Main Options** toolbar.
- If you'd like to record system audio instead of narration, click the **System Audio** button before recording.

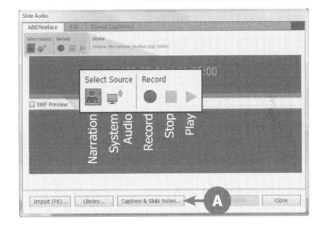

# Record Audio Across Slides

**To record audio across several slides:**

1. Click the **Audio** menu.
2. Select **Record to**.
3. Select **Slides**.
4. Indicate the range of slides you want to record.
5. Click the **OK** button.
6. Click the **Record** button.
7. Speak into your microphone for the first slide.
8. Click the **Stop** button.
9. Click the **Next Slide** button. **(B)**
10. Repeat steps 6-9 until all the slides are done.
11. Click the **Save** button.
12. Click the **Close** button.

# Record Audio While Capturing

If you want to record your narration while capturing a software simulation, you can set that up in your initial recording settings. Simply select the microphone you want to use from the **Audio** drop-down menu. Then, speak into your microphone while you are capturing.

 Recording Settings: p. 22

 **CAUTION**

Recording audio while you capture may seem like a time-saver, but in the long run, it may not be. It can be difficult to perform the steps and record the narration properly at the same time, meaning you may need several "takes" before getting it right. In addition, the editing process may take longer if you have to add or delete slides, change the script, etc. This option is best when you want a quick, casual sound. Add a scripted voice-over later if you want a more polished sound.

## BRIGHT IDEAS

### Setting up the Recording Environment

**Microphone:** Get the best results from a USB, unidirectional, headset microphone with a foam windscreen.

- The headset helps to keep the microphone a uniform distance from the speaker's mouth for a more consistent sound.
- The unidirectional feature helps eliminate background noise.
- The windscreen controls the popping and hissing sounds that come from letters such as "p" and "s."

### Environment:

- Record in a room without a lot of hard, reflective surfaces such as large windows, tile floors, and metal or glass furniture. Instead, pick smaller rooms with carpet, curtains, and upholstered furniture.
- Record away from florescent lighting, electronic equipment, and air vents, which can cause background noise.
- To create a makeshift sound studio, glue "egg crate" foam sheets to a three-sided presentation board and prop it up in front of the speaker.

### Tips for Audio Quality

- Before you spend a lot of time recording, timing, importing, etc., do a quick test of all the settings. Create a single-slide course, record the audio, publish it, and play it. Adjust your tone, compression settings, and other elements until you are happy with the results. Then, proceed to record the rest of the audio.
- Listen to your audio using both your computer speakers and headphones. You may notice different quality issues using each method. Consider what your students will use to help you decide if you are happy with the audio quality.
- If audio quality is extremely important to you, consider recording it outside of Captivate and then importing it. Software made specifically for audio recording (such as Audacity or Wavepad) often provide useful noise filters and more precise editing control.

# Edit Audio

**To edit audio:**

1. Click the **Audio** menu.
2. Select **Edit**.
3. Select the scope of the audio you want to edit. **(A)**
4. Make your changes in the audio editor. (See below.)
5. Click the **Save** button.
6. Click the **Close** button.

**To change the break between slides:**

1. Click and drag the **Slide Divider** to the point where you want the break. **(B)**

**To delete a section of audio:**

1. Click and drag your mouse in the waveform to select the audio you want to remove.
2. Click the **Delete** button.

**To cut or copy and paste audio:**

1. Select the audio you want.
2. Click the **Cut** or **Copy** button.
3. Click in the waveform where you want the new audio to go, or select the audio you want to replace.
4. Click the **Paste** button.

## CAUTION

If you have closed captions, editing the *project* audio will delete the timing of your closed captions.

## BRIGHT IDEAS

Select **Slides** and **Project** if you want to adjust the breaks between slides.

To edit the audio for one slide, just double-click the audio item in the **Timeline**.

You can edit audio in Adobe Audition right from the **Slides Audio** window **(C)**, with Soundbooth, or with the software of your choice via the **Library**.

Library, p. 210

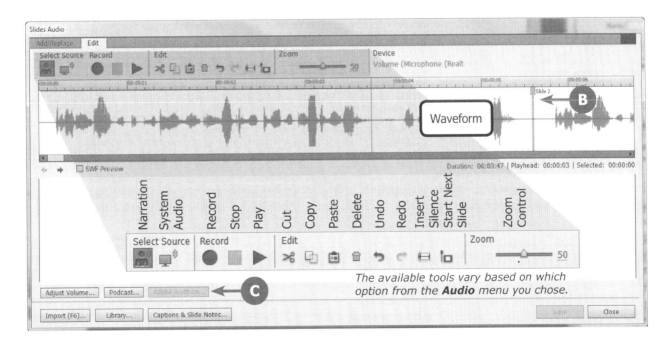

The available tools vary based on which option from the **Audio** menu you chose.

# Edit Audio (cont'd)

**To adjust volume:**

1. In the waveform, select the audio you want to adjust.
2. Click the **Adjust Volume** button. (See previous page.)
3. Click and drag the **Volume** slider up to increase volume or down to decrease volume.
4. Click the **OK** button.

## Audio Processing Options

**Normalize:** Use this option to have Captivate automatically adjust the audio to maintain a consistent volume between slides.

**Dynamics:** Use this option to have Captivate manage volume variations based on your settings. **Ratio** determines how loud to make the most quiet sections (**2** means the volume would double). **Threshold** determines the level of sound that shouldn't be amplified, such as background noise.

**To insert silence:**

1. Click in the waveform where you want the silence.
2. Click the **Insert Silence** button. (See previous page.)
3. Enter the amount of silence you want.
4. Select the location for the silence if you want it at the start or end of the audio instead of at the **Playhead** position.
5. Click the **OK** button.

**To record additional audio:**

1. Click in the waveform where you want the new audio.
2. Click the **Record** button. (See previous page.)
3. Speak into the microphone.
4. Click the **Stop** button.

**To import a new audio file into the waveform:**

1. Click in the waveform where you want the new audio.
2. Click the **Import** button. (See previous page.)
3. Find and select the audio you want.
4. Click the **Open** button.

**To import an audio file from the Library:**

1. Click the **Library** button. (See previous page.)
2. Select the file you want.
3. Click the **OK** button.

 The Library, p. 210

 **BRIGHT IDEA**

One common reason to insert silence is because the length of the slide is longer than the length of the audio. For example, you might try to place a slide break where the playhead is, but the break actually shows up a little bit later.

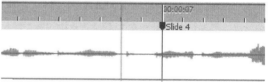

Or, you try to drag a slider to the left, and it won't go any farther.

In both cases, you can insert silence to make the audio for the slide (slide 3 in these examples) longer to fit the timing better.

## Export Audio

Exporting audio can be useful if you want to keep a backup of your audio or want to use it somewhere else.

**To export audio:**

1. Click the **Audio** menu.
2. Select **Audio Management**.
3. Select the slides whose audio you want to export.
4. Check the boxes for the file types you want (**MP3** and/or **WAVE**).
5. Click the **Export** button.
6. Find and select the location where you want to save the audio.
7. Click the **OK** button.
8. Click the **OK** button again.

### BRIGHT IDEA

You can also export the audio for the entire project as a single .wav or .mp3 file.  Go to the **Slides Audio** dialog box for the whole project, and click the **Podcast** button.

## Other Audio Management Options

You are able to perform several other tasks from the **Advanced Audio Management** dialog box.

- **Play**: Select an audio file in the list at the top, and click the **Play** button.
- **Remove**: Select an audio file in the list at the top, and click the **Remove** button.
- **Update**: Click the **Update** button to update the audio file from the **Library**.
- **Add Closed Captioning**: Click the **Closed Caption** button to bring up the **Audio Editor** to the **Closed Caption** tab.
- **Edit**: Click the **Edit** button to bring up the **Audio Editor** to the **Edit** tab.

Closed Captions, p. 84

## Remove Audio

There are many ways to remove audio from a slide:

- Right-click the slide thumbnail, select **Audio**, and then **Remove**.

- Click the audio icon under the slide thumbnail, and click **Remove**. **(A)**

- Right-click the audio in the **Timeline**, and select **Remove**. **(B)**

- Click the **Remove Audio** button in the **Audio Properties** pane. **(C)**

- Go to the **Audio** menu, select **Remove**, and then **Slide**.

- Go to the **Advanced Audio Management** dialog box, select the audio, and click the **Remove** icon.

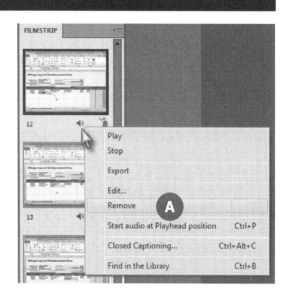

### TIME SAVER

You can also *edit* audio from all of these locations.

## Change Settings in the Audio Pane

The **Audio** pane in the **Properties** panel has a few important slide-level settings.

- **Fade In/Fade Out**: Adjust the number if you want your audio to fade in or out—used more often with music than with narration.

- **Loop Audio**: Check this box if you want the audio to continue playing until the slide is done playing, even if it means playing the audio more than once. Otherwise, the audio will play only once. This is used more often with music than with narration.

- **Stop Background Audio**: If you are using background audio, check this box if you do not want it to play on this particular slide.

- **Edit Audio**: Click this button to go to the **Audio Editor**.

- **Remove Audio**: Click this button to remove the audio for the slide.

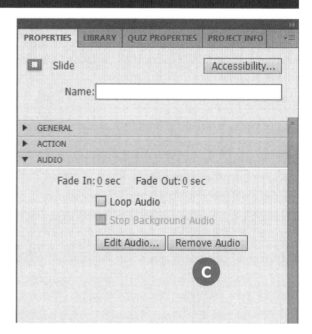

# Create Audio With Text-to-Speech

To use the text-to-speech (TTS) converter, you must first install the conversion software, which is available on your installation CD, if you have one, or from the Adobe website.

**To convert your text to speech:**

1. Add your text in the **Slide Notes** panel for each slide.
2. Check the **Text-to-Speech** box next to each slide note you want to convert. **(A)**
3. Click the **Text-to-Speech** button.
4. Select the voice option you want from the **Speech Agent** drop-down menu.
5. Click the **Generate Audio** button.
6. Click the **Save** button
7. Click the **Close** button.

Slide Notes, p. 39

## CAUTION

If you change the text in your slide notes, the changes are NOT automatically updated in your audio. You need to regenerate the audio anytime you make changes.

## TIME SAVERS

If you'd like to generate audio for the whole project at once, go to the **Audio** menu, and select **Speech Management**. You'll see the same dialog box, but with the selected slide notes from all of your slides.

You can add/delete/edit captions right from the **Speech Management** dialog box without having to go back to the **Slide Notes** panel.

Even if you plan to use "live" narrators for the final product, consider using TTS for early drafts. That way, you can easily make edits during revision cycles, recording the final narration at the very end.

# Closed Captioning

To help make your projects accessible to people who cannot hear your audio, you can convert your slide notes into closed captions that are timed to the audio.

To set up closed captions, you must first have slide notes and audio for your slides. (Closed captioning options are disabled on slides without audio.)

## CAUTION

If you are using closed captions, be sure to enable the **Closed Caption** button on the playbar, which is DISABLED by default. If this button is not on the playbar, your students will not be able to see the closed captions.

 Playback Controls, p. 226

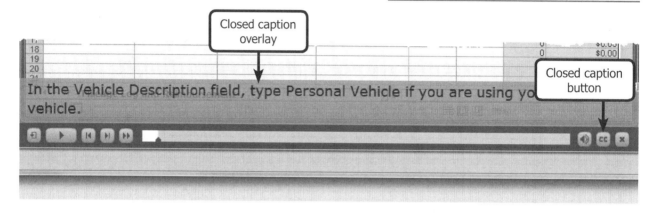

Closed caption overlay

Closed caption button

In the Vehicle Description field, type Personal Vehicle if you are using your own vehicle.

## Create Closed Captions

**To convert your slide notes to closed captions:**

1. Add your text in the **Slide Notes** panel for each slide.

2. Check the **Audio CC** box next to each slide note you want to convert. **(A)**

3. Click the **Closed Captioning** button. **(B)**

4. If you have more than one caption per slide, drag the caption markers in the waveform to where you want each caption to begin.

5. Click the **Save** button.

6. Click the **Close** button.

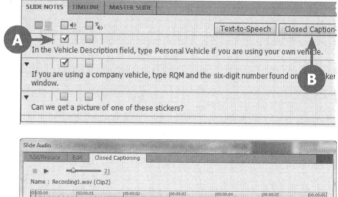

Caption marker

# Change Closed Caption Settings

**To change the closed captioning settings:**

1. Click the **Closed Captioning** button in the **Slide Notes** panel. (B on previous page)

2. Click the **CC Project Settings** button.

3. Change the settings you want.

4. Click the **OK** button.

## Settings

**Lines**: Enter a number or drag your mouse to indicate the maximum number of lines that will show at any one time. This determines the height of the closed caption overlay area.

**Background**: Click the color swatch to pick the color and transparency of the overlay area.

**Font Settings**: Select the font family, size, and color for the closed caption text.

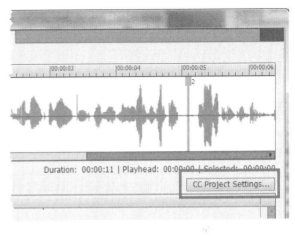

### DESIGN TIP

Consider the space used by the overlay when taking your initial captures. Avoid showing anything important in the space that will be covered by the captions.

# Adding Video

Video is a great way to provide demonstrations of procedures, interviews with experts, scenarios, or visual effects.

Captivate accepts .flv, .f4v, .avi, .mp4, .mov, and .3gp movie types.

You can also use video deployed to a web server, Flash Video Streaming Service, or Flash Media Server.

There are two ways to add video to your projects: multi-slide synchronized video or event video. Both options have their advantages, as listed in the table.

| Use the multi-slide method when you want: | Use the event video method when you want: |
| --- | --- |
| • The video to be distributed over several slides.<br>• The video in the **Library**.<br>• The video on the slide or in the Table of Contents.<br>• Closed captioning.<br>• The video to play in sync with the **Timeline**. | • More than one video on the slide.<br>• Playback controls on the video.<br>• The video to play separately from the **Timeline**. |

## Insert a Multi-Slide Synchronized Video

**To insert a multi-slide synchronized video:**

1. Click the **Insert Video** button on the **Object** toolbar.

2. Select **Multi-Slide Synchronized Video**.
3. Click the **Browse** button.
4. Find and select the file you want.
5. Click **Open**.
6. Select the **Video Type** you want. (See below.)
7. From the **Show Video On** menu, select **Stage** to put the video on the slide or **TOC** to put it in the project's table of contents.
8. Select the timing option you want. (See below.)
9. Click **OK**.

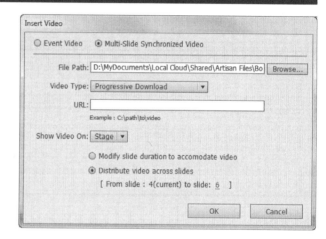

**Video Type:**

By default, video is played via progressive download. If you would instead prefer to host the video on a streaming server, select either **Streaming** or **Flash Video Streaming Service** from the drop-down menu, and then enter the URL for the host location.

**Timing Options:**

- Select **Modify slide duration...** if you want to extend the slide to be as long as the video.
- Select **Distribute video...** if you want to split the video among several slides, based on the current slide durations. For example, a 30-second video might be split across a 10-second slide and a 15-second slide, with the rest going on the following 20-second slide.
- You can go back later and adjust how the video is distributed. (See next page.)

 **POWER TIP**

Captivate can *publish* to YouTube formats, but can you *put* a YouTube video in your project? Yes! A YouTube widget is available as one of the Smart Interactions.

Smart Interactions, p. 115

**DESIGN TIP**

Once the video is on the slide, you can move, resize, rotate, and adjust timing just as with any other object.

# Change Slide Distribution

Whether you choose to extend the slide duration to match the video length or choose to distribute the video across several slides, you can edit how the slide video is distributed. (This option is only available when you add a multi-slide synchronized video.)

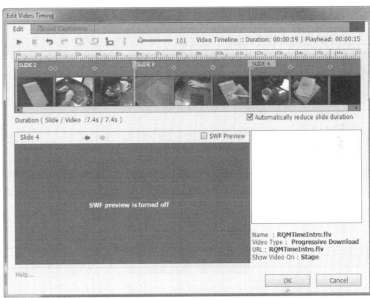

**To change how the video is distributed:**

1. Go to the **Video** menu.
2. Select **Edit Video Timing**.
3. Drag the orange slide markers where you want the slide breaks to happen.
4. Click the **OK** button.

## BRIGHT IDEAS

- Don't worry about adding Flash video to a project that will be viewed on an iPad. If you publish to HTML5, the video is converted to .mp4 format.

- Video closed captions work very much like audio closed captions. Click the **Closed Captioning** tab to enter and time the captions.

Closed Captioning, p. 84

# Insert an Event Video

**To insert an event video from a file:**

1. Click the **Insert Video** button on the **Object** toolbar.

2. Select **Event Video**.

3. Click the **Browse** button.

4. Find and select the file you want.

5. Click **Open**.

6. Click **OK**.

**To insert an event video from a server:**

1. Click the **Insert Video** button.

2. Select **Event Video**.

3. Click the **Already deployed...** radio button.

4. In the **URL** field, enter the web address of the video file.

5. Click **OK**.

---

**Insert Video**

◉ Event Video    ○ Multi-Slide Synchronized Video

Where is your video file?

◉ On your Computer

File Path: [                    ] [ Browse... ]

Examples: C:\path\to\video
server\path\to\video

○ Already deployed to a web server, Flash Video Streaming Service, or Flash Media Server

URL: [                    ]

Examples: http://myDomain.com/directory/video
rtmp://myDomain.com/directory/videostream

[ OK ]    [ Cancel ]

---

## BRIGHT IDEA

If you add video *other* than .flv or .f4v, the files will to be converted to .flv format using Adobe Media Encoder (which is included with Captivate).

**AME Conversion**

The video you have selected is not a Flash file. Adobe Captivate will convert it to FLV or F4V format using Adobe Media Encoder (AME) v5.5.The path of the converted file will be:

C:\Users\Diane Elkins\Documents\PleaseSendBackup.flv    [ Change Path... ]

Do you want to continue launching AME for conversion?

[ Yes ]    [ No ]

When it is done converting, select the insert option you want from the **Progress Indicator** pane.

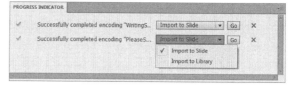

# Event Video Properties

Event video comes with special properties unique to this type of video. Standard object properties are covered in chapter 6.

## Video Type

Use this menu if you want to change how the video is hosted. For example, you may want to use progressive download during the development cycles, but then move the video to a streaming server once the course is ready to go live. Select the video type you want from the drop-down menu. Additional fields will appear based on the type you choose.

## Detect Size

Click this button to adjust the size of the video to be at 100% of its original size.

## Auto Play

By default, the video does not start until the student clicks the **Play** button on the video controls. Check this box if you want the video to play automatically.

## Auto Rewind

Check this box if you want the video to go back to its starting point when it is finished.

## Skin

The skin is the video control toolbar that appears underneath the video. You can select a different look for the controls (or choose not to have one) from this drop-down menu.

## Pause Slide Till End of Video

Because the video is not synchronized to the slide, your slide might finish before the video does. Keep this box checked if you want the slide to pause until the video is done. Uncheck it if you want the slide to finish even if the video is not done.

# Video Management

**Video Management** (available from the **Video** menu), lets you perform a number of functions:

- **Edit the video timing**: Select the video, and click the **Edit Session** icon. **(A)**

- **Delete a video**: Select the video, and click the **Delete Session** icon. **(B)**

- **Move the video to the Table of Contents**: Select the video, and then select **TOC** from the **Show Video on** menu.

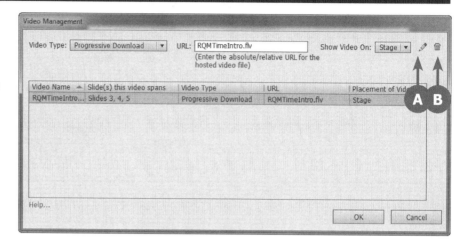

 **DESIGN TIP**

Put the video in the table of contents (TOC) when you want the video to be the secondary visual. For example, you may have an expert explaining a process in the TOC while the main slide area shows a diagram of that process.

**CAUTION**

If you put a video in the table of contents, make sure you enable the TOC for your project.

 Table of Contents, p. 228

# Update Project Video

If you make changes to the video, you can update your project to include the most recent version of the video.

**To update project video:**

1. Right-click the video in the **Library**.
2. Select **Update**.
3. Select the video you want to update.
4. Click the **Update** button.

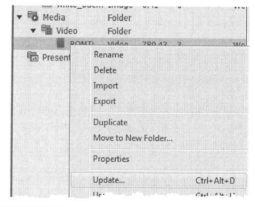

# Managing Objects

## Introduction

Every object has properties—every caption, every graphic, every highlight box.  This chapter focuses on the properties that are common to most object types, whether sizing and rotating, changing colors, or applying styles.

In addition to these common properties, many object types have additional properties unique to that type of object.  For example, captions let you choose fonts and character formatting.  You can learn more about these unique properties in the chapter for that object type, such as:

- Captions and other content objects, ch. 4
- Audio and video, ch. 5
- Interactive objects, ch. 7
- Questions & quizzes, ch. 10

In this chapter, you'll also learn about ways to work more efficiently with objects, such as with layering, alignment, and grouping tools.

## In This Chapter

- Object Properties Panel
- Colors
- Managing Objects
- Styles
- Effects
- Timing

# Notes

# Object Properties

You can find an object's properties by selecting the object in the work area or in the **Timeline**. The **Properties** panel appears on the right side of the interface by default. If you do not see the **Properties** panel, go to the **Window** menu, and select it.

## Object Information

### Accessibility Button

To help make your course accessible to visually-impaired students using screen readers, click this button to add a text description of the object, known as alt text. Alt text is read to the student by the screen reader.

When the **Auto Label** box is checked in the pop-up window **(A)**, the name of the object is read to the screen reader. Uncheck this box if you want to add your own text in the fields provided.

The accessibility text will only appear in your published movie if you enable accessibility for the project.

 Accessibility, p. 245

### Name

In this field, you can enter a name for each object. This makes it easier to identify an object in the **Timeline** or when selecting the object from a drop-down menu. It also serves as the alt text for an object if the **Auto Label** box is checked (see above).

### Visible in Output

By default, all objects are visible. Uncheck this box if you want the object to be initially invisible. For example, you may create a button the student clicks to show the object.

 Show/Hide Actions, p. 124

### Use as Button

You can turn a shape into an interactive object by checking this box. When you do, the **Action** and **Options** panes appear where you can configure the interactivity.

 Action and Options Panes, p. 133

### Style

The bottom half of the options in this section refer to object styles. Styles let you group formatting elements and apply them all at once.

 Object Styles, p. 104

# Fill & Stroke Pane

The **Fill & Stroke** pane is available on smart shapes, highlight boxes, rollover objects, and hot spot areas.

**Fill:** Click the swatch to select the color to fill the shape.

**Fill Alpha (A):** Enter a percentage for the transparency for the fill color.  0% = transparent / 100% = opaque

**Stroke:** Click the swatch to select the color you want to outline the shape.

**Width:** Use the slider or enter the point size you want for the width of the outline.

**Style**: Smart shapes let you select the style of the outline, including **Solid**, **Dash**, **Dot**, **DashDot** and **DashDotDot**.

**Start and End**: With lines, you can choose what the ends look like.  Options include **None**, **Square**, **Round**, **Diamond**, and **Arrow**.

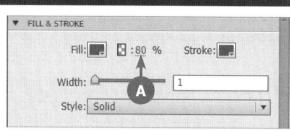

*Rectangle options*

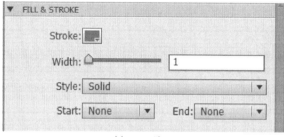

*Line options*

# Colors

Whether you are selecting a fill color, stroke color, slide background color, or any other color in Captivate, the color palette gives you many different ways to select your color.

**Hexadecimal Value (A)**

If you know the six-digit (hexadecimal) value for the color you want, you can enter it in the text field.  Click and drag the text field to find a color similar to the one entered.

**Pre-Set Colors (B)**

Click any of the pre-set colors in the palette.

**Recent Colors (C)**

Click any of the recently-used colors to select that color.

**Pick Color/Eyedropper  (D)**

To match a color somewhere on the screen, click the **Pick Color** button, and click on the color you want to match.

**Color Picker (E)**

If you click the **Color Picker** button, a new window appears with additional color choices.

- Use the slider and the color area to mix any color.
- Enter HSB (hue, saturation, and brightness) values.
- Enter RGB (red, green, blue) values.
- Enter the six-digit (hexadecimal) value.

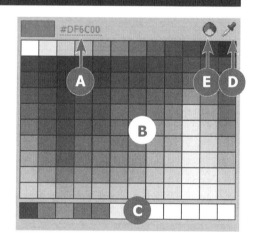

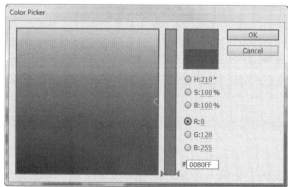

# Color Gradients

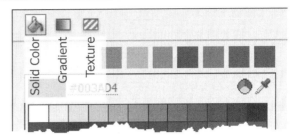

With some fill color palettes (such as for slide backgrounds and smart shapes), you have the option of using a gradient. Click the **Gradient** button at the top to change the palette to show your gradient options.

**Pre-Made Gradients**: Click an icon in the top row of swatches to use one of the pre-made gradients. **(A)**

**Direction**: Click any of the swatches to change the direction of the gradient (horizontal, vertical, diagonal, etc.). **(B)**

**Custom Gradients:** If you have saved any custom gradients, click the swatch to apply that gradient. **(C)**

**Gradient Bar:** Use the gradient bar to customize an existing gradient or create your own. **(D)**

- Click an existing color stop **(I)** to change the color for that stop.

- Click and drag a color stop to change where that color starts/stops.

- Drag a color stop away from the gradient bar to delete it.

- Click below the gradient bar to add a new color stop.

**Linear Gradient and Radial Gradient:** Click either of these icons to indicate the type of gradient you want. **(E)**

**Reverse Colors:** Click this icon if you want the colors on the left to move to the right and vice-versa. **(F)**

**Add to Custom Gradients:** If you create a gradient you want to use again, click this icon to add it to the **Custom Gradients** area. Custom gradients will be available for your other projects. **(G)**

**Remove Custom Gradients:** If you want to remove one or more of your custom gradients, click this icon. This puts a small red x on each of your custom gradients. Click the red **X** on a gradient to delete it from your custom palette. **(H)**

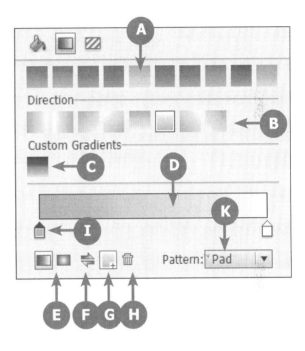

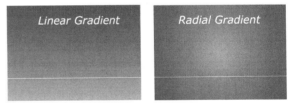

*Linear Gradient*

*Radial Gradient*

---

## POWER TIP

You can edit the direction of a gradient. Right-click a gradient-filled shape, and select **Edit Gradient**. This gives you a controller **(J)** you can click and drag to change the direction and the start/end points.

If the gradient is shorter than the shape, use the **Pattern** drop-down menu **(K)** to determine how to fill the remaining space.

**Pad** *continues the end colors*    **Reflect** *continues the gradient in reverse*    **Repeat** *starts the gradient over at the beginning*

# Fill Texture

With some fill color palettes (such as for slide backgrounds and smart shapes), you have the option of using a gradient.  Click the **Texture** button **(A)** to change the palette to show your fill texture options.

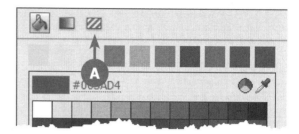

**Pre-Made Textures**: Click an icon in the top row of swatches to use one of the pre-made textures.

**Custom Image**: You can fill your shape with the image of your choice.  Click the **Browse** icon (folder) to find and select the image you want to use.  Click the **Edit** (pencil) or **Delete** (trash can) icons to change or delete the chosen image.

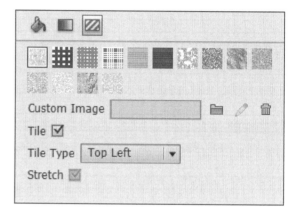

**Tile**: If the image used for the texture is smaller than the shape being filled, the image will be repeated within the shape, creating a tiled effect.  Uncheck this box if you don't want the tiling.  This option is used in conjunction with the next two options below.

**Tile Type**: If you are using the **Tile** option, you can use this drop-down menu to indicate the part of the object where the first tile should be placed.

**Stretch**: If you are not using the **Tile** option and the texture image is smaller than your shape, you can either have the image stretch to fill your shape or have the image stay at its normal size.  Check or uncheck this box based on the option you want.

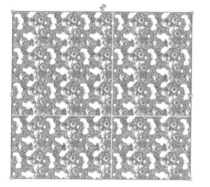

*Tile = yes*

*Tile = no; Stretch = no*

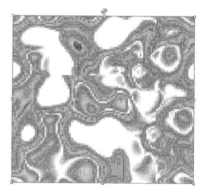

*Tile = no; Stretch = yes*

## Shadow & Reflection Pane

## Shadow

You can add drop shadows to objects such as shapes, captions, and images.

**Shadow**: Check this box to turn on the shadow.

**Direction**: Select **Outer** for a traditional drop shadow or **Inner** for a "sunken" effect.

| What would you do? | What would you do? |
|---|---|
| *Outer shadow* | *Inner shadow* |

**Presets**: Select the angle of lighting you want, which determines on which side of the object the shadow falls.

**Color**: Select the color for the shadow.

**Alpha**: Select the alpha (opacity) of the shadow. **(A)** A lower number gives you a lighter shadow, and a higher number gives you a darker shadow.

**Blur**: Enter a number to indicate how sharp or how blurry the edges of the shadow are. A higher number makes the shadow appear bigger.

| What would you do? | What would you do? |
|---|---|
| *Blur of 3 pixels* | *Blur of 15 pixels* |

**Angle**: If you do not want to use a pre-set direction, you can indicate your own angle for the shadow.

**Distance**: Enter a number to determine how far away from the object you want the shadow. A larger number means it is farther away, making the object look more like it is coming off the surface of the screen.

| What would you do? | What would you do? |
|---|---|
| *Distance of 4 pixels* | *Distance of 15 pixels* |

## Reflection

To add a reflection to an object, check the **Reflection** box, and then select the type you want, based on the size of the reflection and the distance from the object.

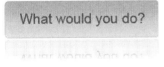

## TIME SAVER

Many of the object properties have an **Apply to All** icon in the top-right corner of the pane. Click the icon, and then select the option you want. You can either apply the new settings to all of that type of item (all captions, all highlight boxes, etc.) or just the items that have the same style (all captions using the "incorrect" style).

# Transition Pane

The settings in the **Transition** pane determine whether an object fades in and fades out or just appears and disappears. First, select the transition you want from the drop-down menu, and then use the **In** and **Out** fields to make any fade longer or shorter.

 **DESIGN TIP**

For a more dramatic entrance or exit (such as flying in and out), use effects instead of transitions.

 Effects, p. 108

# Transform Pane

The **Transform** pane lets you move, resize, and rotate objects numerically. You can also perform these same functions in the work area with your mouse.

## Position

**X**: Enter, in pixels, how far from the right edge you want the object to be.

**Y**: Enter, in pixels, how far from the top edge you want the object to be.

**Mouse equivalent**: Drag the object where you want it.

## Size

**W**: Enter, in pixels, how wide you want the object to be.

**H**: Enter, in pixels, how high you want the object to be.

**Constrain proportions**: If you check this box, when you change the value in width or height, Captivate will automatically adjust the other dimension so that the object keeps its current proportion.

**Mouse equivalent**: Click and drag one of the side or corner handles on the object to resize it. Press and hold the **Shift** key while doing so to constrain the proportions.

## Rotation

**Angle**: Enter, in degrees, any rotation you want to give the object.

**Rotate buttons**: Click either the **Rotate Left** or **Rotate Right** buttons to rotate the object either direction in 90-degree increments. **(A)**

**Mouse equivalent**: Click and drag the rotation handle on top of the object. Press and hold the **Shift** key while dragging to rotate the object in 15-degree increments.

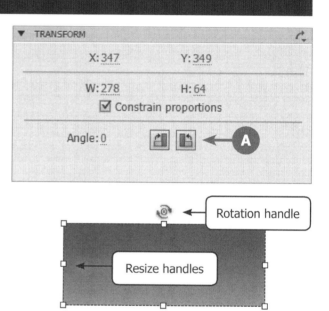

 **TIME SAVER**

To make two or more objects the same size, use the resize tools on the **Align** toolbar. If it is not already showing, select it from the **Window** menu.

| Resize to the Same Height | Resize to the Same Width | Resize to the Same Size | Align and Resize to the Same Size |

# Managing Objects

In this section, you will learn how to:

- Cut, copy, and paste objects.
- Delete objects.
- Group/ungroup objects.
- Show/hide objects.
- Lock/unlock objects.
- Align objects.
- Adjust layering of objects.

## Cut/Copy/Paste/Duplicate Objects

You can cut, copy, and paste objects using the following methods:

- Right-click the object in the work area or the **Timeline**, and select **Cut**, **Copy**, or **Paste**.
- Select the object(s), and press the keyboard shortcut shown to the right of the menu item.

### TIME SAVER

Use the **Duplicate** function to copy and paste all in one step.

| | |
|---|---|
| Cut | Ctrl+X |
| Copy | Ctrl+C |
| Paste | Ctrl+V |
| Duplicate | Ctrl+D |
| Delete | Del |
| Select All | Ctrl+A |
| Convert to freeform | |

## Delete Objects

There are two options for deleting an object.

- Select the object(s), and press the **Delete** key on your keyboard.
- Right-click the object in the work area or the Timeline, and select **Delete**.

# Group/Ungroup Objects

Grouping objects can make them easier to manage. When you group objects, you can:

- Move, resize, and time them all at once.

- Apply certain properties to all objects in the group.

- Expand and collapse the group in the **Timeline**, making it more organized.

- Use the whole group as the target of an action, such as a **Show** or **Hide** action.

**To group objects:**

1. Select them in the **Timeline** or the work area.

2. Right-click any of the selected objects.

3. Select **Group**.

**To ungroup objects:**

1. Right-click any item in the group.

2. Select **Ungroup**.

**To remove a single object from a group:**

1. Click the group.

2. Click the individual object you want to remove.

3. Right-click that same object.

4. Select **Remove From Group**.

## BRIGHT IDEAS

- You can still work with the individual objects in a group. Click the object once to select the whole group, and then click the object again to select just that object. From there, you can move it, resize it, change its properties, etc.

- Click the triangle next to the name of the group in the **Timeline** to expand or collapse the group.

- When the group is selected, any active property in the **Properties** panel can be changed, affecting all the objects in the group.

## Show/Hide Objects in Edit Mode

While you are working on a slide, you can hide certain objects in the work area. This is useful when you have overlapping objects (such as a correct and incorrect caption on a quiz), and you want to more easily work with the one on the bottom.

- To hide an object in the work area, click the dot under the "eyeball" icon for that object in the **Timeline**.

- To bring an object back, click the red X that appears in the dot's place.

- Click the eyeball icon itself to show or hide all objects on the slide.

 **CAUTION**

Hiding an object in the **Timeline** does not change how it appears in the published movie. If you want to hide an object in a published movie, either uncheck the **Visible** check box in **Properties** or use a **Hide** action on it.

 Visibility, p. 93
Hide Actions, p. 124

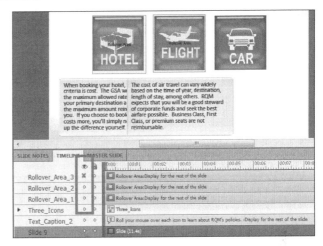

*Rollover caption on the right is hidden, making it easier to work with another caption it was covering.*

## Lock Objects in Edit Mode

When you lock an object, you cannot do ANYTHING to that object. You cannot move, edit, or delete it. You can't even see its properties. This can be useful if you want someone else to work on certain elements of your project but not others, or you just want to keep from accidentally changing an object yourself.

- To lock an object, click the dot under the lock icon for that object in the **Timeline**.

- To unlock an object, click the lock icon that appears in the dot's place.

- Click the lock icon at the top of the column to lock or unlock all objects on the slide.

 **BRIGHT IDEA**

Remember that you can also lock the entire slide. Not only does it lock all the objects on the slide, but it keeps you from deleting the slide or changing the slide properties.

 Lock Slides, p. 46

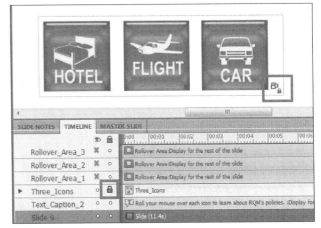

*The group of icon graphics is locked.*

# Aligning Objects

You have several options for aligning objects on the slide to help make your project look more professional.

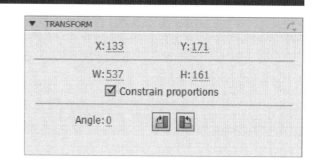

## Transform Pane

You can look at the numerical location of one object in the **Transform** pane, and then enter the number into the **Transform** pane of the other object. This is useful if you want to place an object in the same location on several different slides.

## Alignment Toolbar

Select the objects you want, and then use the buttons on the **Align** toolbar to align them. If the **Align** toolbar isn't showing, go to the **Window** menu, and select it.

These same alignment options are available on the object's right-click menu.

## Show Grid/Snap to Grid/Snap to Object

These three features can be found on the **Main Options** toolbar.

**Show Grid**: You can show a grid on the work area to help you visually align objects. Show the grid from the **View** menu. To change the size of the grid, go to the **Edit** menu, and select **Preferences**.

**Snap to Grid**: In addition, you can turn on the snap feature, which snaps the object into place along one of the gridlines as soon as you get close to it. This prevents your objects from being a pixel or two off.

**Snap to Object:** If you want to draw a line that goes right up to the edge of another drawn object (rectangle, etc.), turn on **Snap to Object**. When you draw a line up to a shape, a small circle appears when you are right at the edge of the object. If you stop the line there, it will be perfectly lined up without a gap or overlap.

*Example of a grid*

## Smart Guides

When you use your mouse to position objects, a blue dotted line appears when the center of that object is aligned with the center of the nearest object. (You can turn this feature off from the View menu if you don't want it.)

*Smart guide showing center alignment of objects*

# Layering

When you have overlapping objects on a slide, you want to make sure they are layered in the right order. For example, you may want the mouse movement to go in front of a caption instead of behind it, or have a text caption appear on top of a colored box.

## Drag-and-Drop Method

In the **Timeline**, the layers at the top appear in front of other layers on the slide. The layers on the bottom appear behind other objects on the slide. To change the layering order, drag and drop the layers up and down in the **Timeline**. Note that changing the top-to-bottom order in the **Timeline** does not affect *when* the objects appear, but rather on *what layer* they appear.

## Right-Click and Toolbar Methods

You can access layering tools from the **Main Options** toolbar and the object's right-click menu, under the **Arrange** sub-menu.

- **Bring Forward**: Bring the selected object one layer forward (up one layer on the **Timeline**).

- **Send Backward**: Send the selected object back one layer (down one layer on the **Timeline**).

- **Bring to Front**: Bring the selected object to the very front layer (very top of the **Timeline**).

- **Send to Back**: Send the selected object to the very back layer (very bottom of the **Timeline**).

*Logo is in front because it is higher in the Timeline.*

*Logo is in back because it is lower in the Timeline.*

Bring Forward   Send Backward   Bring to Front   Send to Back

| Bring Forward | Ctrl+] |
| Send Backward | Ctrl+[ |
| Bring to Front | Shift+Ctrl+] |
| Send to Back | Shift+Ctrl+[ |

| Cut | Ctrl+X |
| Copy | Ctrl+C |
| Duplicate | Ctrl+D |
| Delete | Del |
| Select All | Ctrl+A |
| Find in the Library | Ctrl+Alt+F |
| Lock | Ctrl+Alt+K |
| Hide | Ctrl+Alt+H |
| Arrange | ▶ |
| Align | ▶ |
| Sync with Playhead | Ctrl+L |
| Show for the rest of the slide | Ctrl+E |
| Increase Indent | Ctrl+I |

# Styles

Styles are groups of format settings that can be applied all at once to an object. For example, for a caption, you can create a style that includes the type, font style, size, color, etc. Styles can help you save time and create a consistent look.

You create and modify styles from the **Object Style Manager** (found on the **Edit** menu). Once the style has been created, you then apply it to the object. For most object types, you can apply the style from the **Properties** pane for that object. With some object types, you can also apply a style from the settings for that object. For example, you can select the style of caption during a capture session from the **Recording Settings** dialog box.

## BRIGHT IDEA

Runtime dialog refers to system messages in the published movie.

> Adobe Captivate
>
> Adobe Captivate Message Box
>
> OK

**Styles can be created for:**

| Standard Objects | Quizzing Objects |
|---|---|
| • Captions (text, rollover, success, failure, and hint) <br> • Buttons <br> • Text entry boxes <br> • Text entry box buttons <br> • Highlight boxes <br> • Rollover areas <br> • Rollover slidelets <br> • Slidelets <br> • Zoom area (zoom source and zoom destination) <br> • Smart shapes <br> • Runtime dialog | • Captions (correct, incorrect, retry, timeout, incomplete, partial correct, advance feedback, title, question text, answer/FIB text, header (matching/ Likert), matching entries, Likert question, scoring result, and scoring result label) <br> • Buttons (skip, back, continue, submit, clear, review, retake, and submit all) <br> • Answer area <br> • Progress indicator <br> • Review area <br> • Hot Spot <br> • Short Answer |

## Modify an Existing Style

All object types come with at least one style—the default style. You can modify that default style and any custom styles from the **Object Style Manager**.

1. Click the **Edit** menu.
2. Select **Object Style Manager**. (See next page.)
3. Select the type of object you want to modify. **(A)**
4. Select the specific style you want to modify. **(B)**
5. Make the formatting changes you want. **(C)**
6. Click **OK**.

The options on the right vary based on the object type and contain many of the same options you'll find on that object's **Properties** pane.

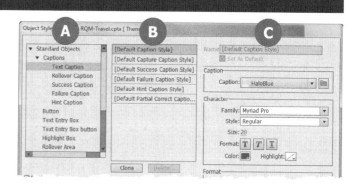

## BRIGHT IDEA

If you make any changes to styles while you are in a project, the style changes affect only that project. But if you modify styles with no project open, the style changes will be available in all future projects.

## Create a New Style

**To create a new style:**

1. Click the **Edit** menu.

2. Select **Object Style Manager**.

3. In the pane on the left, select the type of object you want to modify.

4. In the pane in the middle, select a style that is most similar to the style you want to create.

5. Click the **Clone** button.

6. In the **Name** field, type the name for the new style.

7. In the panes on the right, make the formatting changes you want.

8. Click **OK**.

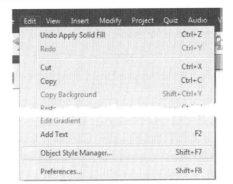

## Set the Default Style

The default style is the style used when an object is first created. For example, when you create a new highlight box or button, it appears on your slide in the default style.

To change the default style, you can go to the **Object Style Manager**, select the default style, and modify it. Or, you can create a new style, and then designate it as the default.

**To designate the default style:**

1. Click the **Edit** menu.

2. Select **Object Style Manager**. (See above.)

3. In the pane on the left, select the type of object you want to work with.

4. In the pane in the middle, select the style you want to use for the default.

5. Check the **Set as Default** box.

6. Click **OK**.

Now when you create a new object of that type, it will automatically use that new style.

 **BRIGHT IDEA**

You can also change the default styles from **Preferences** (on the **Edit** menu).

# Apply Styles to an Object

**To apply a style to an object:**

1. Select an object on the slide.
2. Click the **Properties** tab.
3. Select the style from the drop-down menu.

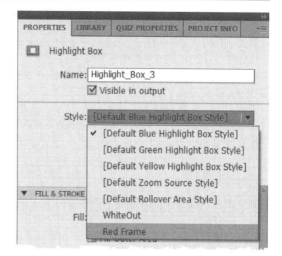

# Additional Style Options

If you make any changes to properties that are governed by a style (caption type, fill color, font, etc.), you are given additional style options in the **Properties** pane.

**Create New Style**: Rather than going to the **Object Style Manager**, you can create a new style right here. Format your object on the slide, and then click this button to create a new style based on that object. For example, if you have a highlight box with a red border, you can give one a blue border and save that as a new style.

**Save Changes to Existing Style**: Instead of making a new style from your revised object, you can override that object's style with the new changes. For example, if your font isn't big enough, you can change the size and resave the style.

**Apply This Style to**: If you change the style of an object, you can apply it to all other objects in the project with any given style. For example, you can apply a new green caption style to all of the objects that currently use the blue caption style.

**Delete Style**: Click this button to delete the style from the project.

**Reset Style**: If you have made changes to the object, click this button if you want to revert back to the original style.

**Replace Modified Styles**: If you change the style-related properties of an object, it is considered modified. Modified objects have a plus sign next to the name of the style. If you make changes to a style, it does not apply to any objects that are overridden, unless you check this box.

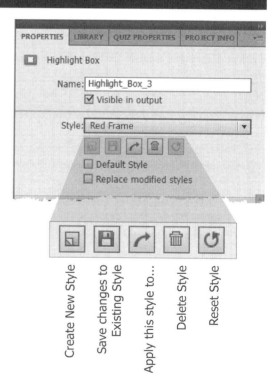

# Import and Export Styles

If you are working on a team, you can share styles with teammates so you maintain a consistent look, and you don't all have to set up the styles individually.  You can also import and export project-specific styles from one project to another.

**To export styles:**

1. Click the **Edit** menu.
2. Select **Object Style Manager**.
3. Click the arrow next to the **Export** button.
4. Select the option for the styles you want to export.
5. Click the **Export** button.
6. Navigate to where you want to save the style.
7. Click **Save**.
8. Click **OK**.

**To import styles:**

1. Click the **Edit** menu.
2. Select **Object Style Manager**.
3. Click the **Import** button.
4. Find and select the style (.cps) you want to import.
5. Click **Open**.
6. Click **OK**.

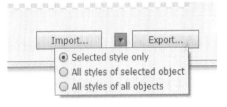

## BRIGHT IDEA

If you manage styles with a project open, the changes affect that project only.  If you manage styles with no projects open, then it affects all future projects.

# Delete Styles

**To delete a style:**

1. Click the **Edit** menu.
2. Select **Object Style Manager**.
3. Select the type of object you want to delete. **(A)**
4. Select the specific style you want to delete. **(B)**
5. Click the **Delete** button.

If there are no objects in the project using that style, that's all you need to do.  If, however, there are any objects in the project that use that style, you need to choose what style you want to give them instead.

6. In the dialog box that appears, select the style you want from the drop-down menu.
7. Click **OK**.

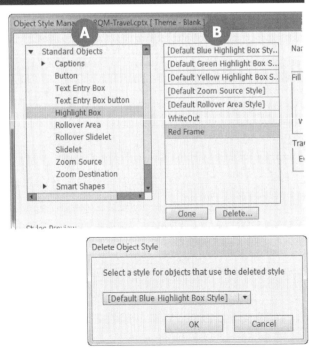

# Object Effects

Object effects let you create visual interest as objects appear, disappear, or move across the slide, similar to animations in PowerPoint. Effects in Captivate can either be triggered based on the **Timeline** (fly in at 3.5 seconds) or based on an action (the page loading or the student clicking a button).

Effects are managed in the **Effects** panel. To show the **Effects** panel, go to the **Window** menu, and select **Effects**.

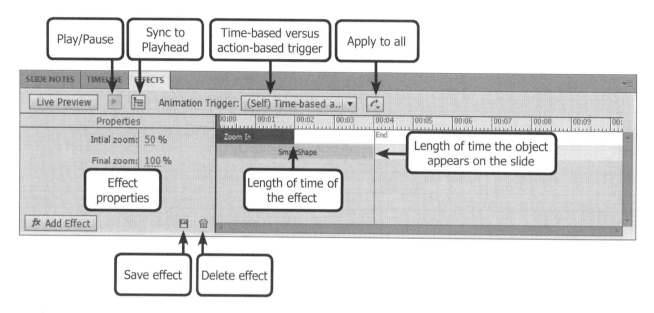

## Add a Time-Based Effect

Time-based effects start and end based on the **Timeline**. When you go to the **Effects** panel for a given object, there is a **Timeline** just for that object. The effects **Timeline** is the same length as the object's duration. In the example above, the rectangle is visible on the slide for four seconds, so its effects **Timeline** is also four seconds. That is the maximum amount of time you have to work with for effects. If you wanted an object to have a five-second effect, then you would first need to extend that object to at least five seconds in the main **Timeline**.

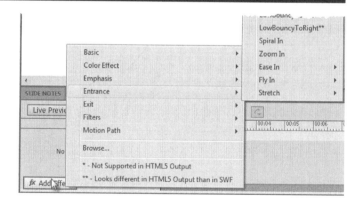

**To add a time-based effect:**

1. Select the object you want to add the effect to.
2. Click the **Effects** tab.
3. Click the **Add Effect** button.
4. Select the effect you want from the pop-up menus.
5. Move and resize the effect item on the **Timeline** to change the starting time, ending time, and duration.
6. Repeat steps 3-5 for additional effects for that object.

## BRIGHT IDEAS

- Some effects have properties that let you customize the effect. For example, the blur filter lets you indicate how much of a blur effect you want. When an object has options, they appear in the **Properties** section of the **Effects** panel.

- Asterisk indicators let you know which effects do not work or do not work the same when publishing to HTML5.

# Add an Action-Based Effect

Setting up an action-based effect starts with the trigger, meaning the item that will trigger the event. For example, if you want the animation to start when the student clicks a button, then you would start by adding a trigger to the button.

**To add an action-based effect:**

1. Select the object that will trigger the effect.

2. In the **Action** pane for that object, click the drop-down menu for the trigger you want, such as **On Success** or **Last Attempt**.

3. Select **Apply Effect** from the drop-down menu.

4. Click the **Object Name** drop-down menu that appears.

5. Select the object you want to apply the effect to.

6. Click the **[ ... ]** button to go to the object that will have the effect (or simply select that object in the work area).

7. In the **Effects** panel, click the **Animation Trigger** drop-down menu.

8. Select the name of the action that will initiate the trigger.

9. Add your effect. (See steps 3-5 on previous page.)

 Actions, ch. 7

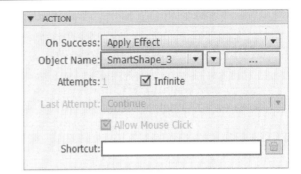

## POWER TIP

In addition to the effects that come with Captivate, you can also create your own effects in Flash and bring them into Captivate. Search Adobe Help for "Creating custom effects in Adobe Flash" for specific guidelines.

# Managing Effects

## Preview Effects

Effects do not show up when you preview a single slide. Instead, use the other preview modes (such as **Next 5 slides**), or you can preview from the **Effects** panel.

To preview effects, click the **Live Preview** button. From there, you can use the playhead and the **Play/Pause** button to view the effect. Then click the **Edit View** button to return to edit mode.

## Remove an Effect

To remove an effect, select the effect in the effects **Timeline**, and click the **Delete** button. **(A)**

## Sync to Playhead

The **Timeline** on the **Effects** tab always starts at zero, even if the object doesn't start at the beginning of the slide. So if you have an effect that finishes two seconds into the object's duration, that doesn't mean the effect finishes two seconds into the slide. This button lets you figure out how the two **Timelines** relate. On the *effects* **Timeline**, put the playhead where you want, and click the **Sync to Playhead** button. This takes you to the *slide* **Timeline**, putting the playhead in the corresponding spot.

## Save and Reuse Effects

You can reuse effects for a given object so that you don't have to set them up over and over again. Effects are saved as XML files. All time-based effects for that object are included in the file.

**To save an object's effects:**

1. Select the object with the effects.
2. In the **Effects** panel, click the **Save** button. **(B)**
3. Designate a name and location for the file.
4. Click the **Save** button.

**To reuse a saved effect:**

1. Select the object you want to give the effects to.
2. Click the **Add Effect** button.
3. Select **Browse**.
4. Find and select the saved effects file.
5. Click the **Open** button.

## Motion Paths

When you add a motion path, you can configure the individual points on the path. For example, if you have a left-to-right motion path, you can modify the path to be a certain length or angle.

**To modify a motion path:**

1. Click the small icon at the bottom-right of the object.
2. Click and drag any of the points on the arrow.

Preview the effect (becomes Edit View button) | Play/Pause | Sync to Playhead

## POWER TIP

Reused effects are also available for use with advanced actions.

Advanced Actions, ch. 9

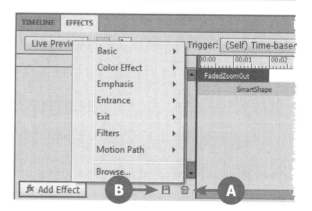

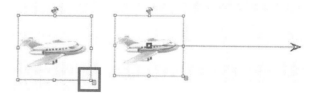

# Timing Slide Objects

A Captivate project plays like a movie along the **Timeline**. Once your objects are on the slide, you may want to time them to appear in the appropriate sequence and to stay on-screen for the appropriate length of time. For example, a caption needs to stay up long enough to be read, and a highlight box or image might need to appear at a certain point in the audio.

On the **Timeline** for each slide, you can quickly adjust the start, duration, and finish of each slide object, as well as the length of the slide as a whole. If your **Timeline** isn't showing, go to the **Window** menu, and select **Timeline**.

## CAUTION

When a slide is finished playing, the movie automatically goes on to the next slide. If you want the student to choose when to advance to the next slide, you'll need to add a button or other object that pauses the slide until the student clicks it.

Buttons, p. 130

---

## Adjust Timing of Slide Elements

**To adjust timing in the Timeline panel:**

- Drag the left edge of an item to adjust the start time.

- Drag the right edge of an item to adjust the end time.

- Drag the entire object to move it to a different place on the **Timeline**.

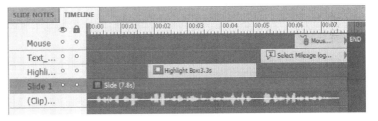

**To adjust timing in the Properties panel:**

1. Select the object in the **Timeline** or the work area.

2. In the **Timing** pane, enter the duration for the object in the **Display For** field.

3. Enter the start time for the object in the **Appear After** field.

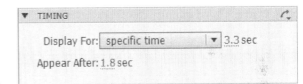

## Timing Options

The **Display For** drop-down menu has some additional timing options.

- **Specific time**: This is the default. This displays the object for the amount of time set in the **Timeline** or in the **Timing** pane of the **Properties** panel.

- **Rest of slide**: This extends the object to the end of the slide and "locks" it in place so that if the slide is extended or shortened, the object is moved to stay at the end of the slide.

- **Rest of project**: This extends the object to the end of the project. The object will only appear on this slide's **Timeline**, but will show up on every other slide for the rest of the project.

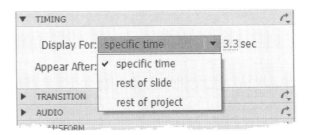

## BRIGHT IDEA

Use the zoom control to zoom the **Timeline** in or out for more or less detail.

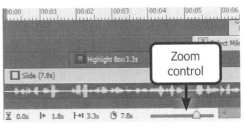

# Notes

# Actions & Interactions

## Introduction

Actions are commands that can either be triggered by the student (such as clicking a button) or triggered automatically (such as reaching the end of a slide). Actions let you customize the functionality of the course and make it more interactive.

In this chapter, you will learn first about pre-made interactive objects and templates, such as rollover captions and interactive diagrams. From there, you'll learn how to build your own custom interactions. You'll learn the individual actions available in Captivate, as well as the interactive objects you can apply them to. These become building blocks that let you create any number of features from branching navigation to games.

The following table describes the action options for the various interactive objects.

| Object | Action options |
|---|---|
| Rollover Caption | A text caption appears when the student rolls over the hot spot. |
| Rollover Image | An image appears when the student rolls over the hot spot. |
| Rollover Slidelet | A mini slide (with text, graphics, audio, etc.) appears when the student rolls over the hot spot area. You can add an additional action for when the student clicks the hot spot. |
| Smart Interactions | Interactive diagrams and other templates you can use with your own text and media. |
| Slide | Even though this technically isn't an interactive object, you can assign an action for when the slide starts and finishes. |
| Text | You can use text hyperlinks to perform most actions. |
| Click Box, Button, Text Entry Box, Quiz Question | Select one action for clicking/answering successfully and/or one action for failing to click/answer successfully after the specified number of attempts. |

Many properties for interactive objects are the same as for other objects (such as size, layering, and shadows). This chapter explains the properties specific to the interactivity. Refer to the Object Properties chapter for information on the standard properties. Quiz questions are covered in the Questions & Quizzes chapter.

Object Properties, ch. 6
Questions & Quizzes, ch. 10

### In This Chapter

- Smart Interactions
- Rollover Objects
- Action Types
- Slide Actions
- Click Boxes
- Buttons
- Text Entry Boxes

# Notes

# Smart Interactions

Smart interactions are pre-built interactive templates that come with Captivate. You can choose over 25 different templates and then customize them to your content.

## BRIGHT IDEA

Even though these interactions are Flash widgets, they will still output to HTML5 format if you select that option when publishing.

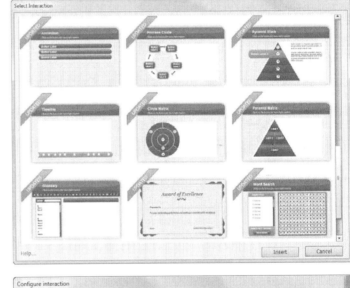

## Add a Smart Interaction

**To add a smart interaction:**

1. Click the **Insert Interaction** button on the **Object** toolbar.

2. Select the interaction template you want.

3. Click the **Insert** button.

4. In the **Configure interaction** dialog box, select a theme from the column on the left.

5. Enter your content. (See next page.)

6. Click the **OK** button.

## DESIGN TIPS

- Captivate 7 has many new and updated templates, including those for YouTube videos, student note-taking, and embedding web pages.

- Click the **Custom** button to configure the colors and fonts used in the interaction.

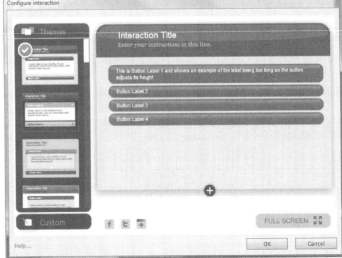

# Configure Interaction Content

**To configure an interaction:**

- Double-click an object to add your content.
- Click the plus button **(A)** to add additional elements, if available.
- Double-click an element, and then click the minus button **(B)** to delete that element.
- Double-click a content area, and click the audio or image icons **(C)** to add media, if available.

**To edit an interaction after it is on the slide:**

- Click the **Widget Properties** button in the **Properties** panel. **(D)**

 **BRIGHT IDEA**

The properties for an interaction are the same for other animations.

 Animation Properties, p. 65

# Interaction Gallery

Checkbox Widget

Timer

Drop Down

Hangman

Hourglass

Image Zoom

Jeopardy

Jigsaw Puzzle

Notes

Radio Button Widget

YouTube

Process Circle

Pyramid Stack

Timeline

Circle Matrix

# Interaction Gallery (cont'd)

Pyramid Matrix

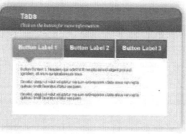
Glossary

Certificate

Word Search

Tabs

Accordion

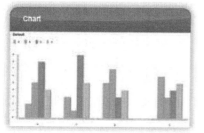
Chart

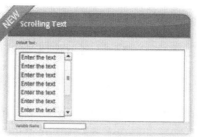
Countdown Timer

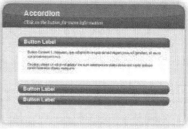
Memory Game

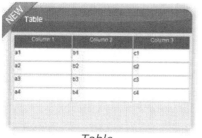
Table

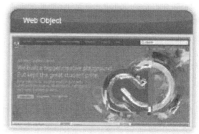
Scrolling Text

Web Object

## BRIGHT IDEA

From time to time, Captivate may make additional templates available. Click the **Download More** link when selecting a template to check for additional options.

# Rollover Objects

The three types of rollover objects let you quickly create interactive objects where students roll their mouse over a hot spot (**A**) to reveal additional content (**B**).

- **Rollover Captions**: Place hot spots on the slide that the student rolls over to view a text caption.

- **Rollover Image**: Place hot spots on the slide that the student rolls over to view an image.

- **Rollover Smart Shape**: Place hot spots on the slide that the student rolls over to view a smart shape.

- **Rollover Slidelets**: Place hot spots on the slide that the student rolls over to view a mini-slide that can contain text, images, audio, etc.

## Insert a Rollover Caption

**To add a rollover caption:**

1. Click the **Insert Rollover Caption** button on the **Object** toolbar.

2. Move and resize the rollover area over the portion of the screen to serve as the hot spot for the caption.

3. Enter text, format, and position the caption.

4. Repeat steps 1-3 for additional rollover captions.

5. Format the objects in the **Properties** panel.

 **TIME SAVER**

If you are placing the rollover area over an object, such as an image, you can save yourself a little time. Right-click the rollover area and select **Auto-adjust Rollover Area**. This "snaps" the rollover area to the same size as the object below it.

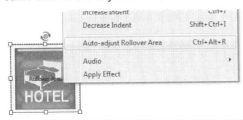

 **CAUTION**

Your movie will not automatically stop so that students can roll over all of the hot spots and read all of the text. To give them enough time, either extend the length of the slide, or add a **Continue** button that pauses the slide until they want to continue.

 Buttons, p. 130

# Insert a Rollover Image

**To add a rollover image:**

1. Click the **Insert Rollover Image** button  on the **Object** toolbar.

2. Find and select the image you want to use.

3. Click the **Open** button.

4. Format and position the rollover area and the image.

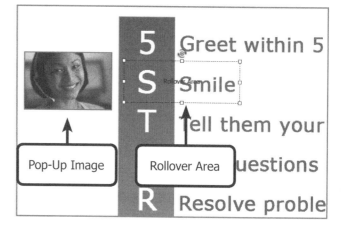

## BRIGHT IDEA

Rollover objects don't actually require a mouse, making them accessible. When a student using keyboard navigation tabs to the rollover area, the caption, image, or slidelet appears.

# Insert a Rollover Smart Shape

**To add a rollover smart shape:**

1. Create the smart shape you want to have appear.

2. Right-click the shape.

3. Select **Convert to rollover Smart Shape**.

4. Move and resize the rollover area that appears.

 Smart Shapes, p. 62

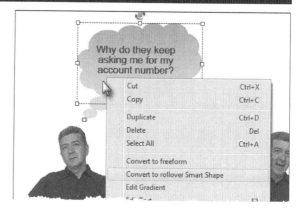

# Insert a Rollover Slidelet

### To add a rollover slidelet:

1. Click the **Insert Rollover Slidelet** button on the **Object** toolbar.

2. Move and resize the rollover area over the portion of the slide to serve as the hot spot.

3. Move and resize the slidelet frame to the size and location you want for the pop-up slidelet.

4. Select the slidelet frame in the work area.

5. Add objects to the slidelet as you would to a regular slide.

The slidelet has its own **Timeline**. To add objects to it, its **Timeline** must be showing. Do this by selecting the slidelet frame on the main slide.

## Rollover Area Properties

Both the rollover area and the slidelet have their own properties, which are similar to other object types. The rollover area has some additional properties. **(A)**

**Show Runtime Border**: If you select this option, a border appears around the rollover area while the student's mouse is over it. This is useful when you have more than one rollover area on a slide as it lets the student know which object they are viewing.

**Stick Slidelet**: By default, the slidelet disappears when the student moves off the rollover area. If you check this box, the slidelet stays up. A close button appears on the slidelet that the student would click to close it.

**On Click**: You can designate an action to execute if the student clicks in the rollover area rather than rolling over it.

**Shortcut**: You can type a keyboard command to run the **On Click** action if the student types it. If there is no **On Click** action, the keystroke does nothing.

**On Rollover**: In addition to having the slidelet appear, you can set an action to execute upon rollover, such as showing an object elsewhere on the slide. Please note, however, that the action does not undo when the student rolls off the rollover area.

 **CAUTION**

If you use an **On Click** action, be sure to test everything carefully to make sure the actions don't contradict with each other.

*Objects as they first appear on the slide*

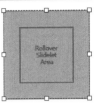

Slidelet    Rollover Area

*Slide Timeline*

*Slidelet Timeline*

# Actions

The following pages describe the types of individual actions you can use to create your own interactivity and custom functionality. Objects that can serve as triggers (such as buttons and hyperlinks) have an **Action** pane in the **Properties** panel. The available actions vary somewhat based on the type of object.

## Action Types

### Continue

The slide continues to play along the **Timeline**. This action is useful if the action is paused, perhaps because of a click box or button.

### Go To and Jump Actions

These actions allow for custom navigation and branching.

**Go to the previous slide**: Go to the beginning of the previous slide.

**Go to the next slide**: Go to the beginning of the next slide.

**Go to the slide last visited**: Go to the beginning of the slide the student was on before the current slide.

**Return to Quiz**: See page 175.

**Jump to slide**: Go to the beginning of the slide specified in the **Action** pane.

### Open URL or File

You can go to a web page (such as a page on your website or a PDF document stored on your intranet). For this action, type the URL in the space provided.

You can link to a file (such as a file on your computer or a network drive). Click the **Browse** button **(A)** to find and select the file you want to link to. The file needs to be included with the published movie, or the link will not work.

For both options, click the drop-down menu **(B)** to indicate how you want the webpage or file to open.

> **Current**: The web page or document replaces the Captivate movie in the current browser window.
>
> **New**: The web page or document opens in a new window.
>
> **Parent and Top**: These only apply if your movie will play on a webpage with frames. **Parent** replaces all the frames in the current frameset, while **Top** opens the webpage or document in the topmost frame.
>
> With all but the **Current** option, you can check the box at the bottom to indicate whether you want the movie to continue playing once the new webpage launches.

### CAUTION

Don't confuse the following actions:

**Go to the previous slide** and **Go to the last slide visited:** Imagine the student is on slide 3 and then goes to slide 6. **Go to the previous slide** takes the student to slide 5. **Go to the last slide visited** takes the student back to slide 3.

**Continue** and **Go to the next slide**: With a **Continue** action, the project keeps playing from that point in the **Timeline**. With a **Go to the next slide** action, it goes immediately to the next slide and does not finish playing the slide it is on.

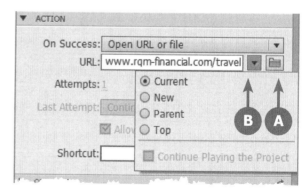

### BRIGHT IDEA

If you use a file with the **Open URL or File** action, you will need to copy the file to the output folder when you publish.

## Open Another Project

Open a Captivate project file, template, or published movie. Click the **Browse** button to find and select the file, and click the drop-down arrow to indicate how you want it to open.

You can use this action for any of the following file types: Captivate project file (.cptx or .cp), Captivate template file (.cptl), RoboDemo file (.rd), Flash output file (.swf), and Captivate video composition file (.cpvc).

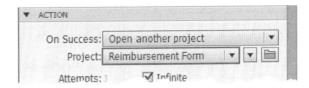

## Send E-Mail To

Open the student's default e-mail program with a message addressed to the address entered in the **Action** pane. Click the drop-down arrow to indicate if you want to continue playing the project or you want to pause the project when the e-mail message opens.

 **CAUTION**

Be sure to test the e-mail function carefully. The configuration of the users' computers and your servers can cause complications.

## Execute JavaScript

Run JavaScript code entered in the **Action** pane. This lets you extend the capabilities of what Captivate can do. For example, you could:

- Manipulate something on the HTML page.
- Create a custom pop-up message window.
- Communicate with other Captivate movies.

To enter your code, click the **Script Window** button, enter your code, and click the **OK** button.

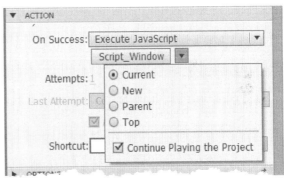

 **BRIGHT IDEAS**

If you don't know JavaScript, you can often find sample code in the Captivate forum or blogs.

JavaScript is interpreted by a browser, so use the **In Web Browser** preview mode to test your work.

## Execute Advanced Actions

Advanced actions let you perform more than one action at once, use conditional actions (only perform an action if something is true), or build customized actions. After you build the advanced action in the **Advanced Actions** dialog box, then you run it with this action.

 Advanced Actions, ch. 9

# Action Types (cont'd)

## Shared Action

In the Advanced Action dialog box, you can create actions that you can save and use over and over again across projects. This action runs one of those saved actions.

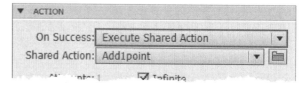

 Saving and Reusing Actions, p. 164

## Play Audio/Stop Triggered Audio

**Play Audio** plays an audio file separate from the **Timeline**. For example, you can add a sound that plays when the student clicks a button or answers a question incorrectly. The **Stop Triggered Audio** action stops any audio that is playing from a **Play Audio** action.

## Show/Hide

The **Show** action makes a hidden object visible. (Objects can be hidden in the **Properties** pane **(A)** or with a **Hide** action.) For example, you could have a hidden hint caption on a question with a **Help Me** button that shows it.

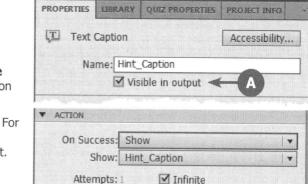

**Hide**: The **Hide** action lets you make an object invisible. For example, you might want the student to click a button to make an image disappear, revealing information beneath it.

## BRIGHT IDEA

If you need to show and hide objects based on time, simply adjust them on the **Timeline**. Use **Show**/**Hide** actions if you want them to appear/disappear based actions or conditions.

## Enable/Disable

**Enable** lets you activate an interactive object (such as a button or click box) that has previously been disabled. For example, a **Next** button might be disabled until certain tasks are performed. Once they are, the button could be enabled.

**Disable** de-activates an interactive object (such as a button or click box). The object will still be visible on the screen, but associated actions will not work.

With **Enable** and **Disable**, select the object you want to enable/disable from the drop-down menu that appears. Only eligible objects appear on the drop-down menu.

## Assign/Increment/Decrement

These actions let you adjust the value of a variable.

 Variables, p. 155

# Action Types (cont'd)

## Pause

This action pauses the **Timeline** for the slide. (You can use a **Continue** action or have the student click the **Play** button on the **Playbar** to resume.)

## Exit

This action closes the published project.

## Apply Effect

You can use this action to trigger an effect, such as a fly-in or fly-out animation.

 Action-Based Effects, p. 109

## No Action

This does nothing—on purpose.

**ACTION**

On Success: Pause ▾

Attempts: 1   ☑ Infinite

**ACTION**

On Success: Exit ▾

Attempts: 1   ☑ Infinite

**ACTION**

On Success: Apply Effect ▾
Object Name: Text_Animation_1 ▾ ▾ ...

Attempts: 1   ☑ Infinite

**ACTION**

On Success: No Action ▾

Attempts: 1   ☑ Infinite

## DESIGN TIP

What's the point of an action that does nothing?!? This is often used for objects, such as a button or click box where there is one option on success and one option for failure, and you don't need both options.

# DESIGN TIPS

## Creating Branching Scenarios

In a branching scenario, students make choices that determine where they go next. For example, in a customer service scenario, the student can choose between several options. Each option takes the student to a different slide for feedback and a continuation of the scenario.

To create a branching scenario, it is usually best to sketch it out first. This will help you make your basic design decisions before you build it.

- Do you want to give students the chance to go back and change their answers?

- After getting feedback, do all students go to the same question next, or do they get different questions based on their responses?

- How many content slides do you need for instructions and to set up the scenario?

- Can the new question be on the same slide as the feedback for the previous question, or do you need separate slides?

Once you have your structure determined, create the slides and give them logical names. Before adding your content, set up the logic: buttons with the branching actions, quiz questions, etc.

Once you have the logic working, then you can add your content.

## Using Branching View

To help you manage the flow of slides in any project with branching, you can use the branching view. Branching view is a flowchart-style view that helps you quickly determine where the student can go from each of the slides.

**To show branching view:**

1. Go to the **Window** menu.
2. Select **Branching View**.

From branching view, you can:

- Create and manage slide groups. **(A)**
- Export the view as a bitmap. **(B)**
- View or change the action of an interactive object. **(C)** Click the navigation line for the action box to appear.
- View success, failure, and navigational paths. **(D)**
- Expand and collapse sections. **(E)**
- View or change the action of a slide. **(F)** Click a thumbnail for the action box to appear.

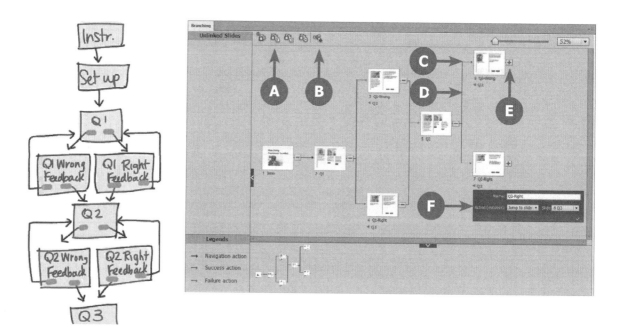

# Adding Actions

Now that you know your options for actions, you can add them to your projects using the various interactive objects, covered on the next few pages.

## Add Actions to a Slide

Actions can be triggered when the project goes to the first frame of a slide (**On Enter**) or the last frame of a slide (**On Exit**). For example, you might want to run an advanced action at the end of the slide that branches to different slides based on whether the student has indicated if he or she is a supervisor.

**To add an action to a slide:**

1. Select the slide(s) you want in the **Filmstrip**.

2. Select the action from the **On Enter** and/or **On Exit** menus in the **Action** pane.

> ACTION
>
> On Enter: Continue
>
> On Exit: Execute Advanced Actions
>
> Script: SupervisorBranching
>
> AUDIO

### CAUTION

An **On Exit** action will only execute if the project reaches the last frame of the slide. It will not execute if the student leaves the slide in the middle, such as by clicking a button that takes them to the next slide.

## Add a Hyperlink to Text

You can add a hyperlink to text in a caption or a smart shape.

**To add a hyperlink to text:**

1. Select the text you want to use for the hyperlink.

2. In the **Format** pane, click the **Insert Hyperlink** button. **(A)**

3. Select an action from the drop-down list that appears.

4. Configure the rest of the action.

5. Click the **OK** button.

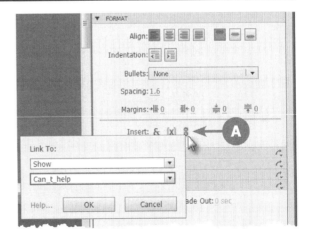

# Add a Click Box

Click boxes are useful for turning images into hot spots. For example, you can show a diagram with a click box over three key parts of the diagram. Each of the click boxes could link to a slide with more information.

Click boxes can have success and failure captions as well as success and failure actions.

**To add a click box:**

1. Click the **Insert Click Box** button on the **Object** toolbar.

# Click Box Properties

## Action Pane

**On Success**: Select an action that executes if the student clicks in the click box.

**Attempts**: Enter the number of attempts the student gets before the interaction is considered incorrect. Either enter a number in the **Attempts** number field or check the **Infinite** check box.

**Last Attempt**: Select an action that executes if the student fails to click inside the click box within the specified number of attempts.

**Allow Mouse Click** and **Shortcut**: Click boxes are designed to be...clicked! However, sometimes you might want to test the student on a keystroke command. There is not a designated Captivate object for that, but you can use a click box object for it.

- Type the keyboard shortcut in the **Shortcut** field.

- If you want the student to be able to use either the keyboard shortcut or a click in the click box as the correct action, then leave the **Allow Mouse Click** box checked. If you only want to consider the keyboard shortcut as correct, uncheck the box.

- To clear the **Shortcut** field, click the **Clear** (trash can) button.

## Options Pane

**Captions**: Check the boxes to select which captions you want to include with the click box.

- **Success** shows when the student clicks in the click box (or presses the corresponding keyboard shortcut).

- **Failure** shows when the student clicks somewhere other than the clickbox.

- **Hint** shows up when the student's mouse hovers over the click box area.

## CAUTION

If you use multiple click boxes on a slide or keyboard shortcuts, be sure to test it carefully to make sure they work, especially in a web browser.

# Click Box Properties (cont'd)

## Options Pane (cont'd)

### Others

- **Pause for Success/Failure Captions**: Success and failure captions are not in the **Timeline**. If you include these captions, you'll need to decide if you want the project to pause long enough to read them or if you want the captions to appear while the project continues. The project pauses by default. Uncheck this box if you don't want the project to pause.

- **Hand Cursor**: Check this box if you want the student's cursor to change from an arrow to a hand when it is over the click box area. This is an indication to students that their cursor is over a hot spot area.

- **Double-Click**: Check this box if you want the student to double-click the box instead of single-click the box. This is most commonly used in computer simulations.

- **Disable Click Sound**: When a student clicks the click box, Captivate plays a click sound. Check this box if you don't want the sound to play.

- **Pause Project Until User Clicks**: When there is a click box on the screen, the project pauses until the student either clicks successfully in the box or uses up all of the incorrect attempts. Uncheck this box if you don't want to pause the project.

- **Right-Click**: Check this box if you want the student to right-click the box instead of the traditional left-click. This is most commonly used in computer simulations.

## Reporting Pane

**Include in Quiz**: Check this box if you want to count the click box interaction as a question in a quiz.

- **Points**: Enter the number of points the student should receive for clicking the click box within the specified number of attempts. The value can be between 0 and 100.

- **Add to Total**: Check this box if you want to include the points in the quiz total.

- **Report Answers**: Check this box if you want to send the scores to a learning management system (LMS). Uncheck it if the score does not need to be reported.

**Interaction ID**: Enter an ID to be used when sending the data to the LMS. This can help you identify the data in the LMS.

 LMS Reporting, p. 234

# Add a Button

Buttons are a very flexible way to add interactivity, because there are so many ways you can format them. Use buttons for course navigation, branching scenarios, questions built outside of the question wizard, pop-up interactions, etc.

Buttons can have success and failure captions as well as success and failure actions. However, the captions are turned off by default.

**To add a button:**

1. Click the **Insert Button** button on the **Object** toolbar.

Continue

*Text button*

*Transparent button*

Continue ➔

*Image button*

Continue

*Widget button*

# Button Properties

Most of the button properties are the same as for a click box. This section covers the properties that are different.

 Click Box Properties, p. 128

**Button Type**: Select from the following options:

**Text Button**: Type the text for the button in the **Caption** field. Format the text in the **Character** pane.

**Transparent Button**: Use the **Fill & Stroke** pane to change the button's fill color, transparency, and stroke color and weight. A transparent button works very similarly to a click box.

**Image Button**: Select a button from the options provided, or click the **Browse** button next to the menu to select your own.

**Make Transparent**: Check this box to make the background of a text button transparent.

## BRIGHT IDEAS

- When you select **Transparent Button**, it doesn't actually make the button transparent! Instead, it enables the **Fill & Stroke** pane that lets you make the button transparent (set **Alpha** to 0%) or any other color.

- When you select **Image Button** and then click the **Browse** button, you are taken (by default) to the Captivate Gallery. If you open the **More** folder, there are a number of other image buttons to choose from.

▼ GENERAL

Button Type: Text Button

Caption: Continue

☑ Make Transparent

Button Widgets

▼ GENERAL

Button Type: Transparent Button

Caption: Button

☐ Make Transparent

Button Widgets

▼ FILL & STROKE

Fill: ⬚ ⬚ :100 % Stroke: ⬚

▼ GENERAL

Button Type: Image Button

blank_silver(93*21)

« Back    back_bluesmall(57*20)

◀◀ Back    back_silver(60*21)

# Button Widgets

Button widgets offer additional button formats and effects. The button widgets come in two forms:

- **Interactive**: Interactive buttons have the same basic action properties as a regular button: action on success, action on failure, and success, failure, and hint captions.

- **Static**: Static buttons have a single action, no failure action, and no captions.

### To add a button from the button widgets:

1. Click the **Insert Button** button on the **Object** toolbar.

2. In the **Properties** pane, click the **Button Widgets** link. **(A)**

3. In the **Widgets** panel, click **Insert** for either the **Static** or **Interactive** button. **(B)**

4. In the **Widget Properties** dialog box **(C)**, select the options, including the success action and button text.

5. Click the **OK** button.

To make changes later, click the **Widget Properties** button in the **Properties** panel. **(D)**

For interactive buttons, use the **Action** and **Options** panes to configure the attempts, captions, etc.

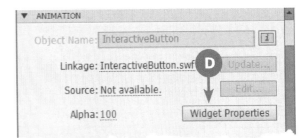

# Add a Text Entry Box

Text entry boxes let the student enter text. This text can then be validated (graded), sent to the LMS, or stored and used later for conditional logic or to display back to the student. Remember that you can also use a fill-in-the-blank question for similar purposes. Text entry boxes can have success and failure actions and captions.

**To add a text entry box:**

1. Click the **Insert Text Entry Box** button on the **Object** toolbar.

# Text Entry Box Properties

## General Pane

**Default Text**: If you don't want the text entry box to appear blank to the student, you can enter default text here. For example, you can add default text that says "Enter name here." This text can be edited by the student.

**Retain Text**: By default, the student's answer stays in the text box if the student navigates away from the page and returns during the same session. Uncheck this box if you want the answer cleared when the student leaves the page.

**Show Text Box Frame**: By default, there is an outline around the entry box. Uncheck this box if you don't want the frame. For example, if you are laying the text box over a shape, you may not need the frame.

**Password Field**: If you are using the entry box as a real or simulated password field, check this box. Then the student's typing is captured as typed but is shown as asterisks.

**Validate User Input**: By default, a text entry box is not graded. However, if you want to grade the answer, check this box. When you do, a small dialog box appears that lets you add one or more correct answers. **(A)**

**More Options:** Click this button for a menu of validation and display options. **(B)** You can specify a maximum number of characters. When you do, you can check the **Auto Submit** box to evaluate the student's answer when that number is reached. Select **Numbers** to only accept numbers. Select **Uppercase** or **Lowercase** to display all characters in the selected format. Select **Allow All** to clear out to reset the radio buttons and accept all text.

**Variable**: A variable is a stored piece of data that you can use later. All text entry boxes are assigned a variable. You can either use the variable name provided, select a variable that already exists from the drop-down menu, or click the **[X]** button to create a new variable name.

 Variables, p. 155

**On Focus Lost**: Select an action to execute when the student clicks off of the text entry box.

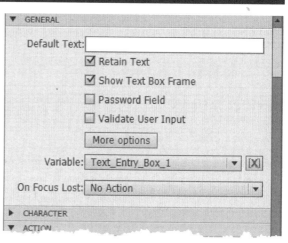

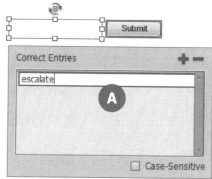

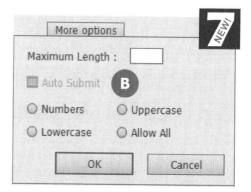

# Text Entry Box Properties (cont'd)

## Action Pane

The **Action** pane for a text entry box is similar as for other interactive objects. The main difference is how the **Shortcut** field works. By default, text entry boxes come with a shortcut of **Enter**.

With non-validated text entry boxes (and most other interactive objects), the keyboard shortcut activates the **On Success** action. But for text boxes that are validated, this shortcut is what triggers the validation. Then the grading logic (**On Success** action, number of attempts, etc.) is activated.

## Options Pane

**Captions**: The success and failure options are only available if you are validating the student's entry. Check the **Hint** box if you want a hint caption to appear when the student hovers over the text entry box. This can be useful for instructions.

**Show Button**: By default, a **Submit** button is added with your text entry box to validate the student's input. Uncheck this box if you don't want this button, for example, if you want to use the keyboard shortcut for validation or don't have any validation. You can click the **Submit** button itself to view and manage its properties.

**Show Scrollbar**: Check this box if you want to add a scrollbar to the text box, letting the student enter more text in a smaller amount of space.

# Notes

# Editing Software Simulations

## Introduction

In chapter 2, you learned how to capture software simulations. Your raw captures get you off to a great start when creating your simulations. However, there is usually a fair amount of clean-up to be done. You will often spend more time on editing than you do on the initial capture. That's why it is important to know what your options are and how to work quickly.

In previous chapters, you learned about many features to edit and customize your recordings:

- Add/modify slides, chapter 3
- Add/modify captions and highlight boxes, chapter 4
- Add audio, chapter 5
- Adjust timing of on-screen objects, chapter 6
- Add rollover objects, chapter 7

This chapter shows you features that are specifically designed to help you edit your captures:

- Add/modify mouse movements
- Add/modify typing
- Make changes to the underlying captures
- Edit a full-motion recording clip
- Recapture additional screen shots or video demo clips
- Manage click box slides and text entry slides for interactive practices
- Edit video demos

### In This Chapter

- The Editing Process
- Editing Typing
- Editing Mouse Movements
- Editing Full-Motion Recording
- Editing Slide Backgrounds
- Recording Additional Slides
- Managing Practice Slides
- Managing Video Demos

# Notes

# The Editing Process

Once you have your "raw" capture, it is time to edit it. You might need to:

- Correct errors, such as multiple or missing captures.
- Refine placement of automatically added elements, such as the exact position of a mouse click.
- Add instructional elements, such as an extra caption.
- Modify underlying images, such as hiding sensitive information or changing the name of a button.
- Recapture new screen shots.

## CAUTION

Always save your raw capture before making edits. That way, you can revert back to your original if you make mistakes during the editing process.

# Editing Typing

By default, when you type during a capture, Captivate captures the keystrokes and plays them back one character at a time in the published movie. If you make a mistake in the typing, it is often easier to re-do the slide while capturing. However, sometimes you don't realize you need to make a change until much later, and recapturing the typing again would be too time consuming. Fortunately, you are able to go in and edit the typing by converting the typing into a text animation.

## Edit Typing

**To edit typing:**

1. Right-click the typing item in the **Timeline**.

2. Select **Replace with Text Animation**. **(A)**

3. In the **Properties** panel, click the **Properties** button. **(B)**

4. In the **Text** field **(C)**, make text edits to the typing.

5. Click **OK**.

Text Animations, p. 66

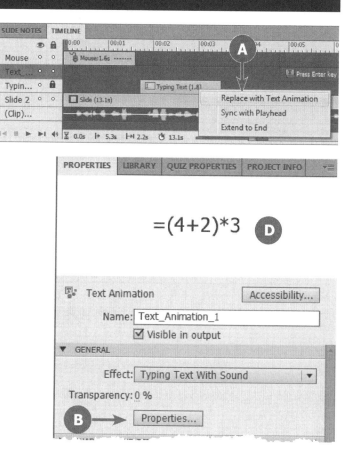

## CAUTION

- Converting the typing to a text animation may change how the characters look. You may need to adjust the formatting or placement of the typing on the screen to make it match.

- Changing the typing on one screen does not change it on later slides, so you may need to do photo editing on the background of later slides. For example, if you changed Excel formula **(D)** to formula **(C)**, the later screens will need to be corrected to show the answer **2** instead of **18**.

# Mouse Movements

When you capture a procedure, you have the option to include the mouse movements. Captivate keeps track of where you click the mouse on each screen and then creates an animated path from point to point on each slide.

Because the mouse movement is "layered" on top of the slides, it is easy to make changes to the movement. For example, you can adjust where the mouse click occurs and what the cursor looks like.

## Move the Mouse Click Position

You may need to adjust where the mouse is positioned when it clicks. For example, you may have clicked a menu item in the empty space on the right of that item, which seemed natural during the capture. However, when you review the movie, it seems odd to click off to the side.

**To move the mouse click position:**

1. Click and drag the mouse cursor to the location you want.

*Mouse position from original capture*

*Mouse position after manual adjustment*

# Change Initial Mouse Position

On each slide, mouse movements start from where they left off on the previous slide. However, on the first slide, there is no such point of reference. Instead, the mouse starts in the upper-left corner. In many cases, this works just fine. However, if your first click is very close to the upper-left corner, your students might not see the mouse move. In cases like this, you might want to change the initial mouse position.

**To change the initial mouse position:**

1. Click and drag the four red dots to the location you want.

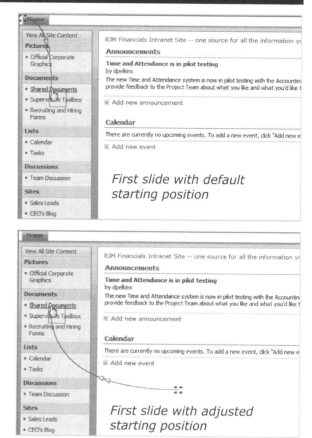

*First slide with default starting position*

*First slide with adjusted starting position*

# Align Mouse Paths

Because the mouse movement on a slide picks up where the previous slide left off, you should get smooth, fluid movement. However, if you have a slide where you don't want the mouse to move at all, there still might be a little jump in movement because the mouse is not in exactly the same place as it is in the previous slide. You can fix this by aligning the mouse to the previous slide or the next slide.

**To align mouse paths with another slide:**

1. Right-click the mouse cursor on the slide.

2. Select **Align to Previous Slide** or **Align to Next Slide**.

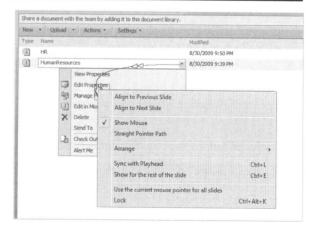

## Hide/Show Mouse Movement

Based on how you configured your recording settings, Captivate automatically includes the mouse movements. However, you may want to hide the movement on certain screens.

If you didn't choose to include the mouse when you initially captured, Captivate still "knows" where you clicked on each slide. This means you can add the mouse movement back to any slide during editing.

**To hide the mouse movement on a slide:**

1. Right-click the mouse cursor on the slide **(A)** or click the mouse icon under the **Filmstrip** thumbnail. **(B)**

2. Deselect **Show Mouse**.

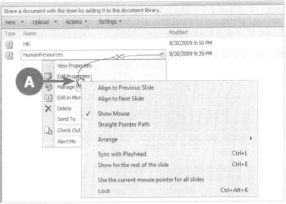
*Right-clicking the mouse*

*Clicking the mouse icon in the **Filmstrip***

**To show the mouse movement on a slide:**

1. Right-click the slide or the thumbnail.

2. Select **Mouse**.

3. Select **Show Mouse**.

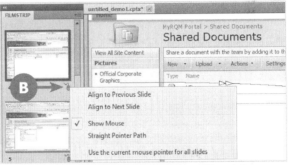
*Right-clicking the slide*

 **TIME SAVERS**

- You can show the mouse by clicking the **Insert Mouse** button on the **Object** toolbar.

- You can hide the mouse for the entire project in the **Publish Settings** section of **Preferences**.

 Publish Settings, p. 232

# Change Mouse Properties

When you select the mouse cursor on a slide, the **Mouse Properties** pane appears, giving you additional options for how the mouse behaves.

### Cursor Type

Captivate adjusts the look of the cursor based on what it looks like in the software. For example, you might see an arrow when clicking a button or an "i-beam" when editing text. You can change the look of the mouse if you need something different.

You can select one of the mouse options shown in the gallery or click the **Browse** button to select from any cursor type included with your operating system.

### Double Mouse Size

If you'd like to give the mouse more emphasis, check this box so the mouse appears larger than normal.

### Straight Pointer Path

By default, the path of the mouse curves slightly. If you would prefer that it be straight, check this box.

### Reduce Speed Before Click

If you check this box, the mouse slows down before the click, which may make the movements appear less abrupt and easier for your students to absorb.

### Mouse Click Sound

By default, a click sound is played for every click in the published movie. If you want to change that setting for a given slide, check or uncheck this box.

In addition, you can select the sound used for the click. From the drop-down menu, you can select a single-click sound or a double-click sound. You can also click the **Browse** button **(A)** to select your own sound. The **Play** button **(B)** lets you hear the selection.

### Show Mouse Click

By default, a small blue glow appears with every click in the published movie. If you want to change it for a given slide, check or uncheck this box. In addition, you can click the color swatch to change the color, select **Custom** from the menu to pick from several other options, or browse for your own .swf file.

### Timing

The **Timing** pane lets you adjust when the mouse moves. This can also be done on the **Timeline**.

 Timing Slide Objects, p. 111

## CAUTION

Don't confuse **Show Mouse** with **Show Mouse Click**. **Show Mouse** determines whether the mouse cursor and movement appear. **Show Mouse Click** determines whether or not there is a glow or other effect associated with the click.

## POWER TIP

In addition to the cursor options shown and those available with your operating system, you can use any .cur file for Windows or .pict file for Mac.

# Editing Full-Motion Recording

During a capture, certain actions (such as a dragging action) trigger a full-motion recording (FMR). You can also manually start FMR in a capture. On screens with FMR, the on-screen action is not presented as an image with the mouse layered on top, but as a video clip in .swf format. On FMR screens, the **Properties** panel has an **FMR Edit Options** pane which lets you perform the steps below.

Recording Settings, p. 23

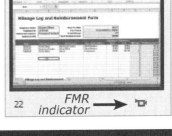

**Edit FMR**

**To insert another .swf file onto the slide:**

1. Click the **Options** drop-down menu.
2. Select **Insert**.
3. Indicate the point when you want to add the clip:
   - Enter the time in the **Insert At** field.
   - Drag the black time marker to the time.
   - Click the **Snap to Playhead** button.
4. Click the **Insert** button.
5. Find and select the .swf file you want to insert.
6. Click the **OK** button.

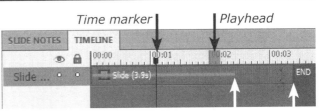

**To split the FMR file into two slides:**

1. Click the **Options** drop-down menu.
2. Select **Split**.
3. Indicate the point when you want to split the clip:
   - Enter the time in the **Split At** field.
   - Drag the black time marker to the time.
   - Click the **Snap to Playhead** button.
4. Click the **Split** button.

**To trim the front and/or end from a clip:**

1. Click the **Options** drop-down menu.
2. Select **Trim**.
3. Enter the times you want to start and end the clip:
   - Enter the start and end points in the **Trim From** and **To** fields.
   - Drag each of the two black time markers to indicate the start and end points.
   - Click the **Snap to Playhead** button for the start or end point.
4. Click the **Trim** button.

**To combine multiple FMR slides into one:**

1. Select the slides you want to combine.
2. Go to the **Modify** menu.
3. Select **Merge FMR Slides**.

# Editing Slide Backgrounds

Each capture in your software simulation is saved as an image. This makes it fairly easy to make changes to those images either using photo editing software or the tools that come with Captivate. For example, you may be creating training for a new software rollout, and at the last minute, the developers change the name of one of the buttons. Instead of redoing the entire capture, you can make background edits to your slides.

## Copy and Paste Backgrounds

You can copy the background image of any slide to either paste into another slide or to edit in photo editing software.

**To copy a slide background:**

1. Right-click the slide.
2. Select **Copy Background**.

**To paste an image as a slide background:**

1. Copy the image you want to use.
2. Right-click the slide.
3. Select **Paste as Background**.

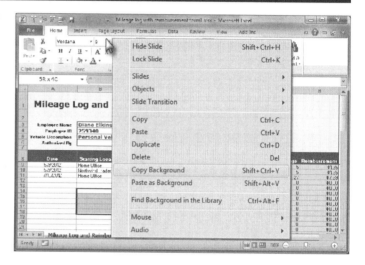

 **CAUTION**

Be careful about using **Paste** instead of **Paste as Background**. When you use **Paste as Background**, the existing background is replaced with the new image. If you use **Paste**, the new background appears as its own item in the **Timeline** on top of the old background. This adds some risk, because that object could be deleted or moved in the **Timeline**, causing the original background to show.

*New background using **Paste as Background***

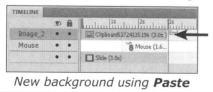

*New background using **Paste***

**POWER TIPS**

- If you ever need to go back to your original background image, you can find it in the **Library**.

- You can save time with photo editing by launching your photo editing software from the **Library**. Right-click the background image you want and select **Edit with**. Then, navigate to your photo editing software. This lets you make edits without having to go through the copy and paste steps.

| Name | | Type | Size(K...| Use C...| St...| Dat |
|---|---|---|---|---|---|---|
| ▶ 🔊 Audio | | Folder | | | | |
| ▼ 📁 Backgrounds | | Folder | | | | |
| 🖼 Backgroun... | | Image | 1753.41 | 1 | | T |
| 🖼 Ba | Rename | | | | | |
| 🖼 Back | Delete | | | | | |
| 🖼 Back | Import | | | | | |
| 🖼 Back | Export | | | | | |
| 🖼 Back | Edit with... | | | | | |
| 🖼 Back | Duplicate | | | | | |

# Merge With Background

In addition to using photo editing software to modify your backgrounds and then pasting them back into your capture, you can also use many of the object tools in Captivate to make simple changes. When you use a rectangle, text box, or small image to modify a section of the screen, you'll usually want to merge that item with the background.

Merging with the background combines the existing background and the new object being merged. This keeps the object from being deleted or moved.

**To merge an item into the background.**

1. Paste or create the object on the slide.
2. Right-click the object.
3. Select **Merge with the background**.

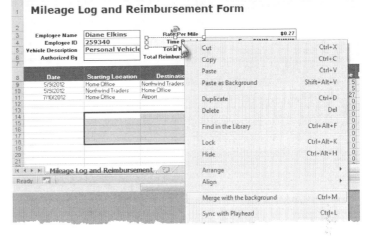

---

## CAUTION

- If your new objects are even a pixel off, your students may notice the "jump" when they are viewing your movie. Before merging, check your edits carefully by going back and forth between the previous and next slides or by toggling the visibility icon for that object to make sure the edit isn't noticeable.

- Use **Merge with the background** when you have an object to add to the background. Use **Paste as Background** when you want to replace the background.

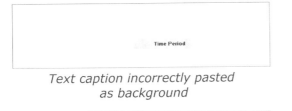

*Text caption incorrectly pasted as background*

*Text caption pasted and then merged into background*

---

## DESIGN TIP

Here are some helpful hints about how to use objects to edit your backgrounds.

### Shapes

Use the shape tools (rectangle, line, etc.) to cover over solid color areas. This is a great way to cover over a tooltip, a feature that shouldn't be showing, or text that you'll be replacing. Use the eye dropper tool to match the background perfectly.

### Captions

Use a transparent caption to replace text. Change sensitive information, such as a customer name, update the name of a feature that has changed, or fix a typo on a non-typing slide.

### Sections of Other Slides

Use a screen capture tool such as TechSmith's Jing to capture a small part of another slide to reuse. For example, if an **Enter** button was renamed **OK**, and you have another slide with a similar **OK** button, capture just the area with the **OK** button and paste it on the slide you need to fix.

# Recording Additional Slides

After your initial capture, you may need to return to your software application and get additional captures. For example, you may have found an error that can't be fixed by photo-editing the background, or you may have missed a few steps. You can record new slides inside an existing capture. You can also add a video demo into an existing project.

## Record Additional Slides

**To record additional slides:**

1. Click the **Record additional slides** button on the **Main Options** toolbar.

2. Select the slide after which the recorded slides should be inserted.

3. Click the **OK** button.

4. Configure your capture settings.

5. Click the **Record** button.

6. Capture your screens as you did before.

7. Press the **End** key on your keyboard.

 Record a Software Simulation, p. 20

## TIME SAVERS

- Set up everything for the new slides before you click **Record**. For example, you may need to undo some of the steps you performed in the original capture, especially if the new slides go in the middle of the project. For example, if you approved a vacation request at the end of a project, you may need to "unapprove" it before you can recapture an earlier step.

- Use the **Snap to window** feature during the initial recording and any additional recording to reduce the chance of your new captures being misaligned with your original captures.

## CAUTION

Not all of the recording options are available when you are adding additional captures. For example, the size of the recording window is locked to the size of the existing project.

# Managing Practice Slides

When you create an interactive practice (such as training or assessment mode), Captivate adds either click boxes or text entry boxes to create the student interactivity. You can manage the properties of the click boxes and text entry boxes, and you can also add your own if you want to.

Here are some special considerations when dealing with practice slides: click boxes and text entry boxes.

## Elements of a Click Box Slide

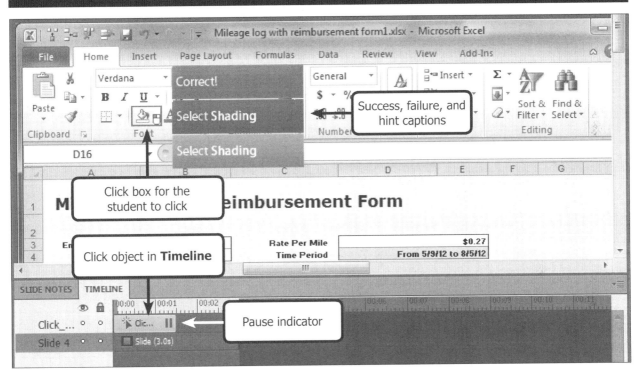

**Placement:** Be sure that the click box fully covers the area that the student should click. In some cases, the default placement only covers half of the button, menu item, etc. Click and drag the click box to move or resize it.

**Action Pane:** By default, students go to the next slide when they click correctly, and the slide continues if they do not click correctly within the designated number of attempts. This means the rest of the slide plays, so you can put an extra caption with feedback after the pause indicator. Only the students who don't click correctly within the set number of attempts will ever see that caption. You can also designate a keyboard shortcut to take the place of a click.

**Options Pane:** Here you can change many of the options you selected in the **Recording Settings**. In addition, you can change a left-click to a double-click or right-click.

 Click Box Properties, p. 128

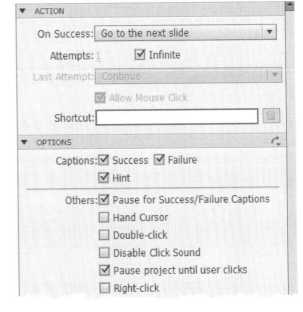

# Elements of a Text Entry Box Slide

## Mileage Log and Reimbursement Form

Text entry area

Submit button to grade the text entry.

Success, failure, and hint captions

Text entry box in Timeline

**Placement**: You may need to adjust the formatting or size of the text entry box to match everything else on the screen.

**Grading the Answer:** When a student types in an answer, Captivate needs to know when to grade it.

- **Keyboard shortcut**: If you enter a shortcut **(A)**, the students' entries are graded when they press that shortcut.

- **Submit button**: If you check **Show Button (B)**, a **Submit** button appears next to the text box. The student's answer is graded when he or she clicks the **Submit** button.

- **Combine the Submit button with the next step**: If the next step in the procedure is a click, add the **Submit** button, but make it transparent and place it over the step. When the student clicks the next step, the text entry will be graded.

- **Grade the answer after a certain limit has been reached**: If you click the **More options** button **(C)**, you can set a character limit and have the answer evaluated when that limit is met.

 Text Entry Box Properties, p. 132

## CAUTION

With the first two options, the student performs a step that is not part of the procedure. The student might get used to pressing **Enter** or clicking **Submit**, and then try to do it in the real system.

---

▼ GENERAL

Default Text:

☑ Retain Text

☐ Show Text Box Frame

☐ Password Field

☑ Validate User Input

More options ← **C**

Variable: Text_Entry_Box_4 ▼ [X]

On Focus Lost: No Action ▼

▶ CHARACTER

▼ ACTION

On Success: Go to the next slide ▼

Attempts: 2 **A** ☐ Infinite

Last Attempt: Continue ▼

Shortcut: Enter 🗑

▼ OPTIONS

Captions: ☐ Success ☑ Failure

☐ Hint

Others: ☑ Pause for Success/Failure Captions

☑ Show Button ← **B**

☐ Show Scrollbar

# Managing Video Demo Projects

As you learned in chapter 2, you can create a screen recording in real-time that works more like a movie than a filmstrip. When you open one of these video composition files, you will not see the **Filmstrip** or individual slides. Instead, your movie appears on a single timeline.

As with any project, you can add audio, captions, shapes, and other static objects to your project and adjust the timing in the **Timeline**. In addition, you can perform special functions available only in a video demo project:

- Trim and split the recording.
- Add transitions.
- Add pan and zoom effects.
- Create a picture-in-picture effect.

## Trim and Split the Recording

**To trim the start or end points:**

1. Click and drag the yellow marker. **(A)**

**To trim a section out of the middle:**

1. Click the **Trim** button. **(B)**
2. Drag the sliders to highlight the portion to be removed. **(C)**
3. Click **Trim**. **(D)**

**To split the recording:**

1. Click in the **Timeline** where you want to split the video.
2. Click the **Split** button. **(E)**

If you have more than one section of video because of splitting and trimming, you can move the individual segments on the **Timeline**.

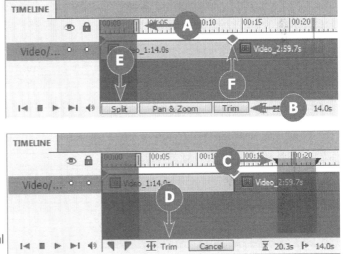

## Add Transitions

At the beginning, the end, and any split or trim point in your video, you can add a transition. A gray diamond or triangle **(F)** indicates a point where you can add a transition.

**To add a transition:**

1. Click a transition marker. **(F)**
2. In the **Transitions** panel that appears, select the transition type you want.
3. From the drop-down menu at the top, select the speed you want.

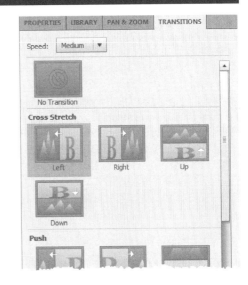

# Add Pan & Zoom Effects

**To add a pan or zoom effect:**

1. Click in the **Timeline** where you want the effect to start.

2. Click the **Pan & Zoom** button. **(A)**

3. In the **Pan & Zoom** panel, position the blue frame to indicate the portion of the screen to zoom into.

## Options:

**Scale**: Rather than manually resizing the blue frame, use the slider or numerical entry box to set the frame based on a scale of the original.

**Speed**: Use the slider or the text entry box to indicate how long it takes to zoom in/zoom out/pan.

**Size & Position**: Use the width and height fields as a different way to adjust the size of the blue frame. Use the X and Y coordinates as a different way to position the frame.

## DESIGN TIPS

- A magnifying glass icon appears in the **Timeline** for each change in pan/zoom. **(B)** Click the icon to change its properties in the **Pan & Zoom** panel. Drag the icon to change when the change happens. Right-click it to delete it.

- To end a zoom effect, click in the **Timeline** where you want to end the effect, and click the **Zoom Out** button in the **Pan & Zoom** panel. **(C)**

- To create a pan effect, put two zoom effects (each focusing on a different part of the slide) next to each other. Captivate will transition between the two with a pan effect.

- If you have splits or trims, the video will zoom out at the end of each segment.

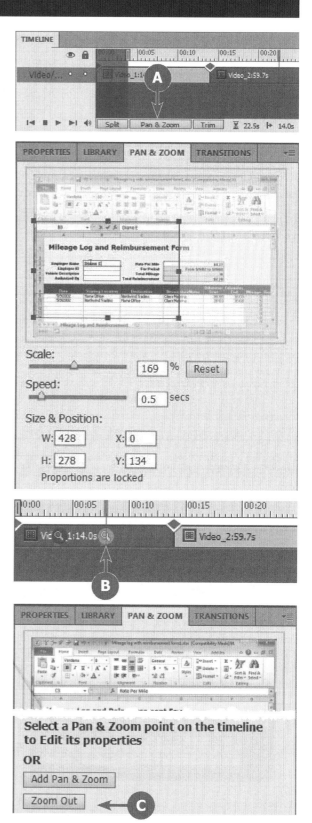

# Create Picture-in-Picture (PIP) Effects

You can add a video that appears in a small window on top of your existing video demo. Acceptable file types include .flv, .f4v, .avi, .mp4, .mov, and .3gp. If you insert one of these file types other than .mp4, the file will be converted to .mp4 for you.

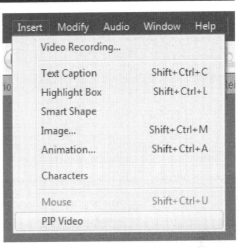

**To add a picture-in-picture effect:**

1. Click in the **Timeline** where you want the PIP to start.
2. Go to the **Insert** menu.
3. Select **PIP Video**.
4. Find and select the video you want to add.
5. Click the **OK** button.
6. Position the video where you want it on the slide.
7. Position the video where you want it in the **Timeline**.

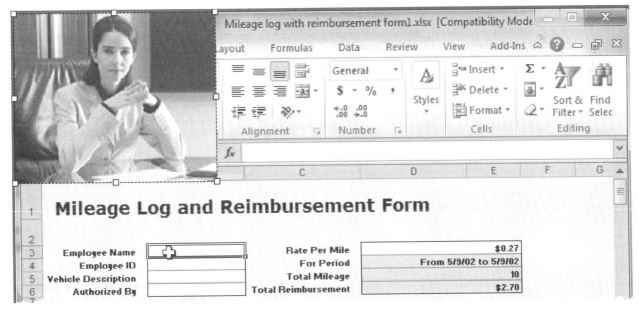

# Add a Video Demo Slide to a Project

In Captivate 7, you can add an existing video demo capture (CPVC) to an existing project. The CPVC file is added as a full-motion recording.

**To add a video demo slide:**

1. Go to the **Insert** menu.
2. Select **CPVC Slide**.
3. Find and select the CPVC slide you want.
4. Click the **Open** button.

**To edit a CPVC file that has been inserted into another project:**

1. Select the CPVC slide.
2. Go to the **Properties** tab.
3. Click the **Edit Video Demo** button.
4. Make your changes.
5. Click the **Save** button.
6. Click the **Exit** button.

Note that the changes you make are saved to the underlying CPVC file.

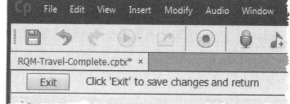

# Variables & Advanced Actions

## Introduction

Variables and advanced actions let you expand and customize the functionality of Captivate. They are like building blocks that you can use however you want to create special features.

A variable is a stored piece of logic within the project that you can use to:

- Track information provided by the student, such as an option that the student selects or text that the student enters.
- Control course functionality, such as turning the audio or the control playbar on and off.
- Display something back to the student, such as the current time or points earned in a test or game.
- Set up conditional logic, such as whether a student is a supervisor or uses a screen reader.

Advanced actions give you more choices than you have in the **Actions** pane of an object's properties. Use the **Advanced Actions** dialog box when you want to:

- Apply more than one action to a single object. For example, in a game, you might want a single button click to show a message, add points to a score, and advance to the next slide.
- Create a conditional action. For example, you can ask students if they are a supervisor or not, and then have a button that branches to one slide if they click **Yes** and a different slide if they click **No**.
- Reuse actions. For example, if you want to add points to a student's score in a game that has several questions, you can set up the action once and then reuse it on each slide.
- Access more action options. For example, you can create calculations from the **Advanced Actions** dialog box.
- Interact with objects on different slides. For example, you can have a button on slide 3 that reveals an object on slide 10.
- Save actions to reuse across multiple slides using different parameters and import/export actions to reuse them in different projects.

### In This Chapter

- Working With Variables
- Advanced Actions
  - Standard
  - Conditional
  - Shared
- Managing Advanced Actions

# Notes

# Working With Variables

Variables, which are stored pieces of information in the project, come in two basic types:

- **System Variables**: System variables are set up by Captivate. They include information about the project (such as the current slide), controls for the project (such as whether the playbar is showing), or quiz information, if there is a quiz. You cannot set up or delete these variables, but you can use them for conditional logic, display them to students, and even modify some of them to control the project.

   Appendix: System Variables, p. 255

- **User Variables**: A user variable is one that you create yourself. You set it up, you define and modify its value, and you decide how it will be used. For example, you can set up a variable to keep score in a game. You can also set up variables that the student controls. For example, you can insert a text box where the student enters his or her name, and then you can use that information later in a certificate.

## Manage Variables

**To view variables:**

1. Go to the **Project** menu.
2. Select **Variables**.
3. Select **User** or **System** from the **Type** drop-down menu to see a list of each type of variable.

System variables can only be viewed, not modified, in this dialog box. Select one from the list to view its current value and the description.

For user variables, you can delete or change the default value of the variable.

**To delete a user variable:**

1. Select a variable.
2. Click the **Remove** button.

**To change the default value of a user variable:**

1. Select a variable.
2. Change the value.
3. Click the **Update** button.

*Button options after initially saving the variable.*

# Add a User Variable

**To add a user variable:**

1. Go to the **Project** menu.
2. Select **Variables**.
3. Click the **Add New** button.
4. In the **Name** field, enter the name for the variable.
5. In the **Value** field, enter the initial value for the variable.
6. In the **Description** field, add a description about the variable or how it will be used, if needed.
7. Click the **Save** button.
8. Click the **Close** button.

Variable names cannot contain spaces or special characters except underscore.

 **TIME SAVERS**

Put an underscore in front of the name of your variables so they'll be easier to find at the top of any variable list.

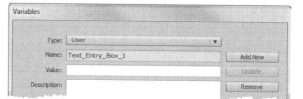

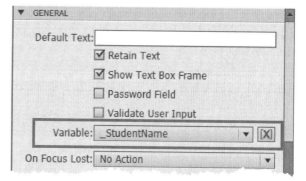

# Add a Text-Entry Variable

When you add a text entry field to a project, the student's entry is saved as a variable. You can then use this for conditional logic or to display back to the student. For example, you may have the student enter his or her name.

In the **General** pane for the text entry box, use the **Variable** field to indicate what variable you want to use to capture the student's answer. Either select an existing variable from the drop-down menu, or click the **[X]** button to create a new variable name.

 Text Entry Boxes, p. 132

# Modify Variables With the Actions Pane

Variables can be modified with simple actions from the **Action** pane of the various trigger objects. More advanced modifications can be done with advanced actions.

## Assign

Use this command to change the value of a variable to an exact value, such as a number or text. For example, you can change the value that controls whether or not the playbar shows, or assign the value for whether or not a student is a supervisor.

## Increment

Use this command to add to a user-defined variable that has a number value. For example, you can add points to a student's score in a game.

## Decrement

Use this command to subtract from a user-defined variable that has a number value. For example, you can subtract points from a student's score.

## Display a Variable

You can display the value of a variable to the student in a text caption or a shape with text. The variable can be included with other text. The text is updated every time the variable is updated.

For example, you might want to display the student's point value during a game or display a name that the student previously entered in a text box.

**To display a variable:**

1. Double-click a caption or shape with text.
2. Click the **Insert Variables** button. **(A)**
3. Select **User** or **System** from the **Variable Type** drop-down menu, based on the type of variable you want to display.
4. In the **Variables** field, select the variable you want.
5. Click the **OK** button.

### Options

Click the **Variables** button if you want to go to the **Variables** dialog box to add or make changes to the variables.

The **Maximum length** field shows the maximum number of characters that will be displayed. If the value of the variable is longer than that, the extra characters will be cut off.

 **POWER TIP**

If you prefer, you can type the variable code into the caption yourself. Type two dollar signs before and after the name of the variable. The variable must be an exact match, including capitalization.

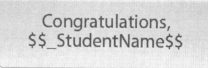

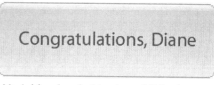

*Variable placeholder in edit mode.*

Congratulations, Diane

*Variable placeholder in published movie.*

# Advanced Actions

The **Advanced Actions** dialog box gives you more options than you have in the **Action** pane in an object's properties, such as grouping actions together or creating conditional actions. You can create a conditional action that only runs if certain conditions are met, or a standard action that runs any time it is executed.

When you create an advanced action, it does not run on its own. You can run that action anywhere in the project (even multiple times) by creating an action that executes it.

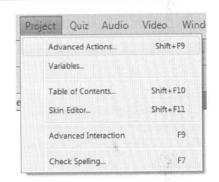

Execute Advanced Actions, p. 123

---

## Add a Standard Advanced Action

**To add a standard advanced action:**

1. Go to the **Project** menu.
2. Select **Advanced Actions**.
3. In the **Action Name** field, enter a name for the action.
4. In the **Actions** list, double-click in the second column.
5. Select the command you want from the drop-down menu.
6. Complete the additional options that may appear in the third column, based on the command you chose.
7. Repeat steps 4-6 for additional commands.
8. Click the **Save as Action** button.
9. Click the **Close** button.

### Special Options

- If you'd like to create a new action based on a previously saved (shared) action, select that shared action from the **Create from** drop-down menu.
- Icons indicate if a command is complete. **(A)** A green check means it is complete. A yellow triangle means there is missing or incomplete information. You cannot save an advanced action with a yellow icon.
- Click the **Variables** button to add or change variables.
- Use the icons just above the **Actions** list to modify individual commands:

    **Add**: Add a new row at the bottom.

    **Remove**: Delete the selected command.

    **Cut**, **Copy**, and **Paste**: Make copies of a command

    **Insert**: Add a line above the selected command.

    **Move Up** and **Move Down**: Change the order of the selected command. On some actions, the order of the commands can be critical.

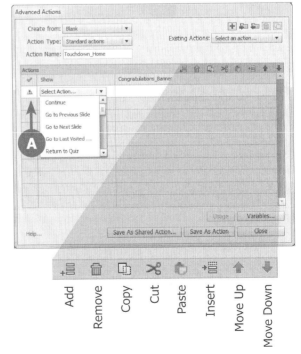

# Advanced Action Commands

Many of the action commands available in the **Advanced Action** dialog box are the same as those available in the **Action** pane. However, some commands are only available here, and some are set up differently here.

## The Same

- **Continue**
- **Go to Next Slide**
- **Go to Previous Slide**
- **Go to Last Visited Slide**
- **Return to Quiz**
- **Jump to Slide**
- **Open URL or File**
- **Open Other Project**
- **Send Mail**
- **Execute JavaScript**
- **Apply Effect**

## Slightly Different

### Enable, Disable, Show, Hide, Play Audio, and Stop Triggered Audio

These work *mostly* the same way as they do in the **Action** pane. In the **Action** pane, you can only select items on that slide. In the **Advanced Actions** dialog box, you can select any eligible object in the project.

### Assign

The **Assign** action still lets you assign a value to a variable. You have some additional choices when you run this action from the **Advanced Action** dialog box.

Once you select **Assign**, you can then select the variable you want from the drop-down menu in the next column.

Next, a new menu appears letting you choose **variable** or **literal**.

- Select **variable** if you want to change the value of the first **variable** to the value of a different variable.
- Select **literal** if you want to use an exact value, such as a number or text.

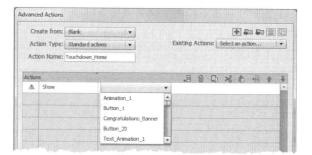

## Only Available Here

The **Expression** action is only available in advanced actions. **Expression** lets you create calculations, taking the place of, and providing more options than, **Increment** and **Decrement**.

First, select a variable that will hold the value of the calculation.

Then, you can make each part of the equation a variable or a literal value. First, select **variable** or **literal** from the menu. If you select **variable**, you get a list of variables to choose from. If you select **literal**, you get a text entry box to enter the literal value.

Finally, you can select from four calculation types: addition, subtraction, multiplication, or division.

*Options for building the expression*

*Finished expression*

# Conditional Actions

With a standard advanced action, all actions run when the advanced action is executed. When a conditional action is executed, the actions only run if certain conditions are met. For example, certain information might be shown if the quiz is passed. A conditional action can have three parts.

- **If**: This is where you set up the conditions that have to be met in order for the actions to run.
- **Actions**: This is where you set up the individual actions that will run when the conditions are met.
- **Else**: Here you can set up an alternate set of actions that will run if the conditions are NOT met. You can leave this section blank, which means that nothing will happen if the conditions are not met.

As with standard advanced actions, you need to first set up the advanced action, and then execute it from the **Action** pane of an interactive object.

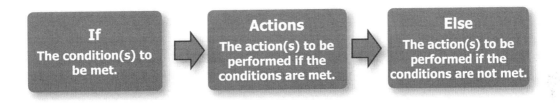

## Add a Conditional Advanced Action

**To add a conditional action:**

1. Go to the **Project** menu.
2. Select **Advanced Actions**.
3. From the **Action Type** drop-down menu, select **Conditional actions**.
4. In the **Action Name** field, enter a name for the action.
5. In the **IF** section, enter the condition(s) that need to occur in order for the action to run.
6. In the **Actions** section, enter the action(s) that will run when the **IF** conditions *are* met.
7. Click the **ELSE** heading.
8. Enter the action(s) that will run if the **IF** conditions are *not* met.
9. Click the **Save as Action** button.
10. Click the **Close** button.

Refer to the next few pages for details on the **IF**, **Actions**, and **ELSE** sections.

# Creating IF Conditions

A condition has three parts: the two items being compared and how they should be compared. Double-click a line in the **IF** section, and enter values for the three parts.

1. Select a variable or literal value for the basis of comparison.

2. Select a comparison operator to determine how the two items will be compared.

   - Is greater than
   - Is less than
   - Greater or equal to
   - Lesser or equal to
   - Not equal to
   - Is equal to
   - Contains

3. Select what the first value should be compared to, either another variable or a literal value.

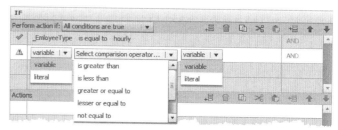

Options for building the conditions

Finished condition

## Multiple Conditions

You can create an advanced action with one or more conditions. If there is only one condition, then you don't need to do anything more. However, if you have multiple conditions, you need to designate how the conditions interact with each other.

For example, you might have a condition about whether an employee is hourly and another about whether an employee is seasonal.

From the **Perform action if** drop-down menu, select one of the following:

**All Conditions Are True**: Select this option if all conditions must be met in order for the actions to be run. For example, an employee must be hourly AND seasonal.

**Any of the Conditions Are True**: Select this option if you only need one of the options to be true for the actions to be run. For example, an employee must either be hourly OR seasonal.

**Custom**: Select this option if you want to use a combination of AND and OR logic. When you use this option, select **AND** or **OR** for each condition in the third column. For example, the employee must be salaried OR hourly AND seasonal.

## Managing Conditions

Conditions can be copied, pasted, moved, etc. just as actions can.

Add   Remove   Copy   Cut   Paste   Insert   Move Up   Move Down

## Creating Actions and Else Actions

In the **Actions** section, add one or more actions, just as with standard actions.

To set up the actions that trigger if the conditions are not met, click the **ELSE** heading. Then, add the actions just as with standard actions.

Click the **IF** heading to return to the original view.

## Creating Multiple Decisions

Just as a standard action can have multiple individual actions, a conditional action can have multiple decisions, meaning multiple if/action/else sets. For example, the advanced action runs one set of logic based on the employee type and a second set of logic based on whether the test was passed. Decisions are managed by the buttons in the middle of the dialog box.

- To view a decision, click the button for that decision.

- To rename a decision, double-click the button for that decision, and type the name.

- To add a new decision, click the **Plus** button.

- To delete a decision, click the button for the decision and then click the **Minus** button.

# Shared Actions

In Captivate 7, actions can be saved as shared actions. When you do this, you can:

- Build new actions based from it, with the shared action acting like a template.

- Import and export them so they can be used in multiple projects and by multiple developers. When exported, shared actions are saved as .cpaa files.

- Reuse the action using different parameters.

You can reuse any advanced action multiple times throughout a project. But when you save an action as a shared action, you can configure slide-specific parameters, making the action more reusable. For example, if you have a course on a time and attendance system, some slides may only be relevant to employees who are supervisors. You can set up an advanced, conditional action to go to slide 3 if the student is a supervisor and slide 6 if the person is not. Later in the course, you might have another situation that needs similar branching. You can't reuse the exact same advanced action, because in this new case, you don't want to branch to slides 3 and 6, you want to branch to slides 14 and 18. This is where a shared action can be useful. If you save the original action as a shared action, it puts placeholders, called parameters, in the saved action. You can then configure those parameters every time you reuse the action—either in the same project or when imported into a different project.

## Save as a Shared Action

**To save an action as a shared action:**

1. Set up your action in the **Advanced Actions** dialog box.

2. Click the **Save As Shared Action** button.

3. In the dialog box, change the name and/or enter a description, if needed.

4. In the **Parameter Description**, describe guidelines for the type of object that should be selected.

5. Click the **Save** button.

6. Click **OK** in the pop-up window that appears.

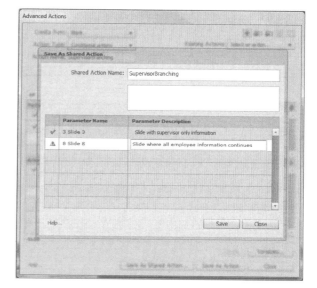

## Create a New Action Based on a Shared Action

**To create a new action based on a shared action:**

1. Go to the **Project** menu.

2. Select **Advanced Actions**.

3. In the **Create From** menu, select the shared action upon which you want to base the new action.

4. Modify and save the action as you normally would.

# Import and Export Shared Actions

**To import a shared action:**

1. Go to the **Project** menu.
2. Select **Advanced Actions**.
3. Click the **Import** button. **(A)**
4. Find and select the shared action you want to import.
5. Click the **Open** button.
6. Click the **OK** button.

**To export a shared action:**

1. Go to the **Project** menu.
2. Select **Advanced Actions**.
3. Click the **Export** button. **(B)**
4. Select the shared action you want to export.
5. Click the **Browse** button.
6. Find and select the location where you want to save it.
7. Click the **OK** button.
8. Click the **Export** button.
9. Click the **OK** button.

# Execute a Shared Action

**To execute a shared action**

1. In any available action menu, select **Execute Shared Action**.
2. In the **Shared Action** drop-down menu, select the shared action you want.
3. Click the **Action Parameter** button.
4. Select the slide-specific elements for the action.
5. Click the **OK** button.

# Managing Actions

## Managing Advanced Actions

From the **Advanced Actions** dialog box, you can manage existing actions.

- To view an advanced action, select it from the **Existing Actions** drop-down menu.

- To add an additional advanced action, click the **Create a new action** button.

- To delete an advanced action, select it, and then click the **Delete action** button.

- To make a copy of an advanced action, select it, and then click the **Duplicate action** button.

- To modify an advanced action (rename it or add or delete actions and conditions), make the changes, and click the **Update Action** button.

## Advanced Interaction Panel

The **Advanced Interaction** panel lets you see all the interactive objects in your project. From this one view, you can see many of the key properties of the interactive objects, such as the action, number of attempts, etc. When you click on an object in the pane, the slide appears with the object selected and the object's **Properties** panel showing.

You can access the **Advanced Interaction** panel from the **Project** menu.

# Questions & Quizzes

## Introduction

Questions, quizzes, tests, scenarios, interactions—these course elements often make the difference between *telling* someone something and *teaching* them something. They allow both you and the students to reinforce and apply the content, assess the learning, uncover opportunities for re-teaching, and evaluate the course effectiveness. Captivate offers nine question types you can insert in a graded format and/or survey format.

In this chapter, you will learn how to add questions to your projects, either for pure reinforcement or as part of a graded quiz that reports to a learning management system (LMS). (You'll learn more about the LMS reporting settings in chapter 12.)

### In This Chapter

- Creating Questions
- Configuring Questions
- Individual Question Options
- Creating Pretests
- Quiz Master Slides
- Question Pools
- Quiz Results Slides
- Quiz Preferences

# Notes

# Creating Questions

## Add a Question

**To add a question to your project:**

1. Go to the **Insert** or **Quiz** menu.
2. Select **Question Slide**.
3. Check the box for the type of question you would like to use.
4. Enter the quantity you want for that question type.
5. Select **Graded, Survey**, or **Pretest** from the drop-down menu.
6. Click **OK**.

## TIME SAVER

You can add several questions at once in this dialog box. Simply select more than one type of question, and enter the quantity you want for each before clicking **OK**.

## POWER TIP

In addition to using question slides, you can make your own questions from scratch using buttons or click boxes. Just check the **Include in Quiz** box in the **Reporting** pane for that object.

Click Boxes and Buttons, pp. 128-130

## DESIGN TIP

Graded vs. Survey vs. Pretest Questions

Use a graded question type when there are right and wrong answers. You can indicate which answer is right vs. wrong and provide separate feedback for right vs. wrong answers. Most knowledge-check questions fall into this category.

Use a survey question when there isn't a right or wrong answer. All students get the same feedback, regardless of their answer. Use this for opinion questions or questions where students self-grade their answers as compared to the answer you provide.

Use a pretest question when you want to assess the student's knowledge before the course and direct them to certain content based on their results.

Pretests, p. 191

# Question Types

## Multiple Choice

Student chooses one or more options among several possible answers.

- Can have up to 15 answer choices
- Available as graded or survey

### When dealing with an angry customer, it is best to:

- ○ A) maintain a calm, soothing voice
- ⦿ B) mirror the client's energy to let him or her know you understand the frustration
- ○ C) speak to the customer firmly telling him or her to calm down
- ○ D) ask the customer to take a few minutes to relax

## True/False

Student decides between two options.

- Can change "true" and "false" labels
- Available as graded or survey

### As an organization, we believe there are opportunities to learn from clients willing to share their complaints.

- ⦿ A) True
- ○ B) False

## Fill in the Blank

Student types a word into the space provided.

- Can be case sensitive or not
- Can allow more than one correct answer
- Can be formatted as a multiple-choice question with a drop-down list
- Available as graded or survey

### Complete the sentence below by filling in the blank.

The first thing we must do with an angry customer is _____ him or her.

### Complete the sentence below by filling in the blank.

The first thing we must do with an angry customer is [ ▼ ] him or her.

| |
|---|
| move |
| listen to |
| calm |

## Short Answer

Student types in a longer answer to a question.

- Available as graded or survey

### What do you believe are the two or three most important qualities a customer service specialist possesses?

# Question Types (cont'd)

## Matching

Student matches items in one column with items in the other.

- Can have up to 8 options per column
- Available as graded or survey

## Hot Spot

Student clicks on one or more designated hot spots on a graphic image.

- Can have up to 10 hot spots
- Available as graded or survey

## Sequence

Student arranges a series of items into the proper sequence.

- Can be formatted as a drag-and-drop or drop-down list
- Available as graded or survey

## Rating Scale (Likert)

Students evaluate statements and rate them on a scale.

- Can have up to 5 points on the scale
- Available as survey only

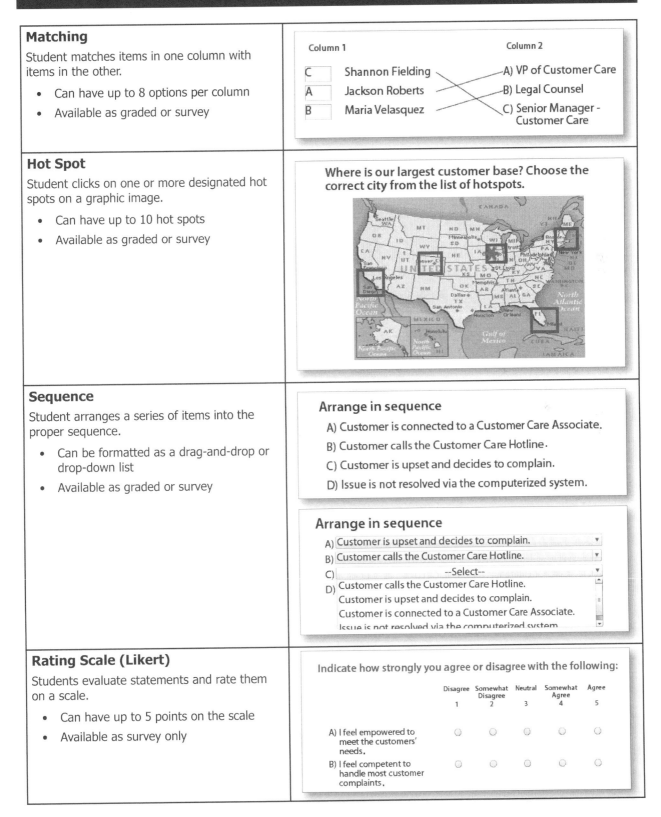

**Matching example:**

Column 1

| C | Shannon Fielding |
| A | Jackson Roberts |
| B | Maria Velasquez |

Column 2

A) VP of Customer Care
B) Legal Counsel
C) Senior Manager - Customer Care

**Hot Spot example:**

Where is our largest customer base? Choose the correct city from the list of hotspots.

**Sequence example:**

Arrange in sequence

A) Customer is connected to a Customer Care Associate.
B) Customer calls the Customer Care Hotline.
C) Customer is upset and decides to complain.
D) Issue is not resolved via the computerized system.

Arrange in sequence

A) Customer is upset and decides to complain. ▼
B) Customer calls the Customer Care Hotline. ▼
C) --Select-- ▼
D) Customer calls the Customer Care Hotline.
Customer is upset and decides to complain.
Customer is connected to a Customer Care Associate.
Issue is not resolved via the computerized system.

**Rating Scale example:**

Indicate how strongly you agree or disagree with the following:

|  | Disagree 1 | Somewhat Disagree 2 | Neutral 3 | Somewhat Agree 4 | Agree 5 |
|---|---|---|---|---|---|
| A) I feel empowered to meet the customers' needs. | ○ | ○ | ○ | ○ | ○ |
| B) I feel competent to handle most customer complaints. | ○ | ○ | ○ | ○ | ○ |

# Configuring Questions

Once you've added your question, you'll need to configure it, changing both the text and the properties. Some options are changed directly on the slide and some are changed on the **Quiz Properties** tab.

The options vary based on question type. The next four pages cover standard properties and options that apply to most questions types. The following pages go into question type-specific options.

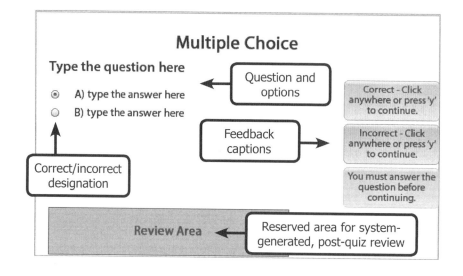

## Add Question Content

Your question slide has placeholders for a title, your question/instructions, and the answer options. To build your question, simply type or paste your text in the placeholders.

**To format the text boxes:**

1. Select the object(s) you want to format.
2. Click the **Properties** tab.
3. Make the changes you want.

 Formatting Caption Text, p. 52

**To add more answer options (except T/F):**

1. Click the **Quiz Properties** tab.
2. Enter the number you want in the **Answers** field.

 **CAUTION**

Don't get confused by the **Properties** and **Quiz Properties** tabs. Use the **Properties** tab for object options, such as font or color. Use **Quiz Properties** for question-specific options, such as the number of correct answers or what feedback options to include.

# Add Standard Feedback

You can have up to five types of feedback captions, which can be turned on and off via the **Quiz Properties** tab. Change the text, formatting, and location of the feedback caption just like you would any other caption.

### Correct (A)
This caption displays when the student answers the question correctly.

### Incorrect (B)
This caption displays when the student answers the question incorrectly.

### Timeout (C)
If you set a time limit for the question, this caption appears when the time runs out.

### Retry (D)
If you allow more than one attempt, this caption appears after each failed attempt (except the last one).

### Required Answer (E)
If the question cannot be skipped, this caption appears if the student tries to leave the page without answering the question.

 Caption Properties, p. 52

Correct - Click anywhere or press 'y' to continue.

Incorrect - Click anywhere or press 'y' to continue.

The time to answer this question has expired. Click anywhere or press 'y' to continue.

Try again

You must answer the question before continuing.

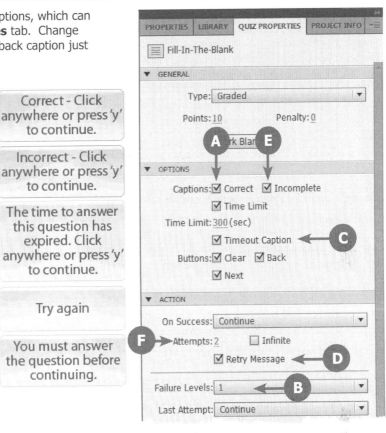

## Set Number of Attempts
By default, quiz questions are set to allow one attempt. That means if the student does not get the question right the first time, the incorrect logic (captions, actions, points, etc.) runs after that attempt. If you'd like to provide more than one attempt, change the number in the **Attempts** field, or check the **Infinite** box for unlimited attempts. **(F)**

 **CAUTION**

When configuring questions, some of the features you want will be on the **Properties** tab and some will be on the **Quiz Properties** tab. Be sure you are looking in the right place!

 **DESIGN TIPS**

- You don't need to make room on your slide for all of these captions. Since most of them will not show up at the same time (such as a success and a failure caption), they can overlap on your slide to save space.

- Use the **Time Limit** option with care. Imposing a time limit has accessibility implications for those with physical, cognitive, or developmental disabilities.

- You can use caption styles to help save time with formatting your feedback captions.

 Styles, p. 104

## Add Progressive Feedback

If you are giving your students more than one attempt at a question, you can give them more than one level of feedback. For example, if they get a question wrong the first time, you can show an incorrect feedback question that simply asks them to try again. Then if they get it wrong again, you can show a different incorrect feedback caption that provides more of a hint. Then the third level of feedback can provide the correct answer.

You can have up to three levels of feedback, and you cannot have more feedback levels than you have attempts.

**To add progressive feedback to a question:**

1. In the **Quiz Properties** panel, enter the number of allowable attempts in the **Attempts** field.

2. In the **Failure Levels** drop-down menu, select the number of failure captions you want.

3. In the work area, add text to each of the failure captions that appear.

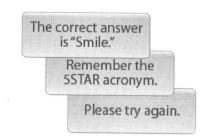

## Set Success and Failure Actions

For any graded question type, you can indicate what you want to have happen when the student answers the question correctly (within the specified number of attempts) or incorrectly (after the maximum number of attempts have been used).

By default, both action fields are set to **Continue**. But you can change either one of those actions to create branching (using any of the **Go to** actions), give audio feedback (**Play Audio**), or create advanced game logic (**Execute Advanced Actions**).

**To set a success action:**

1. In the **Quiz Properties** panel, click the **On Success** drop-down menu.

2. Select the action you want.

**To set a failure action:**

1. In the **Quiz Properties** panel, click the **Last Attempt** drop-down menu.

2. Select the action you want.

 **CAUTION**

You cannot set a **Last Attempt** action if the question is set to unlimited attempts.

## Add Advanced Feedback

### Branching Quizzes

If you want more feedback than fits in a feedback caption, you can branch to a different slide with feedback.

**To branch to a different slide based on answer:**

1. In **Quiz Properties**, add a **Jump to Slide** action in the **On Success** and **Last Attempt** fields.

2. In the **On Success** action, select the slide with the correct feedback.

3. In the **Last Attempt** action, select the slide with the incorrect feedback.

 **POWER TIP**

If your questions branch to other questions based on the student's answer, the student may not take all questions in a quiz, which can affect the quiz score. If you check the **Branch Aware** checkbox in **Quiz Preferences**, Captivate grades the quiz based on the number of questions presented, not the total in the quiz.

### Option-Specific Feedback

On a multiple-choice question, you can have separate feedback and actions for each option. For example, you can have different feedback if A was chosen instead of B.

**To add option-specific feedback:**

1. In the work area, select the individual option you want to work with.

2. In the **Properties** pane, check the **Advanced Answer Option** check box.

3. Configure the action you want, if needed.

4. Check the **Show Feedback Message** box to add a text caption to appear if that option is chosen.

### Remediation Back to Content Slides

If students get a question wrong, you can branch back to one or several slides where the content was taught and then return them back to the quiz to retry the question.

**To add remediation branching:**

1. In the **Last Attempt** field on the question, set a **Jump to slide** action to the first slide with the content.

2. On the last slide with the content, add a **Return to Quiz** action on the slide's next button.

On the content slide, the **Next** button with the **Return to Quiz** action executes a **Continue** action under normal circumstances, but returns students to the quiz if that's where they came from.

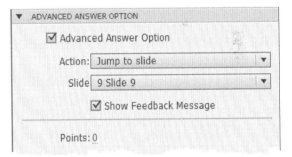

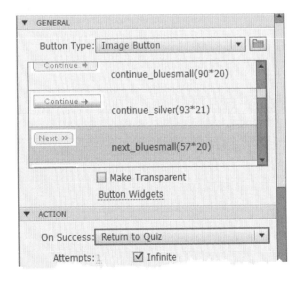

## Assign Points to Questions

When you assign points to a question, by default, the students receive all of the points if they get the question right and none of the points if they get the question wrong.

There are several ways to create more advanced point logic. You can have the student lose points for a wrong answer, and for multiple-choice questions, you can provide partial credit if the student selects a "somewhat correct" option.

**To add standard points:**

1. In the **Quiz Properties** panel, adjust the number in the **Points** field. **(A)**

**To deduct points for an incorrect answer:**

1. In the **Quiz Properties** panel, adjust the number in the **Penalty** field. **(B)**

**To provide points for an incorrect answer:**

1. In the **Quiz Properties** panel, check the **Partial Score** box. **(C)**
2. In the work area, select an individual question option.
3. In the **Properties** panel, adjust the number in the **Points** field. **(D)**

## The Review Area

In addition to feedback given at the time the question is answered, you can also provide a post-quiz review. The **Review Area** is a portion of the slide reserved for system-generated feedback when the student goes back and reviews a quiz. You can move and resize the review area to design your page.

From **Quiz Preferences**, you can enable or disable the review area and change the default text for the entire quiz. If you want to change the text used for a specific question, select the review area for that question, and then go to the **Properties** (not the **Quiz Properties**) tab. You can make edits to the text in the **Review Feedback Messages** pane.

 Quiz Preferences p. 197

## ⓘ CAUTION

Make sure you do not cover up the review area with any of your slide elements.

If you resize the review area, check it in preview mode to make sure it is big enough for all the text.

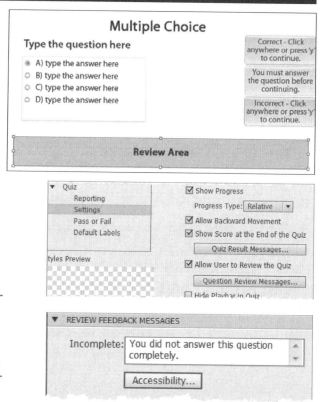

# Additional Quiz Properties

In the previous sections on feedback and score, you've learned about most of the properties in the **Quiz Properties** panel. Here are a few more properties that apply to most question types. The following pages cover the properties that are unique to specific question types.

## General Pane

### Type (A)

When you added the question, you chose **Graded**, **Survey**, or **Pretest**. You can change that here.

### Numbering (B)

Change the type of numbers, letters, and punctuation for the answer options.

## Options Pane

### Buttons (C)

These buttons appear at the bottom of the slide giving students options to maneuver through the training. Check or uncheck the boxes based on which buttons you want to include on the slide.

## Reporting Pane

### Report Answers (D)

If you check this box, question-specific data will be sent to the learning management system (LMS), rather than just the overall test score.

### Interaction ID (E)

If you are sending question-specific data to the LMS, you can enter an interaction number to be sent to the LMS.

# Individual Question Options

The following pages feature elements that are unique to each individual question type.

## Multiple-Choice Question Options

**Shuffle Answers**: Check this box if you want Captivate to shuffle the possible answers so that each student gets the options in a different order. This is great if you don't want your students to "share" answers.

**Multiple Answers**: Check this box if your question has more than one right answer (e.g., Select all that apply...).

 **POWER TIP**

Remember that with multiple-choice questions, you can have option-specific feedback and scoring.

Add Advanced Feedback, p. 175
Assign Points, p. 176

## True/False Question Options

True/False questions do not have any additional properties. You can, however, edit the option text boxes right on the slide to change from **true/false** to **yes/no**, **right/wrong**, etc.

# Fill-in-the-Blank Question Options

## To set up a fill-in-the-blank question:

1. Type your full statement in the text box provided. **(A)**
2. Select the word/phrase you want the student to fill in.
3. Click the **Mark Blank** button. **(B)**

The part that the student fills in appears underlined in edit mode, but appears as a blank in preview mode.

## To enter more than one possible correct answer:

1. Double-click your underlined word or phrase. **(C)**
2. Click the **Plus** button in the pop-up window. **(D)**
3. Type any additional correct answers in the box.
4. Repeat steps 2 and 3 for any other answers you want.
5. Click anywhere on the slide to exit the window.

## To convert to a drop-down multiple-choice question:

1. Double-click your underlined word or phrase. **(C)**
2. Click the **User Input** drop-down menu. **(E)**
3. Select **Dropdown List**.
4. Click the **Plus** button. **(D)**
5. Type an answer option.
6. Repeat steps 4 and 5 for additional answer options.
7. Check the box(es) next to the correct answer(s). **(F)**
8. Click anywhere on the slide to exit the window.

## 💡 BRIGHT IDEAS

- For user input questions, check **Case Sensitive** if you want students to match your capitalization.
- For dropdown list questions, check **Shuffle Answers** if you want to randomize the options.
- Select an option, and click **Minus** button to delete an answer you've entered but don't want.
- Use the drop-down menu **(G)** to switch between blanks if you have more than one blank.

## ⊘ CAUTION

- Be careful about user input questions with many correct answers. For example, if the answer is 12:00 p.m., use a dropdown list because of all the correct ways someone could enter that time.
- You can have multiple correct answers on a dropdown list question. It may not be obvious to the students that they can select more than one answer, so either use very clear instructions, or use the multiple-choice question type.

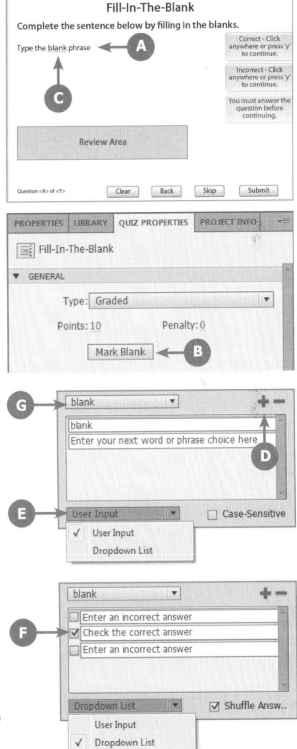

# Short Answer Question Options

**To enter the correct answer for a graded short answer question:**

1. Click the answer text box.
2. Enter the correct answer in the dialog box that appears. **(A)**
3. Click the **Plus** button.
4. Type an additional correct answer in the box.
5. Repeat steps 3 and 4 for any other answers you want.
6. Click anywhere on the slide to exit the window.

## Options

- Select an answer, and click the **Minus** button to delete that possible answer.
- Check the **Case-Sensitive** box if you want the student to match the capitalization you used.

# DESIGN TIPS

- Most short-answer questions are not system-graded because the students are often providing their thoughts and ideas, rather than a specific answer.

- It is best to use a graded short answer test when there is an exact right answer, rather than something subjective. For example, you could use a graded question for "What is our mission statement?" which has only one correct answer, and use a survey question for "How can you put the customer first?" which can have many ways to express the correct answer.

- Even if you have a non-graded survey question, you can still use a single caption with some feedback, or you can take the students to another slide that gives some possible answers for the students to compare their answers to.

# Matching Question Options

**To set up a matching question:**

1. On the **Quiz Properties** tab, enter the number of options you want in each column. **(A)**

2. Type your options in the text boxes on the slides. **(B)**

3. Enter the letter of the correct match from column 2 next to each item in column 1. **(C)**

4. Check **Shuffle Column 1** if you want Captivate to rearrange column 1 to create a different match pattern each time. **(D)**

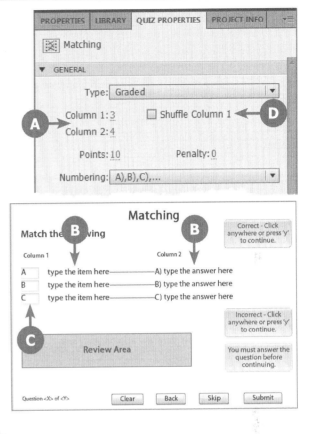

![Design Tips icon] **DESIGN TIPS**

- If you want distractors (items without a match), then have more items in column 2 than column 1.

  Match the following. Not all answers will be used.

  | Column 1 | Column 2 |
  | --- | --- |
  | B Shannon Fielding | A) Legal Counsel |
  | A Jackson Roberts | B) President and CEO |
  | E Maria Velasquez | C) Director of HR |
  | | D) VP of Customer Care |
  | | E) Manager Eastern Region |

- If you want one item to match to more than one answer, enter the same letter in Column 1.

  Match the following. Note: Answers may be used more than once.

  | Column 1 | Column 2 |
  | --- | --- |
  | B Shannon Fielding | A) Legal Counsel |
  | A Jackson Roberts | B) President and CEO |
  | A Maria Velasquez | C) Director of HR |

- Be sure to add instructions to let students know about the unmatched or double-matched options.

# Hot Spot Question Options

## To set up a hot spot question:

1. Place your image(s) on the slide.
2. On the **Quiz Properties** tab, enter the number of hot spots you want to include. **(A)**
3. Position the hot spot areas on the appropriate places on your slide.
4. Select each hot spot individually.
5. On the **Properties** tab, check or uncheck the **Correct Answer** box based on whether or not that hot spot is correct. **(B)**

## Quiz Properties Options

**Hotspot:** When students click on the image, a blue star appears to indicate where they clicked. If you want to change the look of that marker, click the **Browse** button, **(C)** and select a different animation.

Default            Sample options

**Allow Clicks Only on Hotspots (D):** With this box unchecked, students can click anywhere on the slide. With it checked, only clicks in a hotspot count as answers. In the map example, students are only considering the five hot spots. Since they shouldn't be clicking anywhere else, this box could be checked. If you wanted students to consider the whole map, you could add one correct hot spot that was not visible (no stroke or fill) and then check this box. Then, a click anywhere on the map counts as an answer, but only clicks in the one correct hotspot would be correct.

## Individual Hot Spot Properties Options

**Show Hand Cursor Over Hit Area**: Check this box **(E)** if you want the student's cursor to change to a hand when it is over any hot spot, letting the students know it is a hot spot.

**Fill & Stroke**: You can make the hot spots either visible or invisible, based on whether or not you use a fill and stroke. Keep them invisible for a more challenging question that makes the student consider all parts of the image. Make them visible if you only want the students to consider certain areas of the image, as in the example shown on the right.

 **DESIGN TIP**

Be sure to provide clear instructions! For example, let students know if more than one hot spot is correct and that they can undo a selection by clicking the same spot again.

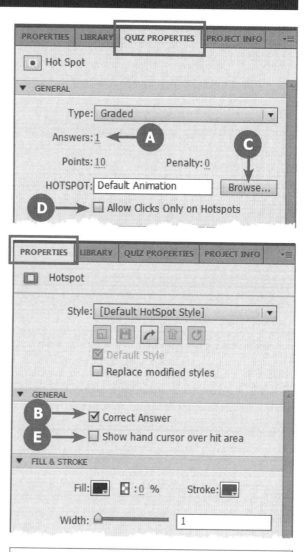

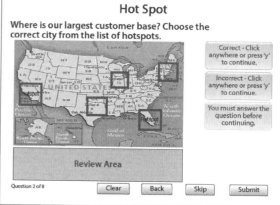

 Fill & Stroke, p. 94

## Sequence Question Options

When you set up a sequence question, you enter the items in the proper order, and then Captivate shuffles the options for the student to see in the published movie.

**To set up a sequence question:**

1. In the **Answers** field, enter the number of items you want to use.

2. In the **Answer Type** drop-down menu, select either **Drag Drop** or **Drop Down** based on the question format you want.

3. On the slide, enter the answer options in the provided text fields in the correct order.

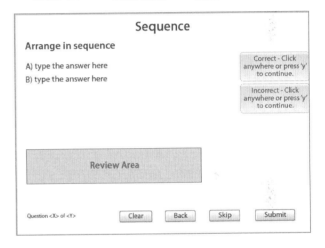

**DESIGN TIP**

As with all question types, include clear directions. Students may not realize they are supposed to drag the items around or select them from a drop-down list.

# Rating Scale (Likert) Question Options

**To set up a rating scale question:**

1. In the **Answers** field, enter the number of statements you want the student to evaluate.

2. In the **Rating Scale** drop-down menu, select the number of options you want on the scale (maximum of 5).

3. On the slide, enter your evaluation items in the text boxes down the side.

4. Change the rating scale text across the top if you want to use a different scale.

Remember that rating scale questions are only available as survey questions. There are no right or wrong answers, grading, or points.

**Rating Scale (Likert)**

Indicate how strongly you agree or disagree with the following:

| | Disagree 1 | Somewhat Disagree 2 | Neutral 3 | Somewhat Agree 4 | Agree 5 |
|---|---|---|---|---|---|
| A) type the item here | ○ | ○ | ○ | ○ | ○ |
| B) type the item here | ○ | ○ | ○ | ○ | ○ |
| C) type the item here | ○ | ○ | ○ | ○ | ○ |

Review Area

You must answer the question before continuing.

Question <X> of <Y>    Clear    Back    Skip    Submit

# Importing Questions

GIFT (General Import Format Technology) is a text file format (.txt) that uses plain text to create quiz questions. Using a text format instead of the wizard might be faster, especially if you have a lot of questions, and may increase your ability to reuse questions in different systems. (For example, you can import GIFT questions into and export them from Moodle.) You can use the GIFT format to create multiple-choice, true/false, short answer, matching, and numerical question types in Captivate.

Here is the format for a multiple-choice question. Refer to the Adobe Captivate Help documentation for more information on creating GIFT files.

```
::Question Title::
Question
{
~incorrect answer
=correct answer
~incorrect answer
~incorrect answer
}
```

## Import GIFT-Format Questions

**To import GIFT-format questions:**

1. Go to the **Quiz** menu.
2. Select **Import GIFT Format File**.
3. Select the .txt file with your questions.
4. Click the **Open** button.

*GIFT file*

*Resulting question in Captivate*

# Drag-and-Drop Interaction Wizard

In addition to the questions you can create from question slides, you can also create drag-and-drop interactions with a wizard.

## Create a Drag-and-Drop Interaction

**To create a drag-and-drop interaction:**

1. Add at least two objects to your slide to be used as drag sources or drop targets.
2. Go to the **Insert** menu.
3. Select **Launch Drag and Drop Interaction Wizard**.
4. On the first page of the wizard **(A)**, select the drag source(s).
5. Click the **Next** button.
6. On the second page **(B)**, select the drop target(s).
7. Click the **Next** button.
8. On the third page **(C)**, drag a line from the plus icon on each drag item to the center of its corresponding drop target.
9. Click the **Finish** button.
10. Configure the properties.
    (See next page.)

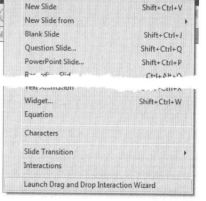

## TIME SAVER

You can group drag or drop items into types to manage the items as a group. This is useful for many-to-one and one-to-many relationships. Select the items, click the plus button **(D)**, and name the group.

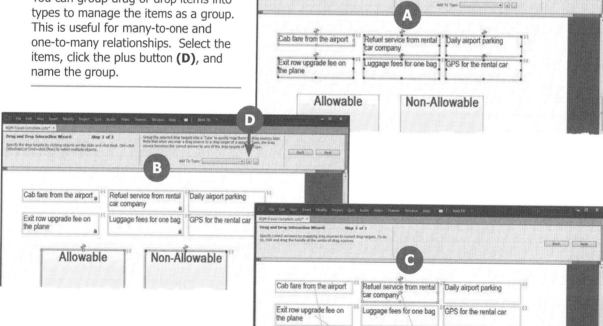

# Drag-and-Drop Interaction Properties

Unlike the other question types, properties for this interaction type appear on their own tab. The **Drag and Drop** tab appears automatically, and you can use the **View** menu to show and hide it.

Many of the properties for drag-and-drop interactions are the same as for any question type. Here are some of the properties that are unique to drag-and-drop interactions.

Configuring Questions, p. 172

## General Pane

**Select**: To manage an individual object in the interaction, select it on the slide or from this drop-down menu. You can also select your groups (custom types) from this menu.

**Mark as**: Here you can change the designation of an item as a drag source or drop target.

**Custom Type**: You manage custom type groups here, including adding new types or deleting types.

## Drag Source

This section is only available if a drag source is selected.

**Effects**: From this menu, you can apply an effect (**Zoom In** or **Glow**) for drag sources while they are being dragged.

## Drop Target

This section is only available if a drop target is selected.

**Accept**: Click this button to bring up a dialog box (A) with extra options for how that drop target accepts drag sources.

**Source check boxes**: By default, any drag source can be dropped in any drop target. (It may be wrong, but the student can do it.) Uncheck the box for any object that you don't want "allowed" in that drop target. If the student drags an unchecked item into that drop target, it will not be accepted and will float back to its original position.

**Action**: You can designate a separate action for each drag source if it is dropped in that drop target.

**Count**: If you uncheck **Accept All**, the **Count** field becomes active. Here you can set a limit for how many drop sources will be accepted. You can then use the radio buttons to indicate what should happen if the count is exceeded. You can have the extra item return to its place or replace an item that's already in the drop target.

**Captions**: Use these check boxes to enable captions that appear when objects are dropped on the drop target you have selected. **On Accept** shows a success message. **On Reject** shows a failure message. **On Hint** shows a hint message.

# Drag-and-Drop Interaction Properties (cont'd)

## Drop Target (cont'd)

**Hit area padding**: You can increase this number if you want to make the live area of the drop target larger than the object itself. This means the student's "aim" doesn't have to be precise.

**Effects**: If you select **Zoom In** from the drop-down menu, the drop target gets larger when the student's mouse gets near it.

**Position**: Use this drop-down menu to control how the drag sources are positioned when dropped.

> **Anchor**: The default option, drag sources are locked to a set point—the point that you select in the thumbnails below the menu. If you have multiple drag sources going to the same drop target, they will overlap.

> **Absolute**: The drag sources stay exactly where the student drops them.

> **Tile**: The drag sources are positioned so they don't overlap.

**Size**: This number controls the size of the drag source after it is dropped. For example, if you set this number to 50%, the drag source will get 50% smaller when dropped into the target.

**Opacity**: Adjust the **Opacity** number to change the opacity of the drag source when it is dropped in the target. Lowering the number makes the object fade.

**Depth**: If your **Position** settings allow drop objects to overlap each other, use this menu to determine whether newly dropped objects appear in front of or in back of the objects already there.

**Audio**: Use the drop-down menu or the **Browse** button if you would like a sound effect to play when an object is dropped in the target.

# Drag-and-Drop Interaction Properties (cont'd)

## Interaction Properties Pane

**Correct Answers**: Click this button for a dialog box with more options for how to grade the interaction. **(A)**

**Type menu**: When **Combination** is selected (the default), the students can drag the objects in any order. If you select **Sequence**, then the objects must be dragged in the order shown in the table.

**Answer1 table**: Use this table to make modifications to the correct answer pairings you set up when you created the interaction.

**Plus button**: Click to add a new row where you can set up a new correct pairing.

**Minus button**: Select a row and click the minus button to remove a correct pairing.

**Arrow buttons**: If you select **Sequence** from the **Type** menu, use the arrow buttons to put the pairings in the order you want the student to use.

**Delete (X) button**: Click this button to delete the entire answer table.

**Rows**: In each row, double-click in the **Drop Target** or **Drag Source** column to reveal a drop-down menu where you can select the objects for each correct pairing. Double-click the **Count** cell to change the maximum number of drop sources for the selected drop target.

**Add New Answer**: Click this button to bring up an extra table where you can set up a completely different set of pairings that would be considered correct.

**Use Hand cursor**: By default, the student's cursor changes from an arrow to a hand when dragging objects. Uncheck this box if you want the cursor to stay as an arrow.

**Send Drag Source to original position**: By default, if a student drops an object outside any of the targets, the object snaps back to its original position. Uncheck this box if you want the drag source to stay wherever it is dropped, even if it is outside the drop targets.

**Play Audio**: Check this box to play a default sound effect when a drop target rejects an answer.

**Redrag the dropped source**: By default, once the student drops an object in one of the targets, the student cannot move it again. Check this box if you want the student to be able to move it again.

# Drag-and-Drop Interaction Properties (cont'd)

## Action Pane

**Reset**: If you allow more than one attempt, use these radio buttons to designate whether the drag sources should stay where they are (**None**) or snap back to the starting position (**Reset All**).

## Options Pane

**Pause After X sec**: By default, the slide's **Timeline** pauses after 1.5 seconds, giving the students time to interact with your content.  You can either change the time for the pause or uncheck the box if you don't want the slide to pause.

**Auto Submit Correct Answers**: Check this box if you want to evaluate the answers without the student having to click the **Submit** button.

**Undo**: Check this box to put an **Undo** button on the slide to undo the student's last action.

**Reset**: Check this box to put a **Reset** button on the slide to reset the entire interaction back to the original state.

## BRIGHT IDEA

Refer to the Adobe Captivate help documentation to review the many hints and cautions around designing a drag-and-drop interaction.

# Creating Pretests

When building questions, you can designate them to be part of a pretest that includes special pass/fail logic. For example, students who achieve an 80% or higher on the pretest can go straight to the main content of the course, and those who don't go to a separate module with some foundational information.  You can have one pretest per Captivate project, and the pretest scores do not affect the quiz results reported to a learning management system.

## Add a Pretest Question

**To add a pretest question:**

1. Go to the **Insert** menu.
2. Select **Question Slide**.
3. Check the box for the type(s) of questions you want to add.
4. In the middle column, enter the quantity for that question type.
5. Select **Pretest** from the drop-down menu.
6. Click **OK**.
7. Configure your question as described in the first part of this chapter.

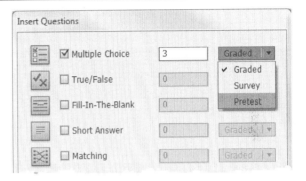

## Configure Pretest Logic

**To configure pretest logic:**

1. Go to the **Quiz Properties** panel of any of your pretest slides.
2. Click the **Edit Pretest Action** button.
3. In the **If** section, adjust the passing percentage, if needed.
4. In the **Actions** section, configure the action that you want if the student passes the pretest.
5. Click the **Else** header.
6. Configure the action that you want if the student does not pass the pretest.
7. Click the **Update** button.
8. Click **OK** in the dialog box.
9. Click the **Close** button.

 Conditional Actions, p. 161

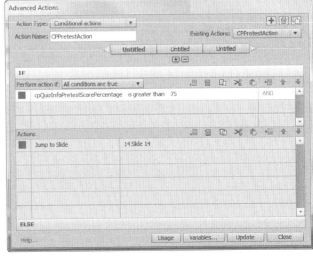

# Quiz Master Slides

When you use a pre-installed theme, it includes master slides for questions.  You don't have to do anything special to use or find them—just apply the theme and add the question.

When creating your own theme and master slides, you can create quiz master slides as part of them.

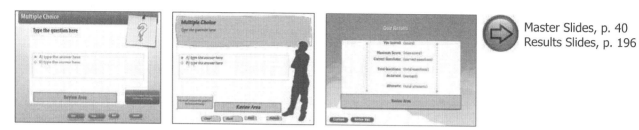

Master Slides, p. 40
Results Slides, p. 196

## Create a Quiz Master Slide

**To create a quiz master slide:**

1. Go to the **Window** menu.
2. Select **Master Slide**.
3. Go to the **Quiz** menu.
4. Select **Quiz Master Slide**.
5. Select the type of question master you want.
6. Go to the **Quiz** menu.
7. Select **Question Placeholder Objects** or **Result Placeholder Objects**.
8. Select the type of placeholders you want.
9. Format the placeholder objects.
10. Add any static objects, such as text and graphics.

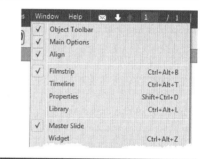

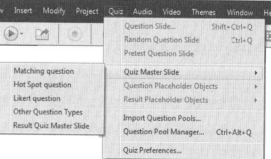

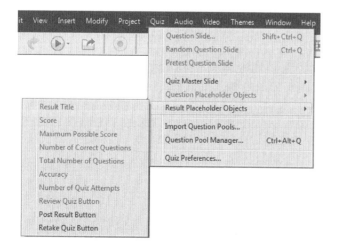

# Question Pools

Question pools let you add questions to your project at random, making each user's experience unique. Rather than entering a specific question at a certain point in the project, Captivate selects a question from a group (or pool) of questions that you've created. You can create as many pools as you'd like.

Use question pools when you want to discourage "sharing" of answers or when you want students to get a different set of questions if they need to retry the quiz.

Question pools are separate entities from the actual presentation. If all you do is create a question pool, no questions will appear in your project. You'll need to insert a random question placeholder into your project that pulls questions from the pool.

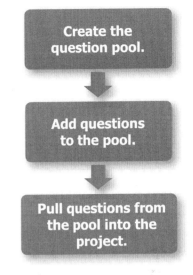

**Create the question pool.**

**Add questions to the pool.**

**Pull questions from the pool into the project.**

---

## Create a Question Pool

**To create a new question pool:**

1. Click the **Quiz** menu.
2. Select **Question Pool Manager**.
3. Double-click the name of the pool to rename it, if needed.
4. Click the **Plus** sign in the upper-left corner to create additional pools.
5. Edit the name of the additional pools.
6. Click **Close**.

## DESIGN TIP

Create a separate pool for each learning objective. That way, you know each objective will be represented in the project.

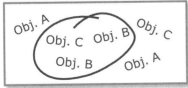

*Three questions pulled randomly from one group*

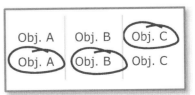

*One question pulled randomly from three groups*

# Add Questions to a Question Pool

**To add a question to a pool:**

1. Click the **Quiz** menu.
2. Select **Question Pool Manager**.
3. Select the pool you want to work with.
4. Click the **Plus** button on the right. **(B)**
5. Select the type and number of questions you want to add.
6. Click **OK** in the **Insert Questions** dialog box.
7. Click **Close** in the **Question Pool Manager**.

You can add and delete pools and questions from the pool using the **Plus** and **Minus** buttons:

- Add and delete pools **(A)**
- Add and delete questions **(B)**

Rather than build questions with the question wizard, you can click the **Import GIFT File** button for step 4 to add your questions.

 Importing Questions, p. 185

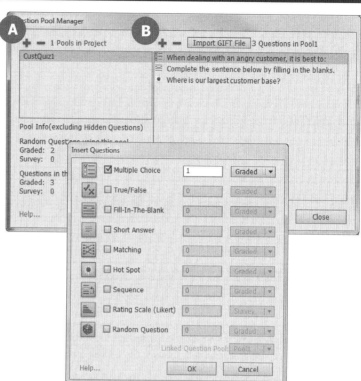

# Manage Questions in the Question Pool

Remember that question pool questions are not added to your project, so they cannot be found in your **Filmstrip**. Instead, you can edit the questions from the **Question Pool** panel, found at the bottom of the interface. If the **Question Pool** panel isn't visible, you can go to the **Window** menu to add it.

From the **Question Pool** panel, you can:

- Select a question to show it in the work area so you can work on the question.
- Click the **Add Questions** link to add a new question to that pool.
- Click the drop-down menu to move between the different pools associated with this project.
- Click the **Browse** button **(C)** to bring up the **Question Pool Manager** dialog box.

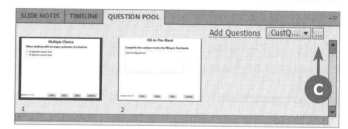

## BRIGHT IDEA

You can move a pool question into another pool or out of the pool to work like a regular question again.

 **TIME SAVER**

Import question pools from other projects from the **Quiz** menu. Select **Import Question Pools**.

# Pull a Question From a Pool to Your Project

**To randomly pull questions from your pool into your project:**

1. Click the **Quiz** or **Insert** menu.

2. Select **Question Slide**.

3. Select **Random Question**.

4. Enter the number of questions from the pool you want to pull.

5. From the **Linked Question Pool** drop-down menu, select the question pool you want to pull from.

6. Click **OK**.

When you add questions to your project from a question pool, they appear as placeholder slides. You are not able to edit the questions from the placeholders, because they do not represent a single question. They merely represent where one of the questions will end up going in the published project. If you want to edit the question, go to the **Question Pool** panel. (See previous page.)

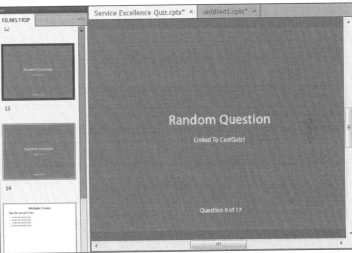

# Quiz Results Slides

When you add the first quiz question to a project, Captivate adds a quiz results slide, showing the users how they did.

There are many things you can do to a results slide in the same way you would for any slide. You can:

- Delete the slide if you don't want it. For example, if you just want a simple reinforcement question, you may not want a results slide.
- Move it to a different location in the project.
- Apply formatting.
- Add, delete, and move elements, such as text and graphics.

Below you will find some of the editing options that are unique to quiz results slides.

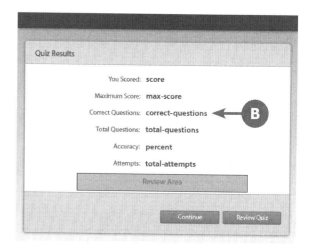

## Manage the Quiz Results Slide

**To turn scoring data on and off:**

1. Go to the **Quiz Properties** tab.
2. Check or uncheck the boxes for the features you want.

**To add custom scoring elements from variables:**

1. Add a text caption or shape to hold the text.
2. In the **Format** pane for that object, click the **Insert Variable** button. **(A)**
3. Find and select the variable you want.

 Display a Variable, p. 158
Quizzing Variables, p. 258

**To change which questions are included in the quiz logic:**

1. Go to the question you want to change.
2. In the **Reporting** pane, check or uncheck the **Report Answers** box.

 **CAUTION**

Be careful about making any changes to the variable placeholders **(B)**. Always preview your work to make sure the variables display properly.

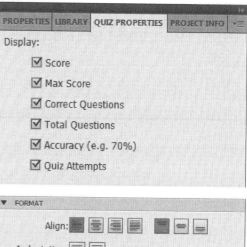

# Quiz Preferences

Quiz Preferences govern the quiz as a whole. They are found in the **Preferences** dialog box, which can be accessed from the **Edit** menu or the **Quiz** menu.

**To change the quiz preferences:**

1. Go to the **Quiz** menu.

2. Select **Quiz Preferences**.

3. In the **Quiz** section, click each category, and change the settings you want.

4. Click the **OK** button.

## Reporting Category

The **Reporting** category governs how the course interacts with a learning management system or other tracking system. This category is covered in the Publishing chapter.

 Publishing, ch. 12

## Settings Category

**Name**: Enter a name for the quiz, if needed.

**Required**: Indicate whether you want the student to be required to take the quiz. Options are:

- **Optional - The user can skip this quiz**

- **Required - The user must take this quiz to continue**: This means the student has to click through all the slides in the quiz—it does not mean the student has to pass or even answer the questions.

- **Pass Required - The user must pass this quiz to continue**

- **Answer All - The user must answer every question to continue**: The student does not have to pass, though.

**Objective ID**: Use this field to identify the quiz to which a question slide belongs.

**Interaction ID Prefix**: To help you manage all the data tracked for quiz questions (answer on first attempt, answer on second attempt, etc.), you can assign a prefix that will go at the beginning of all the interaction IDs that are created for this quiz.

 Interaction ID, p. 177

# Change Quiz Preferences (cont'd)

## Settings Category (cont'd)

### Shuffle Answers

This is a global setting for the entire quiz that shuffles the answers for any question type with multiple answers, such as multiple-choice questions. This can be overridden at the question level.

### Submit All

If you check this box, students' answers are not graded until the end of the quiz. A **Submit All** button appears on each quiz slide, but does not work until all questions are answered. The quiz result is only sent to a learning management system when the **Submit All** button is clicked on the last question slide.

### Branch Aware

If you have branching in your quiz, a student might not take all of the questions in the quiz. If so, check this box so that the student's grade is calculated based on the number of questions taken instead of the total number of questions.

 Add Advanced Feedback, p. 175

### Show Progress

Check this box if you want to include a page count at the bottom of the question slides. Select **Relative** from the **Progress Type** drop-down menu if you want to show the page number and the total number of pages in the quiz. Select **Absolute** if you only want to show the page number.

### Allow Backward Movement:

Uncheck this box if you want to remove the **Back** button from all the slides in the quiz. You can override this at the question level.

### Show Score at the End of the Quiz

Uncheck this box if you do not want to include a quiz results slide. Check it again to bring it back.

### Quiz Result Messages

Click this button to customize the appearance of a quiz results slide.

**Messages**: Check the boxes if you want pass and fail messages to appear, and customize the text, if needed.

**Score**: Check or uncheck the boxes of the slide features you want. These options can also be changed on the **Quiz Properties** tab of the results slide.

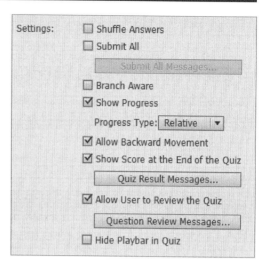

Quiz Results Slide, p. 196

# Change Quiz Preferences (cont'd)

## Settings Category (cont'd)

### Allow User to Review the Quiz

Check this box if you want to add a **Review Quiz** button to the quiz results slide that lets students go back and review the questions, their answers, and the correct answers.

### Question Review Messages

Click this button to customize the text shown to the student during the review. Visual indicators are used to show the students the correct and incorrect answers. To make the course accessible to those using screen readers, you can enter the corresponding text used for the visual symbols.

### Hide Playbar in Quiz

If you enable the playbar in your project's skin, you can check this box if you want to hide the playbar on all quiz questions. This prevents the student from moving forward or backward using the playbar.

 Configure Project Skin, p. 226

---

**Question Review Messages**

Incomplete: You did not answer this question completely.

For Accessibility

Correct: You answered this correctly!

Partial Correct: You answered this partially correct!

Incorrect: Your answer:

The correct answer is:

Help...    OK    Cancel

---

## Sequence

☒ **Arrange in sequence**

- Customer is connected to a Customer Care Associate.
- Customer calls the Customer Care Hotline.
- Customer is upset and decides to complain.
- Issue is not resolved via the computerized system.

☒ A) d decides to complain.

☑ B) istomer Care Hotline.

☒ C) ed to a Customer Care Associate.

☑ D) Issue is not resolved via the computerized system.

*Visual indicators for correct and incorrect answers*

## Change Quiz Preferences (cont'd)

### Pass or Fail Category

**Pass/Fail Options**: Select the first radio button if you want to grade based on percentage or the second radio button to base it on raw score. Then, enter the passing score for the score type you chose.

**If Passing Grade**: Select the action that you want to execute if the student achieves the passing score listed above. For example, you may want to branch to a certain slide.

**If Failing Grade**: Indicate what you want to have happen if the student does not achieve the passing score.

**Attempts**: Enter the number of attempts you want to give the student, or check the box if you want to allow infinite attempts.

**Show Retake Button**: If you allow more than one attempt, check this box if you want to add a **Retake Quiz** button.

**Action**: Select the action you want to execute if the student does not achieve the passing score.

If the student has not passed the test in the designated number of attempts, the **Retake Quiz** button disappears and the failing grade action is executed.

 Actions, ch. 7

### Default Labels Category

This category lets you change all the default styles and messages for the buttons and feedback. For example, if you want to change what the success captions say when they first appear, you can modify the default here so that you don't have to change the text on each and every slide.

 Styles, p. 104

---

**Quiz: Pass or Fail**

Pass/Fail Options: ⦿ [80] % or more of total points to pass

○ [0] points or more to pass (Total Points: 30)

Note: Maximum points to be earned is the sum of all weighted points.

If Passing Grade:

Action: [Continue ▾]

If Failing Grade:

Allow User: [1] Attempts OR ☐ Infinite Attempts

☐ Show Retake Button

Action: [Continue ▾]

---

**Quiz: Default Labels**

Correct Message:
[Default Success Caption Style] ▾
Correct - Click anywhere or press 'y' to continue.

Incorrect Message:
[Default Failure Caption Style] ▾
Incorrect - Click anywhere or press 'y' to continue.

Retry Message:
[Default Hint Caption Style] ▾
Try again

Incomplete Message:
[Default Hint Caption Style] ▾
You must answer the question before continuing.

Timeout Message:
[Default Hint Caption Style] ▾
The time to answer this question has expired. Click anywhere or press 'y' to continue.

Partial Correct Message:
[Default Partial Correct Caption St.. ▾]
Partially Correct - Click anywhere or press 'y' to continue.

Submit:
[Default Quiz Button Style] ▾
Submit

Submit All:
[Default Quiz Button Style] ▾
Submit All

Clear:
[Default Quiz Button Style] ▾
Clear

Skip:
[Default Quiz Button Style] ▾
Next

Back:
[Default Quiz Button Style] ▾
Back

[Create New Style...] [Restore Selected Style] [Restore All Styles]

# Special Tools & Wizards

## Introduction

Adobe Captivate comes with a number of special features designed to save you time and provide more options. In this chapter, you will learn about:

- **Aggregator and Multi-SCORM Projects**: These let you combine multiple projects into one course.
- **Templates**: Templates help you save time and achieve a consistent look.
- **Spell Check**: Use this handy tool to check the spelling in captions, slide notes, slide names, text animations, and quizzes.
- **Find and Replace**: Search for certain words, any type of object, or any style of any object.
- **The Library**: The **Library** provides one convenient place to manage all the assets in your project.
- **Widgets**: Widgets are configurable .swf files that let you extend the capabilities of Captivate.
- **Sharing and Reviewing**: You can share files on Acrobat.com and use Adobe Captivate Reviewer to capture and manage feedback from reviewers.
- **Preferences**: You've learned about many preferences so far in the book. In this chapter, you'll learn about the ones that aren't covered in other chapters.
- **Exporting and Importing to XML**: XML files can let you do things outside of Captivate. For example, you can export to XML, translate your content or do a find/replace to update text, and then import the updated XML back into Captivate.

## In This Chapter

- Aggregator and Multi-SCORM Projects
- Templates
- Text-Editing Tools
- The Library
- Widgets
- Sharing and Reviewing
- Preferences
- Exporting and Importing XML

# Notes

# Aggregator Projects

An aggregator project lets you string together separate Captivate published movies. For example, if you are creating a course on how to use a document management system, you might have five separate screen demonstrations, five practices, and a brief lesson on business rules. Rather than distributing these as individual courses, you can publish them all together as a single, complete course. Aggregator projects can be made up of multiple published .swfs created in Captivate.

## CAUTION

Aggregator projects can only contain published .swf files created in Captivate, not .swf files created elsewhere, such as in Flash. All files must be using the same version of ActionScript. You can see the version of ActionScript in the **Publish** dialog box for that project.

## Create an Aggregator Project

**To create an aggregator project:**

1. Publish all the projects you want to include in the aggregator project.
2. Go to the **File** menu.
3. Select **New Project**.
4. Select **Aggregator Project**.
5. Click the **Add Module** button. **(A)**
6. Find and select the published .swf you want to add.
7. Click the **Open** button.
8. Repeat steps 5-7 to add additional files.
9. Configure the settings. (See below.)
10. Click the **Save** button to save the project.

## Aggregator Project Settings

**Master Movie**: One of the movies can be designated as the master. The table of contents settings and project information for that movie will be used for the entire aggregator project. Select the movie you want to use as the default, and then check this box.

If you want to create movie information specific to this aggregator project and not pull it from any of the existing movies, click the **Info** button, and add the movie information you want to use.

**Movie Titles**: Double-click the movie title in the list to rename it. If you don't want the movie title to appear in the published table of contents, select the movie and uncheck the **Include Module Title** check box.

**Moving and Deleting Movies**: To change the order of the movies, select a movie and click the up or down arrow buttons. To delete a movie, select it, and then click the **Delete** button.

**Preview**: Click this button to preview what the published project will look like.

**Preloader**: Click the **Browse** button **(B)** to select an image to show when the published project is loading.

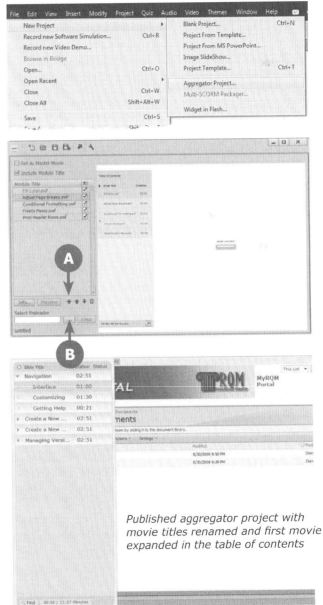

*Published aggregator project with movie titles renamed and first movie expanded in the table of contents*

# Publish an Aggregator Project

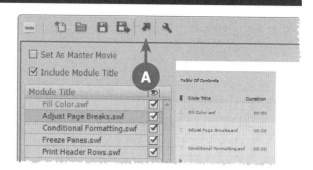

**To publish an aggregator project:**

1. Click the **Publish Aggregator Project** button. **(A)**

2. In the dialog box, select the output format you want.

3. Enter a title for the published project.

4. Enter or browse for the location where you want to save the published project.

5. Select the publish settings you want. (See below.)

6. Click the **Publish** button.

## Publish Settings

**Format**: Select from Flash output (.swf), Windows-compatible executable file (.exe), or Mac-compatible executable file (.app).

**Publish To Folder**: Check this box if you want Captivate to create a separate folder for your published files.

**Export To HTML**: This option, checked by default, creates an HTML page and a JavaScript file that embeds the .swf file into the HTML page. Uncheck it if you only want to publish the .swf file. Having the HTML page may be necessary based on how you plan to display the course.

**Export PDF**: Check this option to create a PDF document that plays the .swf file.

**ZIP Files**: Check this box if you want your published files to be zipped up into a .zip compressed folder.

**Full Screen**: This option includes HTML files that cause the browser window to open up to its maximum size and hide browser elements, such as the toolbar and **Favorites** bar.

**Custom Icon:** If you choose the **Win Executable** format, you can find and select an icon to associate with the executable file. This icon appears in the user's task bar and next to the file name in Windows Explorer.

## POWER TIP

Aggregator projects do not work with learning management systems (LMS). If you need to integrate with an LMS, use the **Multi-SCORM Packager**.

The **Multi-SCORM Packager** lets you combine multiple files into a single shareable courseware object (SCO) to be uploaded to an LMS. The SCO can contain one or more projects from Captivate, Flash, Adobe Presenter, and quizzes made in Dreamweaver with the Coursebuilder extension.

In order to use the **Multi-SCORM Packager**, you must have the Adobe eLearning Suite. Refer to the Adobe eLearning Suite help documentation for more details.

## Aggregator Preferences

There are additional aggregator settings in the **Aggregator Preferences** dialog box, which you can access by clicking the **Publish Settings** button.

**Runtime Option**: If you'd like to enable right-click shortcuts for the student in the aggregator menu, select **Right-click**. However, the special logic needed to enable that right-click menu will disable accessibility features. So if you want the menu to be accessible, select **Accessibility** instead.

Accessibility, p. 245

**Hide Table of Contents**: Check this box if you want to turn off the table of contents completely in the published movie.

## Manage Aggregator Files

You can open existing aggregator files from the main Captivate interface, or from the aggregator window if it is already open. Aggregator projects have a file extension of .aggr.

**To open an aggregator file from Captivate:**

1. Go to the **File** menu.
2. Select **New Project**.
3. Select **Aggregator Project**.
4. Click the **Open Aggregator Project** button.
5. Find and select the project you want.
6. Click the **Open** button.

If the aggregator window is already open, simply start with step 4.

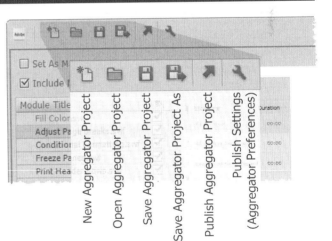

# Templates

Templates help you create a consistent, professional look for your projects and help you save time in the development process. A Captivate template includes slides, objects, placeholder objects, placeholders for recording slides or question slides, master slides, styles, preferences, and slide notes. Project templates have a .cptl extension.

## BRIGHT IDEA

Use **Slide Notes** to provide instructions on how to use the template.

For example, if you are creating a series of computer simulations, you can create a template that is set to the right size, has the toolbar configured the way you want, is set up with all the default styles you want, and has introductory text and closing text placeholders. If you like to create branching scenarios, you can create a template that has all the pages set up with buttons branching to the different pages. Then, all you have to do is add the content to the pages.

## Create a Project Template

**To create a project template:**

1. Go to the **File** menu.
2. Select **New Project**.
3. Select **Project Template**.
4. Select the size for the project. **(A)**
5. Click the **OK** button.
6. Add any slides you want.
7. Add standard project elements. (See below.)
8. Go to the **Insert** menu.
9. Select **Placeholder Objects** or **Placeholder Slides**.
10. Select the placeholders you want. **(B)** (See below.)

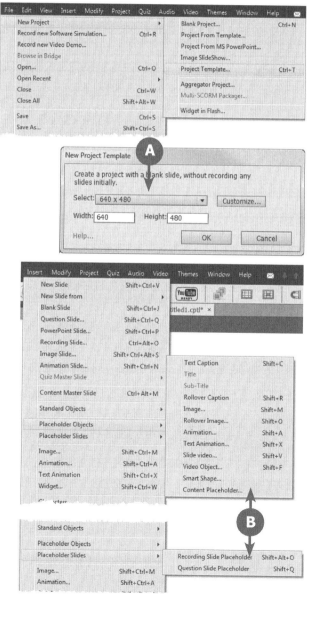

### Standard Project Elements

You can add content and configure settings in a template much the same as any project. For example, you can add and delete slides, create slide masters, add objects to slides, set default styles, etc. These slides and objects appear exactly the same way in any project created from the template. For example, if there is a caption at the end of each simulation that says "Click Next to continue," you could add it as a regular caption object with that text.

### Placeholder Objects

In addition to standard elements, you can add placeholder objects. Placeholder objects put in a gray placeholder that you can fully format and configure properties for, but contains no actual content. When someone creates a project from the template, they can quickly add the project-specific content to the placeholders. For example, if the text of your closing caption varies from project to project, add it as a placeholder caption instead of a standard caption.

### Placeholder Slides

A placeholder slide adds a slide to allow for either screen recording or quiz questions.

# Create a New Project From a Template

**To create a new project from a template:**

1. Go to the **File** menu.
2. Select **New Project**.
3. Select **Project From Template**.

## Modifying Standard Elements

When you create a project from a template, you can still add and modify content and settings like you would with any other project. For example, you can delete unwanted slides or add new ones, change the formatting on objects, etc.

## Modifying Placeholder Objects

To add your content to a placeholder, double-click the placeholder. The resulting steps vary based on the type of placeholder. For example, with a caption or rollover caption, the placeholder converts to an editable caption with proper formatting. With an image placeholder, the **Open** dialog box appears so you can find and select the image you want.

When you add content from placeholders, they appear with the settings from the template. However, you can override those settings if you want to. For example, you could change the size of an image or the caption type of a caption.

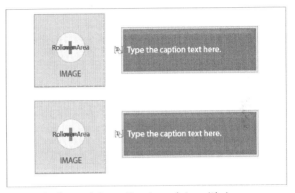
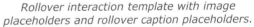

Rollover interaction template with image placeholders and rollover caption placeholders.

## Adding Questions and Screen Recordings

Double-click the placeholder slide to either add questions or initiate screen recording.

# BRIGHT IDEA

How is a template different than a theme?

A *theme* is a set of styles and individual slide templates that can be applied to any project, but it is not a project itself. You need to create a project and add the slides using the options in the theme.

A *template* creates an actual project. When you create a new project from a template, it can have slides already in it—with either actual or placeholder content. For example, you might always have a title slide, an objectives slide, a quiz instructions slide, and a closing slide that are similar. With a template, you can create a new project with those slides already in the project.

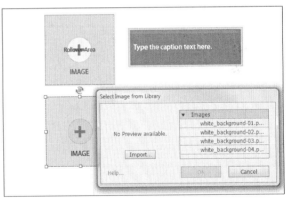

Pop-up window that appears when you double-click an image placeholder.

Themes, p. 42

# TIME SAVER

You can save an existing project as a template. Just use **Save As**, and select **Captivate Template Files** in the **Save as type** drop-down menu.

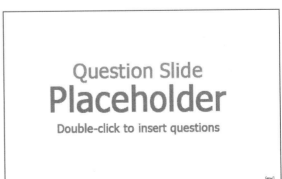

Question Slide
# Placeholder
Double-click to insert questions

# Text-Editing Tools

## Check Spelling

The spell check feature in Captivate checks captions, slide notes, slide names, text animations, and quizzes.

**To check the spelling in your project:**

1. Go to the **Project** menu.
2. Select **Check Spelling**.

Click the **Options** button to change the spell check settings, such as the default language and types of words to ignore.

## CAUTION

The spell checker does NOT check alt text added via the **Accessibility** button.

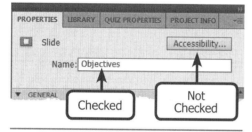

# Find and Replace

**Find and Replace** lets you search for and replace text just like you can in most word processing software.  In addition, you can search for certain types of objects, such as rollover captions.  This can make it easier to find something in a large project.

**To find text or object types:**

1. Go to the **Edit** menu.

2. Select **Find and Replace**.

3. In the **Search In** drop-down menu, select the type of object you want to search in or for, or select **All Object Types**.

4. In the **Style** field, select the styles you want to search in or for, if needed.

5. In the **Find** field, enter the text you want to look for, if needed.

6. In the **Replace** field, enter the text you want to replace the found text with, if needed.

7. Check and uncheck the boxes at the bottom to limit or expand your search.

8. Click one of the four buttons on the right to initiate the search or replacement.

Some fields are only available if your search includes text-related objects.

# The Library

The **Library** contains all the assets of a project: those currently in use, those added but no longer in use, and those added but not yet used. The **Library** is unique to that project. For example, the **Library** contains:

- The background image and audio of all current slides.
- The background image and audio of all deleted slides.
- Every version of the background image and audio of a certain slide.
- An image or audio clip you added to the **Library** and then added to a slide.
- An image or audio you added to the **Library** that has not yet been used on a slide.

**The Library contains:**
- Audio
- Backgrounds
- Equations
- Images
- Media
  - Animations
  - Video
- Presentations

The default location for the **Library** is the panel on the right side of the interface. Look for a tab next to the **Properties** tab. If it is not showing, go to the **Window** menu, and select **Library**.

What can you do with the **Library**?

- Store assets that you know you'll need later.
- Revert back to previous versions of an asset.
- Reuse assets over and over.
- Edit assets.
- Import and export assets.
- Update linked assets, such as a linked PowerPoint or video file.

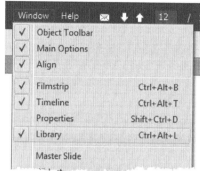

You can also view important information about your project assets from the **Library**. For example, you can:

**Preview the assets**: When you select an item in the **Library**, a preview appears in the pane at the top. For audio, video, and animations, click the **Play** button **(A)** to play the media.

**Determine if assets are currently in use**: The **Use Count** column **(B)** shows you how many times an item is being used in the project. A **0** indicates an unused item.

**Sort the assets**: Click a column heading **(C)** to sort the assets by that heading.

**Organize into folders**: Right-click an item and select **New Folder** to create a new folder. Then drag and drop items into that folder. New folders go inside an existing media type and cannot contain different media types.

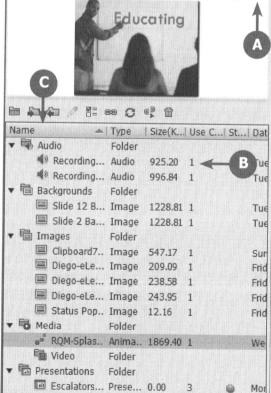

## TIME SAVER

You can import a **Library** from another project. Go to the **File** menu, select **Import**, and then **External Library**.

# Manage Assets in the Library

You can perform these functions in the **Library** by right-clicking an asset or selecting it and using a button at the top.

**To delete an asset:**
- Right-click the asset, and select **Delete**. — or —
- Select the asset, and click the **Delete** button.

**To delete all unused assets:**
- Click the **Select Unused** button, and then click the **Delete** button.

**To edit an asset:**
- Right-click the asset, and select **Edit with**. — or —
- Select the asset, and click the **Edit** button.

**To rename an asset:**
- Right-click the asset, and select **Rename**.

**To update a linked asset:**
- Right-click the asset, and select **Update**. — or —
- Select the asset, and click the **Update** button.

 Update Project Video, p. 90
Update an Imported Slide, p. 35

**To reuse an asset:**
- Drag it to the slide you want.

**To export an asset:**
- Right-click the asset, and select **Export**. — or —
- Select the asset, and click the **Export** button.

**To import an asset into the Library:**
- Right-click any asset, and select **Import**. — or —
- Click the **Import** button.

**To import an asset from another Library:**
1. Click the **Open Library** button.
2. Find and select the Captivate project with the library you want to use.
3. Click the **Open** button.
4. In the pop-up window, find and select the asset you want to import.
5. Drag the asset to a slide or a folder in the **Library**.

Once you import assets from another project, that project is available from a drop-down menu on the **Open Library** button.

## CAUTION

The **Library** contains all versions of all assets. That can cause problems if:

- You deleted an asset from a slide because there was a problem with it, and then accidentally reused it.
- You had sensitive information that you covered with merged objects, but the original image with the sensitive information is still in the **Library**.
- You are concerned about the file size of the .cptx file. (Library size does not affect the published movie, just the .cptx file.)

If these are concerns, it is a good idea to regularly delete unneeded assets.

# Widgets

Widgets are configurable Flash objects that can be configured in Captivate without using Flash. Widgets let you enhance and expand the capabilities of Captivate. You can get widgets in one of three ways:

- Use widgets installed with Captivate.
- Download additional widgets from Adobe or third-party sources.
- Create your own in Adobe Flash.

Widgets are configured in two places. With most widgets, a **Widget Properties** dialog box appears when you add the widget. This lets you choose many of the key settings for that widget. In addition, you can configure many of the regular properties in the **Properties** panel. For example, with a button widget, you designate the style and text in the **Widget Properties** dialog box, but you still designate the button actions in the regular **Properties** panel.

## Add a Widget From the Properties Panel

Certain object types have a link to widgets right in the **Properties** panel. This link lets you select from the widgets installed in the Captivate program files. For example, if you add a caption, the caption's **Properties** panel lets you use a caption widget.

**To add a widget from the Properties panel:**

1. Add the object type you want.
2. Click the widget link in the **Properties** panel. **(A)**
3. In the **Widget** panel that appears, click the **Insert** link for the widget you want to add. **(B)**
4. Configure the properties in the **Widget Properties** dialog box. **(C)**
5. Click **OK**.

# BRIGHT IDEAS

- Pre-installed widgets can be found in the Captivate program files on your hard drive.

    Adobe > Captivate 7 > Gallery > Widgets

- You can bring up the **Widget** panel any time you want by going to the **Window** menu and selecting **Widgets**.

- After you've added the widget, you can still go back and edit the properties found in the **Widget Properties** dialog box. Click the **Widget Properties** button in the object's **Properties** panel.

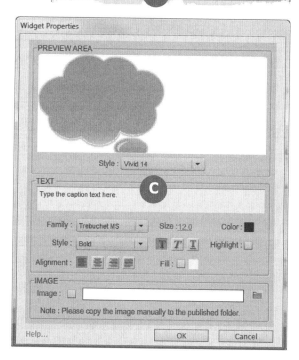

# Add a Widget From the Insert Menu

When you add a widget from the **Insert** menu, you can select any widget on your computer or a network drive. This can include the pre-installed widgets that come with Captivate, third-party widgets you've downloaded, or custom-created widgets.

**To add a widget from the Insert menu:**

1. Go to the **Insert** menu.
2. Select **Widget**.
3. Find and select the widget you want.
4. Click the **Open** button.
5. Configure the widget properties.
6. Click **OK**.

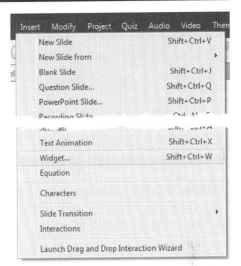

## Options

Use the buttons at the bottom of the **Widget** panel to help manage widgets.

**Change Path**: The **Widget** panel pulls from the widgets stored in the Captivate program files. Click this button if you want to pull from a different file location.

**Adobe Captivate Exchange**: Click this button or the **More** link on the end to go to the Adobe Captivate Exchange website to find additional widgets to download.

**Browse**: Click this button to find and select additional widgets to add to the panel.

**Refresh**: Click this button to refresh the view of available widgets.

**Filter**: Use the drop-down menu to filter the view of available widgets.

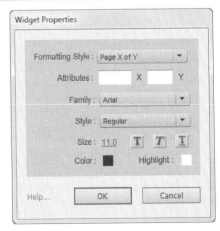

 **POWER TIP**

You can create your own widgets in Adobe Flash. Go to the **File** menu, select **New Project**, and then **Widget in Flash**. This option only works if you have Adobe Flash installed on your computer. Refer to the Adobe Captivate 6 help manual for more information.

# Add the Twitter Widget

Captivate 7 includes a special widget that lets you use Twitter to help students interact with each other and an instructor.

**To insert the Twitter widget:**

1. Go to the first slide of the course.
2. Go to the **Insert** menu.
3. Select **Widget**.
4. Navigate to the **Widgets** folder installed with the program files.
5. Select **A3C.wdgt**.
6. Click the **Open** button.
7. Sign in to your Adobe account.
8. Click the **Login** button.
9. Enter the details about the course.
10. Check the **Twitter Collaboration** box.
11. Enter your Twitter username.
12. Click the **Register** button.
13. Click the **OK** button.
14. Select the widget placeholder on the slide.
15. In the **Timing** pane of the **Properties** panel, select **Rest of Project**.

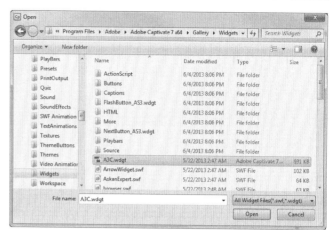

# Add the Twitter Widget (cont'd)

When students launch the course, they need to give Twitter permission to use their account for the course.

**To authorize the Twitter widget in the course:**

1. Launch the published course.
2. In the message box that appears, click the **Generate PIN** button.
3. In the browser window that appears, click the **Authorize app** button.
4. Copy the PIN that is displayed.
5. Return to the published course.
6. Paste the PIN in the message box in the course.
7. Click the **Login** button.

## Options for Students

- A small gray bar appears on the right side of the course. When a student clicks this bar, the full Twitter toolbar appears. Students can click the **Tweets** button to either post a tweet or to view tweets from others.

- If a student right-clicks anywhere on the screen, they can select **Ask a Question** to create a tweet that is anchored to that particular position on the screen, helping to provide context to that tweet.

- Tweets appear in the user's Twitter feed. All course-related tweets have a unique hashtag identifier. Any tweets made through Twitter (or a companion app such as Tweetdeck) using that hashtag will appear in the course's Twitter widget. This lets students (or an instructor) monitor and respond to course comments without having to be in the course.

## Additional Option for Course Administrators

Course administrators can go to cplive.adobe.com to log in and view a dashboard of Twitter activity for their courses.

Student right-clicking content for a context-sensitive comment

**Tweets**

Artisan E-Learning @ArtisanELrng   1m
Testing out the #captivate twitter widget. #CMID_25621
Expand

Student's course tweet appearing in his Twitter feed

Twitter widget as it appears in the published course

Twitter widget when expanded

# Sharing and Reviewing

Acrobat.com is an online collaboration site from Adobe that offers online meetings, document sharing, and file storage. You can either upload or share your Captivate files to Acrobat.com in published format (.swf) or in source file format (.cptx). If you do not already have an Acrobat.com account, you can register for one at www.acrobat.com.

You can also use Adobe Captivate Reviewer to capture comments from reviewers to help you manage the review and editing process more easily. This can either be done through Acrobat.com or your own network.

## Upload Files to Acrobat.com

**To upload files to Acrobat.com:**

1. Go to the **File** menu.
2. Select **Collaborate**.
3. Select **Upload Files to Acrobat.com**.
4. Enter your Adobe ID and password.
5. Click the **Sign In** button.
6. Enter the name you want to use for the file.
7. Check the boxes for the versions of the files you want to upload.
8. Click the **Upload** button.

The files are available from your Acrobat.com home page on the **Files** tab and can be viewed by anyone with access to that page.

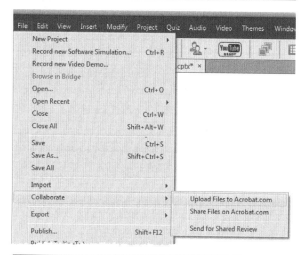

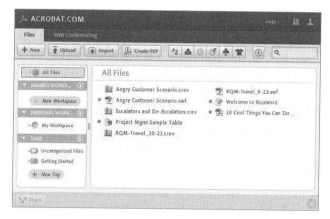

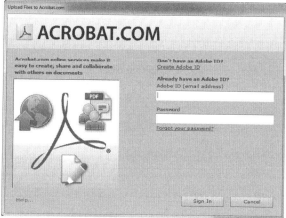

# Share Files on Acrobat.com

The process of sharing files is very similar to the process for uploading files. This difference is that with this procedure, the file is uploaded to your Acrobat.com account, and an email is sent to anyone you want to share the file with.

**To share files from Acrobat.com:**

1. Go to the **File** menu.
2. Select **Collaborate**.
3. Select **Share Files on Acrobat.com**.
4. Enter your Adobe ID and password.
5. Click the **Sign In** button.
6. Enter the name you want to use for the file.
7. Check the boxes for the versions of the files you want to upload.
8. Click the **Next** button.
9. Enter the address, subject line, and message for the email to be sent to the person you are sharing the file with.
10. Click the **SEND** button.

The uploaded file appears on your Acrobat.com home page on the **Files** tab, and the person you are sharing with receives an email with a link to view the file. In order to view it, the person must sign in with their own Adobe ID.

# Adobe Captivate Reviewer

When you send a file for shared review, you are able to collect feedback on the project. Reviewers can view the project in a special interface that lets them add comments. Your reviewers must first install Adobe AIR and then install Adobe Captivate Reviewer to view the project and add comments. You can then accept, reject, or ask for feedback on the comments.

**To send for shared review:**

1. Go to the **File** menu.
2. Select **Collaborate**.
3. Select **Send for Shared Review**. (See pg. 216.)
4. Enter a name for the file.
5. Select the comment collection method you want.
6. Click the **Next** button.
7. Enter your Adobe ID and password. (See pg. 216.)
8. Click the **Sign In** button.
9. Enter the address, subject line, and message for the email to be sent to the people you are sharing the file with.
10. Click the **SEND** button.

## Collection Methods

**Acrobat.com**: With this method, a Captivate review file (.crev) is stored on Acrobat.com, and an email is sent to reviewers with a link to the review file.

**Internal Server**: With this method, you either place the files in a shared location, such as a network drive, or you can email the review file and have the reviewers export their comments and email them back to you. (You can then import them into your review file.)

With this option, there are a few extra steps after step 8. You will pick where to save the review file and comments file and whether or not you want the system to send an email. That email can include the review file as an attachment as well as a link to Adobe Captivate Reviewer.

## BRIGHT IDEA

Refer to the Adobe Captivate 7 help documentation for more information on how to use the Captivate Reviewer. (Search for "Reviewing Adobe Captivate projects.")

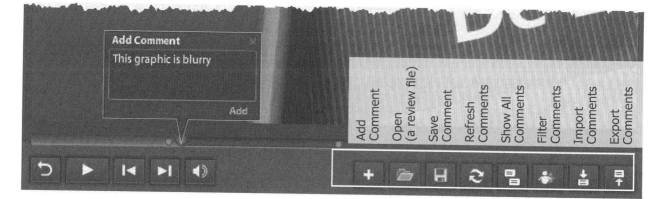

# Adobe Captivate Reviewer (cont'd)

Comments can be managed in the Adobe AIR application or directly in your Captivate project.

**To view comments in Captivate:**

1. Go to the **Window** menu.
2. Select **Comments**.
3. In the **Comments** panel, click the **Refresh Comments** button.
4. Log in with your Adobe ID, if needed.

There are three ways to look at your comments.

- In the **Timeline**, a dot appears for each comment. Hover over the dot to read the comment. **(A)**

- In the **Comments** pane, you can view all the comments for the project using the **View By** drop-down menu to sort by time, reviewer, or status. **(B)**

- In the **Filmstrip**, a comments icon appears to let you know there is a comment for that slide. **(C)**

The **Comments** pane has a number of buttons to help you manage the comments. For some commands, you need to first check the box next to a comment.

**Import Comments**: Use this to incorporate comments that others exported for you.

**Export Comments**: Use this to create a backup file or to share with another user.

**Reply**: Click this button to type a response to a comment.

**Accept**: Click this button to change the status to "Accepted." You can include a message here.

**Reject**: Click this button to change the status to "Rejected." You can include a message here.

**Edit Comments**: Click this button to edit a comment.

**Save Comments**: Click this button to save comments.

| Import Comments | Export Comments | Refresh Comments | Reply | Accept | Reject | Edit Comments | Save Comments |
|---|---|---|---|---|---|---|---|

## ⓘ CAUTION

The **End Review** button **(D)** is not for ending a particular review session. It is for ending the entire review cycle by deleting all of the comments. Only click this button if you are sure you want to delete all of the comments.

# Preferences

**Preferences**, available from the **Edit** menu, has important settings ranging from quality and project defaults to publishing and reporting. You can also get there from a number of other menus, such as from **Quiz Preferences** on the **Quiz** menu.

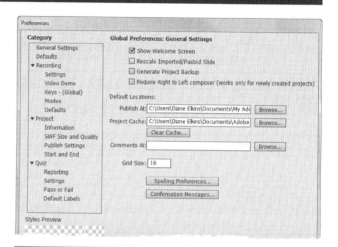

In this book, most of the preferences are covered in the chapter relating to that type of preferences. The remainder are covered here.

- Recording preferences: chapter 2
- Project preferences: chapter 12
- Quiz preferences: chapter 10

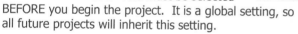

## General Settings

**Show Welcome Screen**: When you have Captivate open but no projects open, you see the **Welcome** screen. If you don't want to see it, uncheck this box.

**Rescale Imported/Pasted Slide**: If you import or paste a slide that's larger than the project it is going into, Captivate asks if you want to resize it. Check this box if you want Captivate to resize it without asking.

**Generate Project Backup**: Check this box if you want Captivate to create a backup file of your project. It is saved with a .bak extension. Change the extension back to .cptx to restore the file.

**Require Right to Left composer**: Check this box to author with right-to-left languages such as Arabic or Chinese. This must be selected BEFORE you begin the project. It is a global setting, so all future projects will inherit this setting.

### Default Locations

**Publish At**: This is where published projects will be saved, unless you change the location. Click the **Browse** button to select a different default location.

**Project Cache**: Software uses cache to temporarily store data to help speed up processing. This field indicates what location is being used for cache.

**Clear Cache**: If you are having performance problems, you can clear your cache by clicking here.

**Comments At**: If you use Adobe Captivate Reviewer, this is where the comments will be saved. Click the **Browse** button to save them to a different location.

**Grid Size**: You can use an on-screen grid to help line up objects on a slide. Change the number to make grid lines closer (smaller #) or farther apart (larger #).

**Spelling Preferences**: Click this button to change spell check preferences.

**Confirmation Messages**: Captivate displays various confirmation messages, such as when you delete a slide or an object. Click this button to get a dialog box where you can turn certain types of messages on or off.

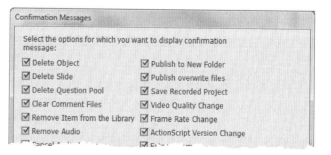

## Default Settings

**Slide Duration**: This is how long all slides are when they are first added to the project. Change the length (in seconds) if you prefer a different default length.

**Background color**: By default, all new blank slides have a white background. Change the color here if you want a different default background color.

**Preview Next**: When you preview a project, one of the options is to preview a small chunk of slides— five by default. **(A)** If you would like that menu option to preview a different number of slides, enter that number here.

**Object Defaults**: In this section, you can designate the length (in seconds) for how long certain objects appear when they are first added to a project. For example, all text captions are three seconds long when they are first added to the project. If you would like to change the default length, select an object from the first drop-down menu, and enter the length just beneath that. You can also designate a default style for the selected object. Click the **Restore Selected** or **Restore All** buttons to go back to the previously saved settings.

 Styles, p. 104

**Autosize Buttons**: When you create a text button, the button resizes automatically based on how long the text is. Uncheck this box if you do not want the buttons to resize.

**Autosize Captions**: When you change the text in a caption, the caption resizes automatically to accommodate the changes in the text. Uncheck this box if you do not want the captions to resize.

**Calculate Caption Timing**: By default, captions use the length specified in the **Object Defaults** section when they are added to a project. Check this box if you want the length to be determined by Captivate based on how much text is in the caption. A caption with more text will stay up longer, giving the student more time to read it.

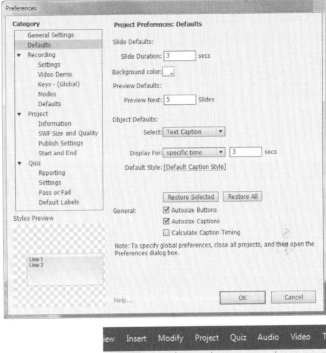

 **BRIGHT IDEA**

If you have a project open when you change the defaults, the changes apply only to that project. If you change them when there are no projects open, they become global preferences for all new projects.

 **TIME SAVER**

You can export preferences from one project/ computer and import them into another project/ computer. On the **File** menu, go to the **Export** or **Import** sub-menu, and select **Preferences**. Preferences are saved as a .cpr file.

# Exporting and Importing XML

Exporting to XML, or extensible markup language, is a way to convert your Captivate project to a text-based form that can be translated, imported into other software applications, or re-imported back into Captivate.

```
<group datatype="plaintext" cp:datatype="x-property" restype="x-cp-slide-label" extype="337">
    <trans-unit id="911-337">
        <source>Standard Fill</source>
    </trans-unit>
</group>
<group datatype="plaintext" cp:datatype="x-property" restype="x-cp-slide-accessibility"
extype="1285">
    <trans-unit id="911-1285">
        <source> </source>
    </trans-unit>
</group>
<group cp:datatype="x-object" restype="x-cp-audio-item" id="1409" extype="275">
    <group cp:datatype="x-object" restype="x-cp-closed-caption-items" id="1410" extype="113">
        <group cp:datatype="x-object" restype="x-cp-closed-caption-item" id="1442"
        extype="114">
            <group datatype="plaintext" cp:datatype="x-property" restype="x-cp-closed-caption-
            name" extype="207">
                <trans-unit id="1442-207">
                    <source>Adding a fill color to your cells can make your spreadsheets more
                    visually interesting. But it can also make them easier to understand. By
                    adding a fill color to header rows or cells with key information, you can
                    make the important elements stand out. </source>
                </trans-unit>
            </group>
        </group>
    </group>
</group>
<group cp:datatype="x-object" restype="x-cp-items" id="912" extype="69">
    <group cp:datatype="x-object" restype="Text Caption" id="1462" extype="19">
        <group cp:datatype="x-paragraph" css-style="line-spacing:1.00;line-indent:0.00">
            <trans-unit id="1462-19-1">
                <source>
                    <g id="1462-19-1-1" css-style="font-family:'Myriad Pro';font-
                    face:'Regular';color:#333333;font-size:18.0pt" ctype="x-cp-font">Select
                    the cells you want to format.</g>
                </source>
```

## Export to XML

**To export a project to XML:**

1. Go to the **File** menu.
2. Select **Export**.
3. Select **To XML**.
4. Find and select the location where you want to save the file.
5. Click the **Save** button.

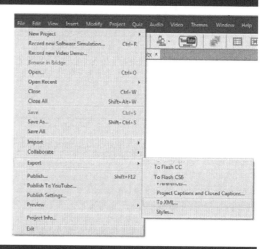

## Import From XML

**To import a project from XML:**

1. Go to the **File** menu.
2. Select **Import**.
3. Select **From XML**.
4. Find and select the file you want to import.
5. Click the **Open** button.

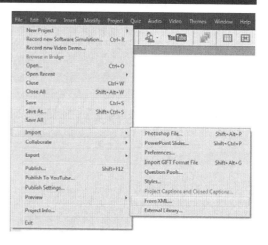

# Publishing

## Introduction

In this chapter, you will learn about the various settings that affect your finished output, such as:

- Whether to include a control toolbar that lets the student control the progress of the finished movie.
- Whether to send tracking data to a learning management system (LMS).
- How much to compress the output to accommodate slow connection speeds.

In addition, you'll look at the specific publishing formats:

- Flash (.swf)
- HTML5
- Adobe Connect
- Media (.exe, .app, .mp4)
- E-mail or FTP delivery of files (published files or source files)
- Print (Microsoft Word)

### In This Chapter

- Rescale a Project
- Project Skins
- Project Settings
- Reporting and Tracking
- Publishing Options

# Notes

# Output-Related Options

Before you publish your project, you'll want to configure a number of settings that affect your finished output.

## Rescale a Project

When you publish your project, the output size is the same as the project size. If you need your published movie to be a different size, you need to resize the entire project.

**To rescale a project:**

1. Go to the **Modify** menu.
2. Select **Rescale project**.
3. Set the new size by width/height dimensions, width/height percentage, or preset sizes from a menu.
4. Set the options for larger or smaller projects.
5. Click **Finish**.

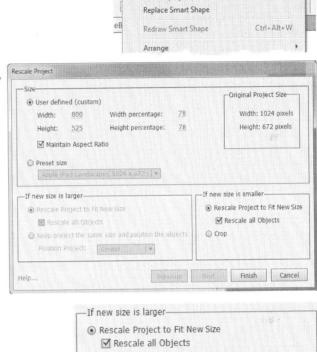

### If New Size Is Larger

**Rescale Project**: Select this option if you want to enlarge the entire background image to fill the new larger slides. Check the box underneath to resize all objects accordingly. Otherwise, they will stay the same size on the larger slide.

**Keep project the same size**: Select this option if you want to keep the background image and objects at their current size, meaning they will be smaller than the slide. Use the **Position Project** menu to indicate where on the larger slide you want the background and objects to appear (center, top left, etc.).

### If New Size Is Smaller

**Rescale Project**: Select this option if you want to scale down the background image to fit in the new smaller size. Check the box underneath to resize all objects accordingly. Otherwise, they will stay the same size.

**Crop**: Select this option if you want to keep the background image and objects at 100% of their current size and instead crop off whatever doesn't fit on the new smaller slide. If you select this option, the **Next** button becomes active, letting you indicate what part to keep and what part to crop.

## CAUTION

- If you select the crop option, make sure you are not cropping out key areas of the slide.
- Be careful about resizing a project to be larger. You will lose resolution, and the resulting quality may not be what you want.

## BRIGHT IDEAS

- Make sure you really need to resize your Captivate output, as you might be able to resize it in its final destination. For example, if you place your movie in another e-learning authoring tool, you may be able to resize it in that tool.

- Cropping is helpful if you want to remove part of a capture, such as menus and toolbars at the top of a browser window.

- For screen simulations, it is a good idea to keep a copy of your Captivate file at full size. After you resize, it may be difficult to get additional captures if you need changes.

# Configure Project Skin: Playback Controls

The project skin controls three features: the playback controls, a border, and a table of contents.

**To select an existing skin:**

1. Click the **Project** menu.
2. Select **Skin Editor**.
3. Select an option from the **Skin** drop-down menu.
4. Close the window.

**To change the elements of a project skin:**

1. Click the **Project** menu.
2. Select **Skin Editor**.
3. Configure the playback control settings. (See below.)
4. Click the **Borders** button.
5. Configure the border options.  (See next page.)
6. Click the **Table of Contents** button.
7. Configure the table of contents options. (See p. 228.)
8. Close the window.

## Playback Control Options

**Show Playback Control**: Check this box if you want to provide the student with a toolbar that controls the movie.

**Hide Playbar in Quiz**: Check this box to hide the playbar on a quiz question slide.  This is useful if you don't want students to move forward or back on a quiz slide.  (The playbar is always hidden on pre-test slides.)

**Playbar Overlay**: By default, the playbar appears under the published movie.  If you check this box, the playbar is placed over the movie.  This covers up part of the content area, but it keeps the published size exactly the same as the project size.

**Show Playbar on Hover**: This option is enabled if you select **Playbar Overlay**.  With this option, the playbar hides if the student's mouse is inactive for two seconds, and then reappears when the mouse is active again.

**Playbar**: From the drop-down menu, select the playbar style you want.

**Playbar Widgets**: Click this link to open the **Widgets** pane in the **Properties** dialog box to find other playbar styles.

**Playbar Two Rows:** When you check this box, the buttons appear on one row and the seekbar appears on a bottom row.  This is useful for projects that are very small.

**Playback Colors**: To further customize the playbar, check this box, and then use the color swatches to adjust the color of the different elements.

## TIME SAVER

If you customize your skin settings, you can save them to reuse over and over.  Click the **Save** button next to the name of the skin to add it to the drop-down list for later use.

# Configure Project Skin: Playback Controls (cont'd)

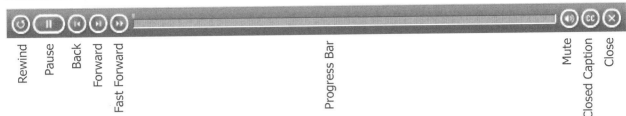

Rewind  Pause  Back  Forward  Fast Forward  Progress Bar  Mute  Closed Caption  Close

**Position**: Indicate where in the movie you want the playbar to appear: top, left, bottom, or right.

**Layout**: Indicate the size and more specific position of the playbar, such as stretched across the screen or over to the left or right. Options vary based on what you choose in the **Position** menu.

**Button Options**: Check the box for each option you want to include on your playbar. (See examples above.)

**Alpha**: Indicate how opaque or transparent you want the playbar to be. 100% is fully opaque. Lower numbers are semi-transparent.

**No Tooltips at runtime**: By default, when a student rolls his or her mouse over a toolbar button, a small tooltip appears, explaining what the button is for. Check this box if you don't want the tooltips.

## POWER TIP

You can make your own custom playbar in Flash. See the Captivate User's Manual for specifications.

## CAUTION

Tooltips are also read by screen readers. If you turn off the tooltips, then your course will not be Section-508 compliant.

Be sure to enable the **Closed Caption** button for projects with captioning.

Accessibility, p. 245

# Configure Project Skin: Border Options

Click the **Borders** button **(A)** to configure a border around the published movie. The skin you have selected in the **Skin** drop-down menu affects what the default options are.

**Show Borders**: Check this box if you want to have a border around your project. Then, click the button for each side you want to give a border to. (Click all four for a full border.)

**Style**: Indicate if you want the border to have square or rounded corners.

**Width**: Enter the point size for the border width.

**Texture**: For a patterned border, select from one of almost 100 texture/pattern options, such as brushed metal or wood grain.

**Color**: Click the swatch to change the color of the border. (The color chosen here does not affect any textures used.)

**HTML Background**: Click the swatch to change the color of the background area around the project on an HTML page.

# Configure Project Skin: Table of Contents

Click the **Table of Contents** button **(A)** to configure the table of contents. The skin you have selected in the **Skin** drop-down menu affects what the default options are.

**Show TOC**: Check this box if you want your published file to have a table of contents that lets the student move freely around the course.

**Title**: Double-click a slide title to edit the name as it will appear in the TOC.

**Show/Hide TOC Entries**: Check or uncheck the box in the show/hide column **(B)** to show or hide that slide in the table of contents.

### Buttons

These options change how your slides appear in the table of contents. They do not affect how the slides appear in the project itself.

**Folder**: Click the **Folder** button to create an entry in the TOC that isn't tied to a slide.

**Reset TOC**: Click this button to return the entries to their original configuration.

**Move TOC Entry Left/Right**: Use the left and right arrows to indent or outdent the selected slide.

**Move TOC Entry Up/Down**: Use the up and down arrows to change the order of the entries. You can also click and drag the slides to rearrange them.

**Delete TOC Entry**: To delete a topic name, select that line item, and then click the **Delete** button. You cannot delete a slide from your project here, you can only hide them.

## ! CAUTION

Changes made to your project after you create the table of contents are not automatically updated in the TOC. Instead, come back to this dialog box and click the **Reset TOC** button.

### Project Info

Click the **Info** button to add project information, such as project name, author, and description. This information appears in a pop-up window at the top of the TOC.

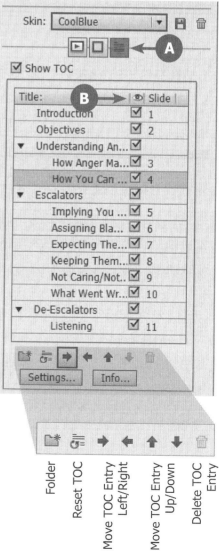

Folder | Reset TOC | Move TOC Entry Left/Right | Move TOC Entry Up/Down | Delete TOC Entry

# Configure Project Skin: Table of Contents (cont'd)

## TOC Settings

Click the **Settings** button to bring up the **TOC Settings** dialog box. (See previous page.)

**Style**: Select **Overlay** to have the TOC appear on the slide with a small show/hide icon that lets the student show or hide it. Select **Separate** if you want the TOC to appear to the side of the slide.

**Position**: Indicate if you want the TOC to be on the left or right side of the slide.

**Stretch TOC**: With this option, the TOC is as long as the slide plus the playbar. If it is unchecked, it is only as long as the slide.

**Alpha**: By default, the TOC is fully opaque. Enter a lower number for semi-transparency.

## Runtime Options

**Collapse All**: When checked, all folders in the TOC will be collapsed when the project plays.

**Self-Paced Learning**: When checked, students' status flags are not reset when the project is closed, and, upon return, the student may resume where he or she left off previously.

**Show Topic Duration**: Check this box if you want the slide duration to appear next to each slide. Uncheck it if you don't.

**Enable Navigation**: When checked, the student can move around freely using the TOC. Uncheck this if you do not want the student to be able to navigate via the TOC.

**Navigate Visited Slides Only**: When checked, students can navigate freely around any slide they have already visited, but can't jump ahead in the course. This option is only available if you have **Enable Navigation** checked.

**Show Search**: Check this box if you want a search box in the TOC. Check the **Search Quiz** box if you want to include quiz slides in the search.

**Status Flag**: When this option is selected, a check mark appears next to each slide that the user has completed viewing. Check the **Clear Button** box if you want the student to be able to clear his or her status.

**Show Movie Duration**: Check this box to show the total time of the movie at the bottom of the TOC.

**Expand/Collapse Icon**: When there are folders, the TOC uses traditional triangle icons for expanding and collapsing the sections. If you want to import your own image, you can do that here.

**Width**: Enter the width you want for the TOC, in pixels.

**Theme**: Use these fields to adjust the font and color settings of the various TOC elements, including font choices for up to five levels in the TOC hierarchy.

**Auto Preview**: Uncheck this option if you do not want to see the changes in the preview panel while you are making them.

# Change Project Preferences

The **Preferences** dialog box has a number of settings that affect your output. You can:

- Add information about the project, such as the title, author, and description.

- Adjust size and quality settings.

- Indicate which features you want to include, such as audio and mouse click sounds.

- Indicate how you want the published movie to start and end.

- Configure options for reporting scores and completion status to a learning management system or other reporting system.

**To change the project preferences:**

1. Go to the **Edit** menu.
2. Select **Preferences**.
3. Click the category you want to change.
4. Make your changes.
5. Click **OK**.

| Edit | View | Insert | Modify | Project | Quiz | Audio | |
|---|---|---|---|---|---|---|---|
| Undo Insert Slides | | | | | | Ctrl+Z | |
| Redo | | | | | | Ctrl+Y | |
| Cut | | | | | | Ctrl+X | |
| Copy | | | | | | Ctrl+C | |
| Copy Background | | | | | | Shift+Ctrl+Y | |
| Paste | | | | | | Ctrl+V | |
| Paste as Background | | | | | | Shift+Alt+V | |
| Duplicate | | | | | | Ctrl+D | |
| Delete | | | | | | Del | |
| Select All | | | | | | Ctrl+A | |
| Group | | | | | | Ctrl+G | |
| Convert to rollover Smart Shape | | | | | | | |
| Edit Points | | | | | | Ctrl+Alt+E | |
| Edit Gradient | | | | | | | |
| Edit Text | | | | | | F2 | |
| Object Style Manager... | | | | | | Shift+F7 | |
| Preferences... | | | | | | Shift+F8 | |

# Project Information Settings

Project information provides data about the project, such as the title, author, etc. This can be used as internal information for the developers, included in a table of contents for students to see, or read by screen readers in an accessible project.

Table of Contents, p. 228
Accessibility, p. 245

**Preferences**

**Category**
- General Settings
- Defaults
- ▼ Recording
  - Settings
  - Video Demo
  - Keys - (Global)
  - Modes
  - Defaults
- ▼ Project
  - Information
  - SWF Size and Quality
  - Publish Settings
  - Start and End
- ▼ Quiz
  - Reporting
  - Settings
  - Pass or Fail
  - Default Labels

**Project: Information**

Author: Diane Elkins
Company: Artisan E-Learning
E-mail: info@artisanelearning.com
Website: www.artisanelearning.com
Copyright: Artisan E-Learning
Project Name: Escalators and De-Escalators
Description: Learn how the little things you say or do can make a customer conflict situation better (de-escalators) or worse (escalators).

Time: 33.0secs (990 frames)
Resolution: 640 x 480
Slides: 11
Hidden Slides: 0

# SWF Size and Quality Settings

When publishing your project, you'll want to balance quality with file size. A high-quality output may look good, but may be too large for remote viewers to access easily. Conversely, a small output file may be easy to access but may not look or sound good.

**Compress Full Motion Recording SWF file**: If you have any full-motion recording in your project, then your movie contains video. Check this box if you want to compress that video.

**High, Medium, and Low**: Set the slider at any of these positions for settings which provide that level of quality for audio and video.

**Custom**: Set the slider at this level if you want to set each quality setting individually.

> **Retain Slide Quality Settings**: Check this box if you want to manage quality at the slide level. Or, uncheck it and enter settings for the entire project here.

 Slide Quality, p. 38

**Bmp**: Select high or low quality for the screenshots taken during your capture session.

**Audio**: Click the **Settings** button to change the audio quality of any voice-over, music, etc.

 Configure Audio Compression, p. 75

**Jpeg**: Select a compression percentage for any .jpg images you placed on your slides.

**Advanced Project Compression**: If you check this option, Captivate looks for similarities between slides and publishes only the differences as the project goes from slide to slide. Be sure to check your output with this option to make sure everything renders properly.

**Compress SWF File**: If you select **High**, **Medium**, or **Low**, this box is checked, meaning additional compression is used (other than the options listed above). If you don't want that extra compression, uncheck the box.

# Publish Settings

**Frames Per Second**: To create the movie effect, Captivate publishes at 30 frames per second. You may need to change this if you are embedding your .swf movie into another file that uses a different rate.

**Publish Adobe Connect metadata**: Selecting this option makes it easier to integrate your movie with Adobe Connect.

**Include Mouse**: Keep this checked if you want the slide mouse movements to appear in the published movie.

**Enable Accessibility**: Check this box to make your movie compatible with screen readers and to enable any other accessibility features you set up.

 Accessibility, p. 245

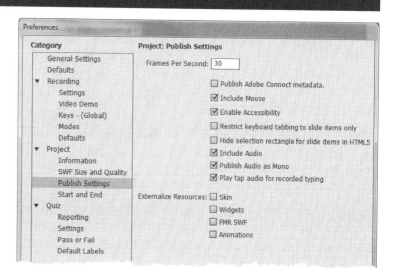

**Restrict keyboard tabbing to slide items only**: When you check this box, the TOC and playbar are skipped when students use the **Tab** key to navigate a course.

**Hide selection rectangle for slide items in HTML5**: When students use the Tab key to navigate the course, a yellow rectangle appears around the active object. Check this box if you want to hide that rectangle for HTML5 publishing.

**Include Audio**: Keep this checked if you want to publish any audio that you've added to the project.

**Publish Audio as Mono**: This setting converts stereo audio to mono audio, resulting in a smaller file size. With voice-over narration, mono audio is a good way to reduce file size without sacrificing audio quality.

**Play tap audio for recorded typing**: If you captured any typing in your project, keep this box checked if you want the published file to play keyboard tapping sounds. Uncheck this box if you don't want to hear those sounds.

**Externalize Resources**: By default, your movie publishes as a single .swf file that includes the skin, widgets, full motion video, and added animations. If you prefer to have these objects published as separate files (referred to by the .swf file), then check the box for that object type. This can help with download times for extremely large files.

# Start and End Settings

**Auto Play**: By default, a published movie starts playing immediately. Uncheck this box if you don't want it to autostart. If it is not set to autostart, a play button appears on the first frame for the student to click. If you want to select your own play button, click the **Browse** button.

**Preloader**: The preloader is a small image or animation that plays while the movie is downloading. With larger movies or slower connections, preloaders are helpful as they let students know that the movie is downloading.

**Preload %**: This indicates the percentage of the movie that must be downloaded before it starts playing.

**Password Protect Project:** Use this option if you want students to enter a password before they can view the movie. Click the **Options** button to change the system messages regarding the password.

**Project Expiry Date**: Check this option and enter a date if you want your movie to expire after a certain date. An expired movie cannot be viewed. This can be useful for limited-time offers or policy/legal information that changes yearly.

**Fade In on the First Slide**: Select this option to have the first frame of your movie fade in.

**Project End Options**: Use this drop-down menu to designate what action should happen when the movie is finished, such as stop, loop back to the beginning, go to a website, etc.

**Fade Out on the Last Slide**: Select this option to have the last frame of your movie fade out to white.

# Reporting and Tracking

If you want to publish your movie to a learning management system (LMS) and have it track usage on the course, you need to configure the **Reporting** settings in **Preferences** based on the needs of your LMS.

Once the settings are configured, you will need to publish your project using the **SWF/HTML5** option with **Zip Files** checked.

 SWF/HTML5 Publishing, p. 237

## Quiz Reporting Preferences

**Quiz:** Check this box to enable reporting. You can use these settings for tracking even if your course does not include a quiz.

**LMS**: Use this menu to select from a list of LMS types. **(A)** Choose from **Moodle**, **Acrobat.com**, **Internal Server**, **Other Standard LMS**, **Adobe Connect**, or **QuestionMark Perception.**

**Standard**: Select the LMS standard you want to use for the reporting. This list may not be active based on what you chose in the **LMS** menu. Choose from **SCORM 1.2**, **SCORM 2004**, **AICC**, or **Tin Can**. The Tin Can standard is new in Captivate 7.

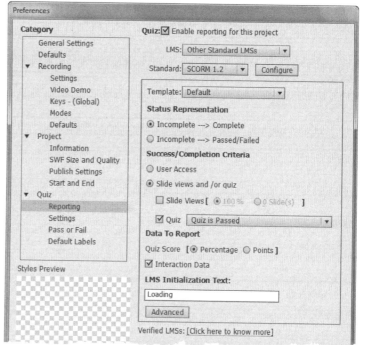

**Configure**: Click this button to provide details about the movie, such as title, description, and length. **(A)** These details will go into the project's manifest file for communication with an LMS. The options will vary based on which standard you have chosen.

**Template**: This drop-down menu is still included for legacy purposes and is rarely needed.

**Status Representation:** Indicate if you want to send a status **Complete** or **Passed** and **Failed**. Your LMS may require one set or the other.

**User Access:** With this option, the course is considered completed as soon as it is launched.

**Slide views and/or quiz**: Select this option if you want to base completion on the amount of slides viewed and/or the status of the quiz. Once selected, check the box for one or both of the options below.

> **Slide Views**: Enter the percentage or number of slides the student needs to view for the course to be complete.

> **Quiz**: Select one of the options from the drop-down menu: **Quiz is attempted**, **Quiz is Passed**, or **Quiz is passed or the quiz attempt limit is reached**.

**Quiz Score**: Indicate if you want to send the raw score (number of points) or the percent score for the quiz.

# Quiz Reporting Preferences (cont'd)

**Interaction Data**: Check this box if you want to include data about each individual question in addition to data about the overall quiz results.

**LMS Initialization Text**: Type the text you'd like to have appear to the student while the course is opening.

**Advanced Button**:  When you click this button, the **LMS Advanced Settings** dialog box appears.

> **Never Send Resume Data**:  Most LMSs offer bookmarking, which keeps track of where the students left off and asks them if they want to resume from that spot.  If you check this box, Captivate will not send information about where the students leave off.

> **Set exit to normal after completion**: In SCORM 2004 courses, check this box to have the course restart from the first slide when the user launches it again after successfully completing it once.

> **Escape Version and Session ID**: This option converts the version and session ID to its URL encoded values, which is sometimes necessary for AICC publishing.  For example, certain LMSs might have issues if there are special characters in the title name.

> **Don't Escape Characters**: If you use the **Escape Version** option, use this field to enter any characters that should not be used.

**Verified LMSs**: Click this link to go to Adobe's website to see which LMSs have been verified to work with Captivate.

## BRIGHT IDEA

What are SCORM, AICC, and Tin Can?

These are industry standards that govern interoperability between a course and an LMS, ensuring that the two can "talk" to each other.

Tin Can is a newer standard, releasing its 1.0 version in Spring of 2013.  Find out from your LMS provider which standard they use so that you can publish your movie accordingly.  They may also have suggestions about what other settings work best for their LMS.

When integrating with an LMS for the first time, it is best to conduct a test early to make sure everything works properly.

## CAUTION

- If you have any branching in your course, be careful about requiring 100% slide views, as the student may not ever get to all the slides. In these situations, determine the shortest path through the course, and use that as the minimum number of slides.

- Just because you choose to send all interaction data doesn't mean your LMS is able to report on it.  Captivate only controls what is sent, not what your LMS chooses to receive and/or display to you.

## POWER TIP

The **Internal Server** option on the **LMS** menu is a way to track student data without having an LMS.  You can either report data to acrobat. com or your own internal server.  Refer to the Captivate 7 help documentation for full technical details.

# Publishing

This first page outlines the high-level procedure for publishing.  The following pages outline the various options for each of the publishing formats.

## Publish Your Project

**To publish your project:**

1. Click the **Publish** button on the **Main Options** toolbar.

2. Select **Publish**.

3. Select the publish format you want down the left-hand side.

4. In the **Project Title** field, enter the name for the published movie.

5. In the **Folder** field, click the **Browse** button to find and select the location for the published files.

6. Check the **Publish to Folder** box if you want Captivate to create a separate folder for your published files.

7. Change the publishing settings, as needed. (See remaining pages of the chapter.)

8. Click **Publish**.

## Sample Output Files

| Name | Type |
|------|------|
| Escalators and De-Escalators.htm | HTML Document |
| Escalators and De-Escalators.swf | SWF File |
| captivate.css | Cascading Style Sheet Docu... |
| standard.js | JScript Script File |

*SWF option only*

| Name | Type |
|------|------|
| Escalators and De-Escalators.htm | HTML Document |
| Escalators and De-Escalators.swf | SWF File |
| imsmanifest.xml | XML Document |
| metadata.xml | XML Document |
| SCORM_utilities.js | JScript Script File |
| captivate.css | Cascading Style Sheet Docu... |
| standard.js | JScript Script File |
| adlcp_rootv1p2.xsd | XSD File |
| browsersniff.js | JScript Script File |
| ims_xml.xsd | XSD File |
| imscp_rootv1p1p2.xsd | XSD File |
| imsmd_rootv1p2p1.xsd | XSD File |
| scormdriver.js | JScript Script File |
| ScormEnginePackageProperties... | XSD File |
| Utilities.js | JScript Script File |

*SWF option only with SCORM 1.2 reporting*

| Name | Type |
|------|------|
| assets | File folder |
| dr | File folder |
| ar | File folder |
| callees | File folder |
| vr | File folder |
| Escalators and De-Escalators.htm | HTML Document |
| Escalators and De-Escalators.swf | SWF File |
| multiscreen.html | HTML Document |
| index.html | HTML Document |
| Project.js | JScript Script File |
| captivate.css | Cascading Style Sheet Docu... |
| standard.js | JScript Script File |

*SWF  and HTML5 options*

# SWF/HTML5 Publishing Options

## Output Format Options

**SWF**: Check this box to output to the traditional Flash format. In addition, an HTML file will be generated that plays the .swf file.

**HTML5**: Check this box to publish to HTML5 format, which plays on devices without the Flash player, such as iPhones and iPads.

 Publishing to HTML5, p. 238

## Output Options

**Zip Files**: Check this box if you want your published files to be zipped up into a .zip compressed folder. This is useful if you are uploading your files to an LMS.

**Fullscreen**: This option includes HTML files that cause the browser to open to its maximum size and hide browser elements, such as the toolbar and **Favorites** bar.

**Generate Autorun For CD**: If you check this box, the published files include a setup file that autoruns the movie on a CD. That way, when a student puts the CD into his or her computer, the published files run automatically.

**Flash Player Version**: You can select the version of Flash player needed to view the project.

**Export PDF**: Check this box to create a PDF document that plays the movie, which is a great way to send it via e-mail.

## Project Information

For any of the information shown in blue in the dialog box, you can click the setting information to make changes. These settings are managed in the **Preferences** dialog box and were covered earlier in this chapter.

## Advanced Options

**Force re-publish all the slides**: For any publish after the initial publish, Captivate detects what has changed and re-publishes only the slides that have changed. Check this box if you want to republish everything instead.

**Scalable HTML content:** Check this box if you want the contents of HTML5 projects to scale based on the size of the window they are viewed in. This option is not recommended for iPad viewing.

**Seamless Tabbing:** Check this box if you want students using the **Tab** key for navigation to be able to tab out of the Flash movie and into the surrounding HTML. Leave it unchecked to have all **Tab** navigation to stay within the movie.

# DESIGN TIPS

## Best Practices for HTML5 Output

- If you select both the **SWF** and **HTML5** options, the output files include logic that helps the published course determine which version to play for the student—based on what type of device the student is using.

- HTML5 is still an emerging standard. Be sure to test your HTML5 output thoroughly on the type of devices your students are likely to use.

- HTML5 output is supported on iPhones/iPads using OS version 5 or later. The output must be viewed through a browser. The following browsers are supported for iPhone/iPad viewing:
  - Internet Explorer 9 or later
  - Safari 5.1 or later
  - Google Chrome 17 or later

- If your project contains links to external files, you'll need to manually move those files to your published output files. If you are using the **Open URL or file** action, include the document in the main folder. If you are using the **Open another project** action, put the file in the **Callees** folder.

- Not all features in Captivate are HTML5-compatible. If any of these features are used in your course, you will receive the following message when you publish to HTML5.

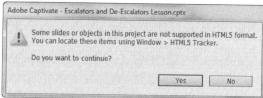

- Show the **HTML5 Tracker** from the **Project** or **Window** menu at any time to see which included course features are not HTML5-compatible.

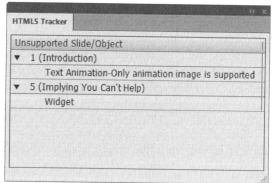

- Some of the most commonly used features that are not HTML5-compatible are:
  - Text animations.
  - SWF animations.
  - Mouse click animations.
  - .swf files used as a slide background.
  - Slide transitions.
  - Mouse right-click and double-click.
  - Reporting to an internal server or Acrobat.com.
  - Some effects (designated by ** in the menu).

Captivate 7 supports more features for HTML5 publishing than Captivate 6 did. Refer to Captivate's help documentation for more details on what is and isn't supported.

- Some features will only display properly in HTML5 if viewed from a web server but will not display properly if run from your local computer.

- Be sure to test your audio and video carefully. There are a number of specific situations that may not work as expected, such as having more than one audio or video file playing, having button click sounds, or having audio attached to invisible objects. Refer to the Captivate help documentation for more information.

# Other Publishing Options

## Adobe Connect

Use this option if you plan to upload your published movie to Adobe Connect. Captivate 7 supports HTML5 publishing for Adobe Connect.

## Media

The media options let you publish your project in formats other than .swf: .mp4, .exe (executable for Windows), and .app (executable for Mac). For example, .mp4 video files work well in iOS environments where Flash output does not work.

When publishing to .mp4, additional options appear that let you select the platform it will be viewed on (such as iPad, YouTube, etc.). Making this selection optimizes the output size for the platform you are using. YouTube publishing is also available from the **File** menu.

When creating a .exe file, you can designate your own icon to appear in the taskbar, Windows Explorer, and other locations. Refer to the Captivate user manual for details about what is needed.

## CAUTION

Only use .mp4 if your project is non-interactive. Any interactivity will be lost when publishing to this format.

## E-Mail

This option lets you publish to a number of formats and automatically adds them as attachments to an e-mail. Once the files are generated, your default e-mail program opens a message (with the files attached) for you to address and send.

## FTP

You can use this option to publish your file and send it directly to a website via FTP (File Transfer Protocol). You can publish to .swf, .exe, or .app formats, or instead send XML files or your project files (.cptx).

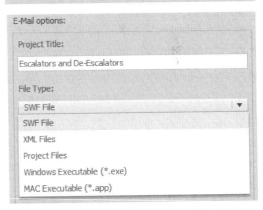

# Publishing to Print/Microsoft Word

When you publish to print, you create Word documents that can be used as handouts, storyboards, job aids, etc.

**Export range**: Specify which slides you want to include in the output.

**Type**: Select the format you want from the drop-down menu. The options in the bottom half of the panel vary based on the format you select.

> **Handouts**: Create a format similar to the PowerPoint handouts where you specify the number of slides per page and include either the slide notes or blank lines for note taking.
>
> **Lesson**: Create a document with the background image, text captions, the image of anything covered by a highlight box, as well as the questions and answers for any quizzes.

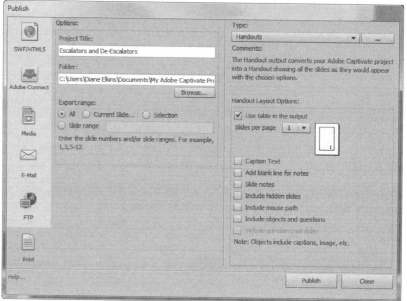

**Step-by-Step**: This format lists all caption text and the portion of the slide under a highlight box. For screen simulations, use this format to create a job aid that lists all the steps (caption text) and highlighted features (such as the **OK** button). Use the automatic highlight box feature during capture if you want to create a job aid such as this.

**Storyboard**: Create a document to help you manage production. It includes slide count, preferences, and settings for the whole project as well as slide-specific information, such as timing, audio, and objects.

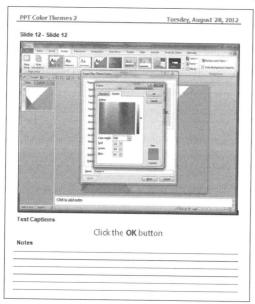

*Handouts including caption text and blank lines for notes; table output turned off.*

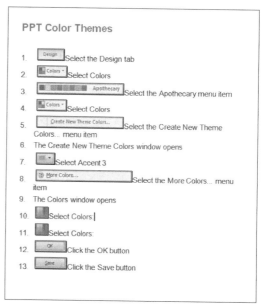

*Step-by-Step output, which includes caption text and the portion of the slide covered by a highlight box.*

## Publish to YouTube

The option for publishing to YouTube is not found in the **Publishing** dialog box with the other formats. When you use this option, the project is published to .mp4 output.

**To publish to YouTube:**

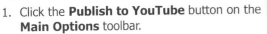

1. Click the **Publish to YouTube** button on the **Main Options** toolbar.

2. Enter your YouTube username and password.

3. Check the **Privacy Policy** check box.

4. Click the **Log In** button.

5. Enter the requested details about the project.

6. Check the box agreeing to the terms and conditions.

7. Click the **Upload** button.

8. Use the information in the final dialog box to share the link to your uploaded movie.

9. Click the **Close** button.

# POWER TIP

## Adobe App Packager

Captivate 7 comes with a companion application that lets you publish your Captivate project as an app for Android, iOS, and similar devices. While the App Packager is installed with Adobe Captivate 7, you will also need to use the Adobe Phone Gap service, which is separate. The high-level process is explained here. Refer to the Adobe Captivate help documentation for full technical details.

Step 1: Publish your project to HTML5.

Step 2: Go to your **Start** menu and launch **Adobe Captivate 7 App Packager**.

Step 3: Find and select your published files.

Step 4 (Optional): Import any additional HTML5 animations, such as those created with Adobe Edge.

Step 5: Publish the project for the devices you want.

Step 6: Download the app from Phone Gap.

# Appendix A

In addition to the cool tools found here in the Appendix, be sure to check out the additional tools on this book's companion website:

**www.elearninguncovered.com.**

## In This Chapter

- Accessibility
- Tips for Using Captivate for Mac
- Menus for Mac
- Menus for PC
- Keyboard Shortcuts
- System Variables

# Notes

# Accessibility

Accessibility in e-learning refers to making courses compatible with various assistive technology devices used by people with disabilities. There are three main classes of disability that affect e-learning: visual, auditory, and motor.

| Impairment | Common Assistive Devices | Considerations for E-Learning |
|---|---|---|
| **Visual**<br><br>Low vision<br><br>No vision<br><br>Color blindness | Screen readers that read information about what is happening on-screen to the user<br><br>Refreshable braille displays that create dynamic braille descriptions of what is happening on screen<br><br>Screen magnifiers that enlarge all or part of what is happening on screen | In order for screen readers and braille displays to describe what is happening on screen, they need to be "told." Therefore, you'll need to add descriptive text, known as "alt text," to course elements for these assistive devices to read.<br><br>Be sure that there are no elements that require recognition of color. Color can be used, as long as it is not the only way to tell what something means. For example, you can include a green check and a red X to indicate right or wrong, because the check and the X alone can convey the meaning. But a red and a green dot would not work, since the student would need to distinguish between the colors to determine meaning.<br><br>Use strong value contrast (light vs. dark) so those with low vision or color blindness can recognize on-screen elements. For example, a light blue caption on a light background may be hard to read for those with vision challenges.<br><br>Vision is required in order to use a mouse properly. Visually impaired students generally do not use a mouse, instead relying on keyboard navigation through their screen reader. Therefore, course elements must be keyboard-accessible. |
| **Auditory**<br><br>Hard of hearing<br><br>Deafness | Closed captioning systems | For individuals with auditory impairments, it is necessary to provide a transcript of any important audio elements in the course. For static content, this can be done with a static transcript text box. For multimedia content timed to audio, the closed captioning should also be timed to audio. |
| **Motor**<br><br>Limited dexterity<br><br>No manual skills | Alternate navigation devices such as keyboards, joysticks, trackballs, and even breathing devices | For those with limited mobility, be sure that any interactive element (such as a button) is large enough for someone with rough motor skills to use.<br><br>Make sure all course elements are keyboard-accessible. If a course is keyboard-accessible, then it will work with most other mobility-assistive devices. |

Another factor to consider is cognitive impairments such as learning disabilities or dyslexia. Courses are more accessible to those with cognitive impairments when there are no time constraints. For example, you can include play/pause/rewind controls and avoid timed elements, such as a timed test.

## Accessibility Requirements and Guidelines

There are two main reasons to make your courses accessible:

1. You want your courses to be available for those in your target audience who may have a disability.
2. You may be required by law.

Internationally, the World Wide Web Consortium (W3C) provides web content accessibility guidelines. In addition, many countries have their own standards and requirements. In the United States, Section 508 of the Rehabilitation Act of 1973 (and later amended) requires that information technology (including e-learning) used by the federal government be accessible to those with disabilities. Many other organizations choose to adopt that standard on their own. Go to www.section508.gov for more detailed information on the standards and the requirements.

# Steps for Creating a Section 508-Compliant Project in Captivate

The following pages contain the accessibility standards for web pages from the Section 508 requirements for web-based intranet and internet information and applications, along with the corresponding procedures in Captivate.

*This guide is not intended to be a stand-alone guide, but rather to be used in conjunction with other educational resources (such as www.section508.gov) and thorough accessibility testing.*

### Section 508 - 1194.22

**(a) A text equivalent for every non-text element shall be provided (e.g., via "alt", "longdesc", or in element content).**

- In order for alt text to be published with a movie, you must first enable accessibility in the project's preferences.

- Add alt text to each slide that conveys content.

- Add alt text to each object that conveys content. For example, if you have an image of a diagram, you'll need to add a text description of that diagram for screen readers to read.

Change Publish Settings, p. 232
Slide Properties, p. 37
Object Information, p. 93

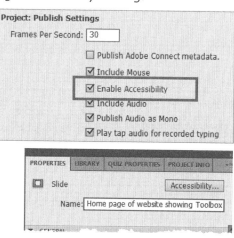

**(b) Equivalent alternatives for any multimedia presentation shall be synchronized with the presentation.**

Add closed captioning timed to audio (if audio is used) or add caption objects timed to audio.

Closed Captioning, p. 84
Timing Slide Objects, p. 111

**(c) Web pages shall be designed so that all information conveyed with color is also available without color, for example from context or markup.**

This is done through your own design of the course. Avoid any element in which color is the only way of communicating information. As a test, print out screens in grayscale to determine if the course elements can still be understood.

**(d) Documents shall be organized so they are readable without requiring an associated style sheet.**

**(e) Redundant text links shall be provided for each active region of a server-side image map.**

**(f) Client-side image maps shall be provided instead of server-side image maps except where the regions cannot be defined with an available geometric shape.**

Captivate does not use style sheets or image maps, so these standards are not applicable.

**(g) Row and column headers shall be identified for data tables.**

**(h) Markup shall be used to associate data cells and header cells for data tables that have two or more logical levels of row or column headers.**

Tables can be created in Captivate with a widget. These tables are not Section-508 compliant. Also realize that if you insert a table as a graphic, you'll need to provide detailed alt text for the content in the table.

**(i) Frames shall be titled with text that facilitates frame identification and navigation.**

Captivate does not use frames, so this part of the standard is not applicable for a Captivate project.

# Steps for 508-Compliance (cont'd)

**(j) Pages shall be designed to avoid causing the screen to flicker with a frequency greater than 2 Hz and lower than 55 Hz.**

Anything that flashes or flickers needs to be either slower than 2 times per second or faster than 55 times per second. Anything in between that range could cause seizures in some people. If you incorporate text animations, check to see how quickly any elements flash. Plus, if you import animations, animated gifs, videos, or use show/hide actions to make something flash, make sure you work outside of the prohibited range.

**(k) A text-only page, with equivalent information or functionality, shall be provided to make a web site comply with the provisions of this part, when compliance cannot be accomplished in any other way. The content of the text-only page shall be updated whenever the primary page changes.**

You can provide text equivalents through closed captioning, caption text, or links to a document. You can link to a document using the **Open URL/File action**. Just be sure that the document in question is also accessible.

 Action Types, p. 122

**(l) When pages utilize scripting languages to display content, or to create interface elements, the information provided by the script shall be identified with functional text that can be read by assistive technology.**

This standard means that in addition to the alt text you set up as part of (a), system controls need to be understandable by screen readers and accessible using keyboard navigation. When you enable accessibility for the project (a), it converts the buttons and other interface/navigation features to be accessible. However, there are a few features that are not accessible that cannot be used in a 508-compliant course. In a quiz, you can only use multiple choice, true/false, and rating scale question types. The other types of questions are not accessible.

**(m) When a web page requires that an applet, plug-in or other application be present on the client system to interpret page content, the page must provide a link to a plug-in or applet that complies with §1194.21(a) through (l).**

Be sure to include links to the Adobe Flash Player BEFORE the student launches the course. (If they don't have the Flash player, they cannot access a Captivate page with the link!) Also, be sure to provide links to Acrobat Reader and any other plug-ins required to view content.

**(n) When electronic forms are designed to be completed on-line, the form shall allow people using assistive technology to access the information, field elements, and functionality required for completion and submission of the form, including all directions and cues.**

When creating forms to capture information from a student, be sure to use only accessible options. Use buttons; multiple-choice, true/false, and rating scale questions; and text entry boxes. Do not use other question types.

**(o) A method shall be provided that permits users to skip repetitive navigation links.**

When students visit multiple web pages, they have to listen to (with a screen reader) and/or tab through (with keyboard navigation) all the main navigational elements each time they visit a new page. This standard requires that a link be provided that lets the user skip these items that appear on every page. In **Preferences**, you can enable **Restrict keyboard tabbing to slide items only**, which skips the TOC and playbar.

 Publish Settings, p. 232

**(p) When a timed response is required, the user shall be alerted and given sufficient time to indicate more time is required.**

If you use a timed test or add/build any content with a time limit, be sure to build in an extension system.

# Accessibility Design Considerations

Accessibility guidelines are subject to interpretation, and there is much debate about what makes a course usable and compliant.  Therefore, it is extremely important that you carefully evaluate the standards and guidance provided by the government, accessibility groups, and your own organization (legal, HR, I.T., etc.).  Here are some additional tips to help make your courses more accessible and more usable to those with disabilities.

- There is no substitute for thorough testing.  Test with accessibility devices to ensure everything works properly.

- Make sure you check the **HTML5** option when you publish.  If you only publish to .swf, the accessibility features will not work properly.

- Add project information.  The data found in the **Project Information** panel is read by screen readers, so be sure to enter your data there.

 Project Information, p. 230

- Give screen-reader students full control over the audio.  If the audio plays automatically while the screen reader is reading slide information, the student may not be able to understand what is happening.

- Screen readers tend to register each slide better if there are interactive elements that let the student move from slide to slide (such as a **Next** button), rather than having the slides play continuously.  If you do have the slides advance automatically, make sure each slide is up long enough for students to tab through all the content.

- Consider the order of a slide's objects.  Screen readers read objects from left to right and from top to bottom.  Use a logical order so screen-reader students can follow the content easily.  For example, you would want instructions to be read before the elements of an interaction.  You can click the **Tab Order** button in the slide's **Properties** panel to manually override the tab order of any interactive elements on a slide.

 Tab Order, p. 37

- When adding buttons or other interactive objects, don't just call them buttons in the alt text.  Provide a description of what the buttons do.

- Do not enable looping on animated objects, such as text animations.  This can cause a screen reader to reload the page over and over again.

 Animation Properties, p. 65

- Captivate lets you use a larger-than-normal mouse cursor in your projects.  This can be helpful for those with low vision.

 Double Mouse Size, p. 142

- Remember that, by default, the closed caption button is NOT included on the playbar.  If you are using captions, be sure to enable the **CC** button, or create your own logic using advanced actions.

 Configure Project Skin, p. 226

- Be careful about assigning keyboard shortcuts to interactive objects, such as buttons.  Those shortcuts might conflict with the shortcuts that a screen reader uses.

- Make sure any elements you add to your course—such as animations, widgets, or JavaScript commands—are accessible as well.

- If you are teaching computer procedures, consider very carefully what the best design will be for students using assistive devices.  For example, is the software you are teaching accessible?  And, would someone using assistive technology be using the software the same way as someone who is not?  Consider creating separate courses based on how the student will be accessing the software being taught.

# Mac and PC Interface Tools

## Tips for Using Captivate for Macintosh

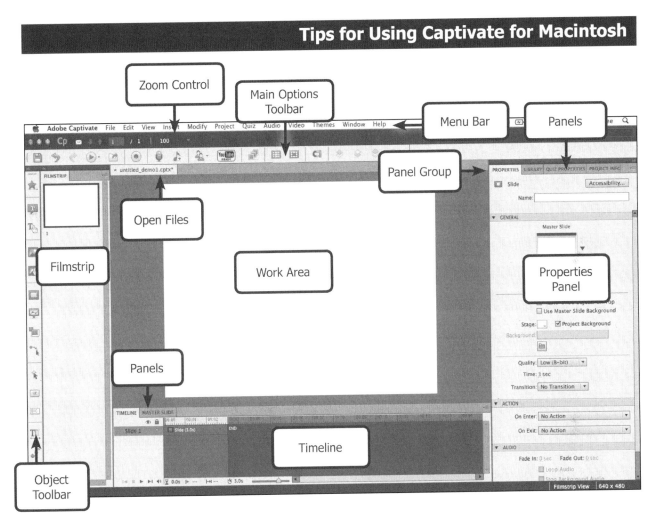

## Interface & Navigation

The Mac interface is very similar to the PC interface. Key differences include:

- The toolbars are arranged slightly differently, with fewer buttons on the **Main Options** toolbar.
- In most dialog boxes for the PC, **OK** (or similar) is on the left and **Cancel** is on the right. They are usually reversed on the Mac.
- Right-click commands on the PC are control-click commands on a Mac.
- The **Preferences** dialog box is on the **Adobe Captivate** menu instead of the **Edit** menu.

Many of the keyboard shortcuts are the same between Mac and PC. The one major exception is that you would use the **Command** key instead of the **Control** key. See page 254 for commonly-used shortcuts.

*Please note: This is not intended to be a comprehensive list of differences between Captivate for Mac and Captivate for PC. While most of the capabilities between the two will be the same, you may encounter some differences.*

# Captivate for Mac Menus

**Adobe Captivate** | File | Edit

About Adobe Captivate...

Preferences...                     ⌘,

Hide Adobe Captivate      ⌘H
Hide Others                      ⌥⌘H
Show All

Quit Adobe Captivate      ⌘Q

---

**File** | Edit | View | Insert | Modify | Pro

New Project                                          ▶
Record new Software Simulation...   ⌘R
Record new Video Demo...
Browse in Bridge
Open...                                               ⌘O
Open Recent
Close                                                  ⌘W
Close All                                            ⌥⇧W

Save                                                   ⌘S
Save As...                                          ⇧⌘S
Save All

Import                                                 ▶
Collaborate                                          ▶

Export                                                 ▶

Publish...                                         ⌥⇧F12
Publish To YouTube...
Publish Settings...
Preview                                               ▶

Project Info...

---

**Edit** | View | Insert | Modify | Project | Qu

Undo                                                  ⌘Z
Redo                                                  ⌘Y

Cut                                                    ⌘X
Copy                                                  ⌘C
Copy Background                              ⇧⌘Y
Paste                                                 ⌘V
Paste as Background                          ⌥⇧V

Duplicate                                          ⌘D
Delete                                               ⌫
Select All                                          ⌘A

Group                                                ⌘G
Find and Replace                              ⌘F
Ungroup                                           ⇧⌘G
Remove From Group
Edit with Microsoft®PowerPoint        ▶

Find Background in the Library           ⌥⌘F

Edit PSD Source File

Convert to freeform
Convert to rollover Smart Shape
Edit Points                                        ⌥⌘E
Edit Gradient
Edit Text                                            F2

Object Style Manager...                      ⇧F7

---

**View** | Insert | Modify | Project

Zoom In                                            ⌘=
Zoom Out                                          ⌘−
Magnification                                      ▶

Hide Comments
Hide Slide                                         ⇧⌘H
Lock Slide                                         ⌘K

Lock                                                 ⌥⌘K
Hide

Show Grid
Snap to Grid
Snap to Object
✓ Show Drawing/Smart Guides

---

**Insert** | Modify | Project | Quiz | Audio

New Slide                                          ⇧⌘V
New Slide from                                    ▶
Blank Slide                                        ⇧⌘J
Question Slide...                                 ⇧Q
PowerPoint Slide...                            ⇧⌘P
Recording Slide...                             ⌥⌘O
Image Slide...                                   ⌥⇧⌘S
CPVC Slide...
Animation Slide...                             ⇧⌘N
Quiz Master Slide                               ▶

Content Master Slide                        ⌥⌘M

Standard Objects                                ▶

Placeholder Objects                            ▶
Placeholder Slides                              ▶

Image...                                            ⇧⌘M
Animation...                                      ⇧⌘A
Text Animation                                   ⇧⌘X
Widget...                                           ⇧⌘W
Equation

Characters

Slide Transition                                   ▶
Interactions

Launch Drag and Drop Interaction Wizard

---

**Modify** | Project | Quiz | Audio | Vide

Rescale project...
Replace Smart Shape

Redraw Smart Shape                         ⌥⌘W

Arrange                                              ▶
Align                                                 ▶

Move Question to                               ▶

Merge with the background              ⌘M
Merge FMR Slides

Sync with Playhead                           ⌘L
Show for the rest of the slide            ⌘E

Increase Indent                                  ⌘I
Decrease Indent                                ⇧⌘I

Auto–adjust Rollover Area                 ⌥⌘R

Update from Source

Mouse                                               ▶

Group                                                ▶

# Captivate for Mac Menus

**Project**   Quiz   Audio   Video

| | |
|---|---|
| Advanced Actions... | ⇧⌘F9 |
| Variables... | |
| Table of Contents... | ⇧⌘F10 |
| Skin Editor... | ⇧⌘F11 |
| Advanced Interaction | ⌘F9 |
| HTML5 Tracker | |
| Check Spelling... | F7 |

**Quiz**   Audio   Video   Themes   Window

| | |
|---|---|
| Question Slide... | ⇧Q |
| Random Question Slide | ⌥⇧R |
| Pretest Question Slide | |
| Quiz Master Slide | ▶ |
| Question Placeholder Objects | ▶ |
| Result Placeholder Objects | ▶ |
| Import Question Pools... | |
| Question Pool Manager... | ⌥⇧Q |
| Quiz Preferences... | |
| Import GIFT Format File | ⌥⇧G |

**Audio**   Video   Themes   Window

| | |
|---|---|
| Import to | ▶ |
| Record to | ▶ |
| Edit | ▶ |
| Remove | ▶ |
| Audio Management... | ⌥⇧A |
| Speech Management... | ⌥⇧S |
| Settings... | |

**Video**   Themes   Window

| | |
|---|---|
| Insert Video... | ⌥⌘V |
| Edit Video Timing... | |
| Video Management... | |

**Window**   Help   ⊕   ✳   ⌘

| | |
|---|---|
| ✓ Object Toolbar | |
| ✓ Main Options | |
| Align | |
| ✓ Filmstrip | ⌥⌘B |
| ✓ Timeline | ⌥⌘T |
| ✓ Properties | ⇧⌘D |
| Library | ⌥⌘L |
| Master Slide | |
| Widget | ⌥⌘Z |
| Question Pool | |
| Quiz Properties | |
| Slide Notes | ⌥⌘N |
| Branching View | ⌥⇧⌘B |
| Skin Editor | ⇧⌘F11 |
| Advanced Interaction | ⌘F9 |
| HTML5 Tracker | |
| Comments | ⌥⌘X |
| Project Info | |
| Find and Replace | ⌘F |
| Progress Indicator | |
| Drag and Drop | |
| Effects | ⌥⇧⌘E |
| Workspace | ▶ |

**Help**   ⊕   ✳   ⌘   ⏚   ◀)   ▣(3:19)   Sat Jun 15   21

Search

| | |
|---|---|
| Adobe Captivate Help | F1 |
| Adobe Product Improvement Program... | |
| Adobe Captivate Blog | |
| Complete/Update Adobe ID Profile... | |
| Sign Out | |
| Updates... | |
| Access Adobe Resources... | |

**Themes**   Window   Help

| | |
|---|---|
| Show/Hide Themes Panel | |
| Master Slide | |
| Apply a New Theme... | |
| Save Theme | |
| Save Theme As... | |
| Recording Defaults | |
| Object Style Manager... | ⇧F7 |
| Table of Contents... | ⇧⌘F10 |
| Skin Editor... | ⇧⌘F11 |
| Help | |

# Captivate for PC Menus

**File**

| | |
|---|---|
| New Project | ▶ |
| Record new Software Simulation... | Ctrl+R |
| Record new Video Demo... | |
| Browse in Bridge | |
| Open... | Ctrl+O |
| Open Recent | ▶ |
| Close | Ctrl+W |
| Close All | Shift+Alt+W |
| Save | Ctrl+S |
| Save As... | Shift+Ctrl+S |
| Save All | |
| Import | ▶ |
| Collaborate | ▶ |
| Export | ▶ |
| Publish... | Shift+F12 |
| Publish To YouTube... | |
| Publish Settings... | |
| Preview | ▶ |
| Project Info... | |
| Exit | |

**Edit**

| | |
|---|---|
| Undo | Ctrl+Z |
| Redo | Ctrl+Y |
| Cut | Ctrl+X |
| Copy | Ctrl+C |
| Copy Background | Shift+Ctrl+Y |
| Paste | Ctrl+V |
| Paste as Background | Shift+Alt+V |
| Duplicate | Ctrl+D |
| Delete | Del |
| Select All | Ctrl+A |
| Group | Ctrl+G |
| Find and Replace | Ctrl+F |
| Ungroup | Shift+Ctrl+G |
| Remove From Group | |
| Edit with Microsoft® PowerPoint | ▶ |
| Find in the Library | Ctrl+Alt+F |
| Edit PSD Source File | |
| Convert to freeform | |
| Convert to rollover Smart Shape | |
| Edit Points | Ctrl+Alt+E |
| Edit Gradient | |
| Add Text | F2 |
| Object Style Manager... | Shift+F7 |
| Preferences... | Shift+F8 |

**View**

| | |
|---|---|
| Zoom In | Ctrl+= |
| Zoom Out | Ctrl+- |
| Magnification | ▶ |
| Hide Comments | |
| Hide Slide | Shift+Ctrl+H |
| Lock Slide | Ctrl+K |
| Lock | Ctrl+Alt+K |
| Hide | Ctrl+Alt+H |
| Show Grid | |
| Snap to Grid | |
| Snap to Object | |
| ✓ Show Drawing/Smart Guides | |

**Insert**

| | |
|---|---|
| New Slide | Shift+Ctrl+V |
| New Slide from | ▶ |
| Blank Slide | Shift+Ctrl+J |
| Question Slide... | Shift+Ctrl+Q |
| PowerPoint Slide... | Shift+Ctrl+P |
| Recording Slide... | Ctrl+Alt+O |
| Image Slide... | Shift+Ctrl+Alt+S |
| CPVC Slide... | |
| Animation Slide... | Shift+Ctrl+N |
| Quiz Master Slide | ▶ |
| Content Master Slide | Ctrl+Alt+M |
| Standard Objects | ▶ |
| Placeholder Objects | ▶ |
| Placeholder Slides | ▶ |
| Image... | Shift+Ctrl+M |
| Animation... | Shift+Ctrl+A |
| Text Animation | Shift+Ctrl+X |
| Widget... | Shift+Ctrl+W |
| Equation | |
| Characters | |
| Slide Transition | ▶ |
| Interactions | |
| Launch Drag and Drop Interaction Wizard | |

**Standard Objects**

| | |
|---|---|
| Text Caption | Shift+Ctrl+C |
| Smart Shape | |
| Rollover Caption | Shift+Ctrl+R |
| Rollover Image... | Shift+Ctrl+O |
| Highlight Box | Shift+Ctrl+L |
| Click Box | Shift+Ctrl+K |
| Button | Shift+Ctrl+B |
| Text Entry Box | Shift+Ctrl+T |
| Rollover Slidelet | Shift+Ctrl+Z |
| Zoom Area | Shift+Ctrl+E |
| Mouse | Shift+Ctrl+U |

# Captivate for PC Menus (cont'd)

## Modify

Rescale project...
Replace Smart Shape
Redraw Smart Shape                     Ctrl+Alt+W

Arrange                                      ▸
Align                                        ▸
Move Question to                             ▸

Merge with the background              Ctrl+M
Merge FMR Slides

Sync with Playhead                     Ctrl+L
Show for the rest of the slide         Ctrl+E

Increase Indent                        Ctrl+I
Decrease Indent                        Shift+Ctrl+I

Auto-adjust Rollover Area              Ctrl+Alt+R

Update from Source

Mouse                                        ▸

Group                                        ▸

## Project

Advanced Actions...                    Shift+F9
Variables...

Table of Contents...                   Shift+F10
Skin Editor...                         Shift+F11

Advanced Interaction                   F9

HTML5 Tracker

Check Spelling...                      F7

## Audio

Import to                                    ▸
Record to                                    ▸

Edit                                         ▸
Remove                                       ▸

Audio Management...                    Shift+Alt+A
Speech Management...                   Shift+Alt+S

Settings...

## Quiz

Question Slide...                      Shift+Ctrl+Q
Random Question Slide                  Ctrl+Q
Pretest Question Slide

Quiz Master Slide                            ▸
Question Placeholder Objects                 ▸
Result Placeholder Objects                   ▸

Import Question Pools...
Question Pool Manager...               Ctrl+Alt+Q

Quiz Preferences...

Import GIFT Format File                Shift+Alt+G

## Video

Insert Video...                        Ctrl+Alt+V
Edit Video Timing...

Video Management...

## Themes

Show/Hide Themes Panel
Master Slide

Apply a New Theme...
Save Theme
Save Theme As...

Recording Defaults
Object Style Manager...                Shift+F7
Table of Contents...                   Shift+F10
Skin Editor...                         Shift+F11

Help

## Window

✓ Object Toolbar
✓ Main Options
✓ Align

Filmstrip                              Ctrl+Alt+B
✓ Timeline                             Ctrl+Alt+T
Properties                             Shift+Ctrl+D
Library                                Ctrl+Alt+L

Master Slide
Widget                                 Ctrl+Alt+Z

Question Pool
Quiz Properties

Slide Notes                            Ctrl+Alt+N
Branching View                         Shift+Ctrl+Alt+B
Skin Editor                            Shift+F11
Advanced Interaction                   F9
HTML5 Tracker
Comments                               Ctrl+Alt+X
Project Info

Find and Replace                       Ctrl+F

Progress Indicator

Effects                                Shift+Ctrl+Alt+E

Workspace                                    ▸

## Help

Adobe Captivate Help                   F1

About Adobe Captivate...
Adobe Product Improvement Program...
Adobe Captivate Blog

Complete/Update AdobeID Profile...

Sign In
Updates...
Access Adobe Resources...

# Useful Keyboard Shortcuts

There are over one hundred keyboard shortcuts in Captivate, all of which can be found in the Adobe Captivate Help documentation.  Here is a list of the shortcuts that the authors find most useful to memorize.

## Insert

| | PC | Mac |
|---|---|---|
| New Slide | Shift + Ctrl + V | Shift + Cmd + V |
| Blank Slide | Shift + Ctrl + J | Shift + Cmd + J |
| Question Slide | Shift + Ctrl + Q | Shift + Q |
| Text Caption | Shift + Ctrl + C | Shift + Cmd + C |
| Mouse | Shift + Ctrl + U | Shift + Cmd + U |

## Editing

| | PC | Mac |
|---|---|---|
| Undo | Ctrl + Z | Cmd + Z |
| Redo | Ctrl + Y | Cmd + Y |
| Cut | Ctrl + X | Cmd + X |
| Copy | Ctrl + C | Cmd + C |
| Paste | Ctrl + V | Cmd + V |
| Duplicate | Ctrl + D | Cmd + D |

## File Management

| | PC | Mac |
|---|---|---|
| Save | Ctrl + S | Cmd + S |
| Publish | Shift + F12 | Option + Shift + F12 |

## Formatting

| | PC | Mac |
|---|---|---|
| Bold | Ctrl + B | Cmd + B |
| Underline | Ctrl + U | Cmd + U |
| Italics | Ctrl + I | Cmd + I |

## Timing

| | PC | Mac |
|---|---|---|
| Sync Object to Playhead | Ctrl + L | Cmd + L |
| Show for Rest of Slide | Ctrl + E | Cmd + E |
| Start Next Slide (in Edit Slides Audio) | Ctrl + S | |

## Play/Preview

| | PC | Mac |
|---|---|---|
| Play Slide | F3 | F3 |
| Preview Project | F4 | F4 |
| Preview From This Slide | F8 | Cmd + F8 |
| Preview Next 5 Slides | F10 | |
| Preview In Web Browser | F12 | Cmd + F12 |
| Preview in HTML5 | F11 | Cmd + F11 |
| Toggle Play/Pause | Space | Space |

## View

| | PC | Mac |
|---|---|---|
| Zoom In | Ctrl + = | Cmd + = |
| Zoom Out | Ctrl + - | Cmd + - |

*Default recording shortcuts for PC*

General:
To Stop Recording: End
To Pause/Resume Recording: Pause

Manual Recording:
To Capture a Screenshot: Print Screen

Full Motion Recording:
To Start Full Motion Recording: F9
To Stop Full Motion Recording: F10

Panning:
For Automatic Panning: F4
For Manual Panning: F3
To Stop Panning: F7
To snap recording window to mouse: F11

To toggle mouse capture in Video Demo: F12

To insert an UNDO Marker: Ctrl+Shift+Z

*Default recording shortcuts for Mac*

General:
To Stop Recording: Cmd-Enter
To Pause/Resume Recording: Cmd-F2

Manual Recording:
To Capture a Screenshot: Cmd-F6

Full Motion Recording:
To Start Full Motion Recording: Cmd-F9
To Stop Full Motion Recording: Cmd-F10

Panning:
For Automatic Panning: Cmd-F4
For Manual Panning: Cmd-F3
To Stop Panning: Cmd-F7
To snap recording window to mouse: Cmd-F11

To toggle mouse capture in Video Demo: Cmd-F12

To insert an UNDO Marker: Shift-Cmd-Z

# System Variables

In **Advanced Actions**, you can assign the value of these variables for custom navigation and interface elements.

| Variable | Definition | Default | Comments |
|---|---|---|---|
| cpCmndCC | Enable/disable closed captioning. Set value to 1 to display closed captions. | 0 | Rather than just adding a closed captioning button to the Playback Control bar, you can add your own buttons or logic by setting this variable to 1 vs. 0. |
| cpCmndExit | Use this variable (set to 1) to exit the movie. | 0 | Rather than just adding an exit button to the Playback Control bar, you can add your own button or logic by setting this variable to 1. |
| cpCmndGotoFrame | Specify a frame number for the movie to jump to and then pause. | -1 | These let you create navigation to a specific point in a slide. One option pauses the movie when the student arrives; the other plays the movie. Temporarily display the **cpInfoCurrentFrame** variable at the point where you want to jump so that you can determine the frame number. |
| cpCmndGotoFrame-AndResume | Specify a frame number for the movie to jump to and then play. | -1 | |
| cpCmndGotoSlide | Assign the slide number that the movie should move to before pausing. | -1 | This works the same as a **Jump to Slide** action. You can use it as part of an advanced action or when integrating with Flash or JavaScript. |
| cpCmndMute | Mute the audio. Set to 1 to mute and 0 to unmute. | 0 | Rather than just adding an audio on/off button to the playbar, you can add your own buttons or logic by setting this variable to 1 vs. 0. |
| cpCmndNextSlide | Set the value to 1 to jump to the next slide. | | This works the same as a **Go to the Next Slide** action. Use it with Flash or JavaScript. |
| cpCmndPause | Set the value to 1 to pause the movie. | | Rather than just adding a pause button to the Playback Control bar, you can add your own buttons or logic by setting this variable to 1. |
| cpCmndPlaybarMoved | Set to 1 if the playbar has moved. | 0 | Use this to find out if students use the playbar to move around (other than **Play/Pause**) |
| cpCmndPrevious | Set the value to 1 to jump to the previous slide. | | This works the same as a **Go to the Previous Slide** action. |
| cpCmndResume | Set the value to 1 to resume play of the movie. | 0 | If the movie is paused, create a button or logic to unpause it by setting this variable to 1. |
| cpCmndShowPlaybar | Set to 1 to show the playbar or 0 to hide the playbar. | 1 | Use this variable to create show/hide controls for the playbar, or to hide the playbar on certain slides, such as the final quiz. |
| cpCmndTOCVisible | Set to 1 to show the TOC or 0 to hide the TOC. | 0 | Use this variable to create show/hide controls for the table of contents, or to hide the TOC on certain slides. |
| cpCmndVolume | Control the movie's volume, from 0 to 100. | 50 | You can change volume throughout the movie or create a control that lets the student do it. |
| cpLockTOC | Enable/disable user interaction on TOC. Set to 1 to disable. | 0 | If you want the table of contents to be for information only and not for navigation, you can lock it so that it isn't interactive. Or you can lock it just for certain slides, such as quiz slides. |

# Movie Information Variables

| Variable | Definition | Default | Comments |
|---|---|---|---|
| CaptivateVersion | Current version of Captivate. | v7.0.0 | This might be useful if you are working in Flash or JavaScript and want the behavior to be different based on which version of Captivate you are using. |
| cpInfoCurrentFrame | Returns the current frame number. | 1 | Use this to identify the frame you want when using the **cpCmndGotoFrame-AndResume** and **cpCmndGotoFrame** variables. |
| cpInfoCurrentSlide | Current slide number. Index begins with 1. | N/A | Use this to display a page counter to the student. |
| cpInfoCurrentSlideLabel | Name of the Current Slide. | N/A | Use this to create a caption that displays the slide label as a heading for the slide. |
| cpInfoCurrentSlideType | Type of the slide that plays now. This can be Normal Slide, Question Slide, or Random Question Slide. | Normal | Use this information for if/then logic based on slide type. For example, enable TOC navigation on normal slides but disable it on quiz slides. |
| cpInfoElapsedTimeMS | Time elapsed (in milliseconds) since the movie started playing. | 0 | This information might be useful if you are working in Flash or JavaScript. |
| cpInfoFPS | The frame rate of the movie in frames per second. | 1 | |
| cpInfoFrameCount | Returns the total number of frames in the project. | 1 | |
| cpInfoHasPlaybar | Provides information about the visibility of the playbar. Returns 1 if the playbar is visible, else 0. | 1 | Use this to create a toggle to show or hide the toolbar. Add a show action if this is 0 and a hide action if this is 1. |
| cpInfoIsStandalone | This value would be set to 1 when published as .exe or .app. Otherwise, it is set to 0. | 1 | This information might be useful if you are working in Flash or JavaScript. |
| cpInfoLastVisitedSlide | The slide last visited. | 0 | Use these variables as conditions based on navigation. For example, you might want to show something different on slide 6 if they are coming from the home page versus coming from slide 5. |
| cpInfoPrevSlide | The previous slide. | -1 | |
| cpInfoSlideCount | The total number of slides in the project. | N/A | Use for a page counter showing x of xx pages. |

## Movie Metadata Variables

| Variable | Definition | Default | Comments |
|---|---|---|---|
| cpInfoAuthor | Name of the Author. | N/A | These variables pull information from the **Project Information** tab in **Preferences**. |
| cpInfoCompany | Name of the Company. | N/A | |
| cpInfoCopyright | Copyright Info. | N/A | |
| cpInfoCourseID | ID of the Course. | | These variables are no longer used by Captivate. |
| cpInfoCourseName | Name of the Course. | | |
| cpInfoDescription | Description of the Project. | | These variables pull information from the **Project Information** tab in **Preferences**. |
| cpInfoEmail | E-mail Address. | | |
| cpInfoProjectName | Name of the Adobe Captivate Project. | | |
| cpInfoWebsite | URL of the company website, starting with www. | | |

## System Information Variables

Use the date information to display on a certificate or to create your own expiration feature. Comments below reflect what would show on: Saturday, Aug. 11, 2012 at 8:02 p.m.

| Variable | Definition | Default | Comments |
|---|---|---|---|
| cpInfoCurrentDate | Day of the month. | Format: dd | 11 (11th day of the month) |
| cpInfoCurrentDateString | Current date in the format mm/dd/yyyy. | Format: mm/dd/yyyy | 8/11/2012 |
| cpInfoCurrentDay | Current day of the week. | Format: 1 | 7 (7th day of the week) |
| cpInfoCurrentHour | Current Hour: Hour set on user's computer. | Format: hh | 20 (military time for 8:00 p.m.) |
| cpInfoCurrentMinutes | Current Minutes: Minutes set on user's computer. | Format: mm | 2 (2 minutes after the hour) |
| cpInfoCurrentMonth | Current Month: Month set on user's computer. | Format: mm | 08 (8th month of the year) |
| cpInfoCurrentTime | Current Time in the format hh:mm:ss. | Format: hh:mm:ss | 20:02:36 |
| cpInfoCurrentYear | Current Year: Year set on user's computer. | Format: yyyy | 2012 |
| cpInfoEpochMS | Time elapsed, in milliseconds, since January 01, 1970. | 0 | 1344729953402 |

# Quizzing Variables

| Variable | Definition | Default | Comments |
|---|---|---|---|
| cpInQuizScope | If the student is currently in a quiz. | 0 | The quizzing variables cannot be set with an **Assign** action, but can be used for conditional logic or displayed to the student. |
| cpInfoPercentage | Scoring in percentage. | 0 | For example, you can: |
| cpQuizInfoAnswerChoice | Student's answer to the current question. | | • Create custom certificates displaying information about the total quiz. |
| cpQuizInfoAttempts | Number of times the quiz has been attempted. | 0 | • Display question-by-question information, such as the number of points at stake or the number of points earned. |
| cpQuizInfoLastSlidePointScored | Score for last quiz slide. | 0 | |
| cpQuizInfoMaxAttempts OnCurrentQuestion | Maximum attempts allowed on a question. | 0 | |
| cpQuizInfoNegativePoints onCurrentQuestionSlide | Negative points for the current slide. | 0 | • Set up conditional logic based on the points earned or the type of question. |
| cpQuizInfoPassFail | Quiz result. | 0 | • Set up conditional logic based on the quiz score as a whole. |
| cpQuizInfoPointsPerQuestionSlide | Points for the question slide. | 0 | |
| cpQuizInfoPointsscored | Points scored in the project. | 0 | |
| cpQuizInfoPretestPointsscored | Points scored in the Pretest. | 0 | |
| cpQuizInfoPretestScorePercentage | Percentage scored in the Pretest. | 0 | |
| cpQuizInfoQuestionPartialScoreOn | If partial scoring is turned on for a question.  1 equals yes; 0 equals no. | 0 | |
| cpQuizInfoQuestionSlideTiming | Time limit in seconds for the current question. | 0 | |
| cpQuizInfoQuestionSlideType | Question slide type, such as multiple-choice or true/false. | choice | |
| cpQuizInfoQuizPassPercent | Percentage needed to pass the quiz. | 80 | |
| cpQuizInfoQuizPassPoints | Points needed to pass the quiz. | 0 | |
| cpQuizInfoTotalCorrectAnswers | Number of correct answers. | 0 | |
| cpQuizInfoTotalProjectPoints | Total project points possible, including those that are excluded from reporting. | 0 | |
| cpQuizInfoTotalQuestions PerProject | Number of questions in the entire project. | 0 | |
| cpQuizInfoTotalQuizPoints | Total quiz points possible, including those that are excluded from reporting. | 0 | |
| cpQuizInfoTotalUnanswered Questions | Number of unanswered questions. | 0 | |

# Index I

# Index

## Symbols

.3gp files, 86, 151
16- and 32-bit color, 24
508 requirements and guidelines, 245–248. *See also* accessibility
* (effects indicator), 108
+ (plus sign), 106

## A

absolute drag-and-drop positioning, 188
absolute page counts, 198
Accept captions, 187
accepting comments, 219
Access Adobe Resources button, 4
accessibility
    alt text, 93, 199, 245
    audio, 248
    closed captions, 39, 227, 245
    enabling, 232
    looping actions and, 248
    navigation, 248
    objects, 93, 248
    requirements and guidelines, 245–248
    right click menus and, 205
    screen readers, 248
    slide text descriptions, 37
    spellchecking alt text, 208
    text in rectangles, 63
    time limit issues, 173
Accessibility button, 93
accordion widgets, 118
Acrobat.com, 216–219, 234
action-based effects, 109
Action pane
    click boxes, 128
    enter and exit settings, 38
    feedback captions, 173
    incorrect clicks, 147
    text entry boxes, 133
    variables, 157
actions. *See also* interactions
    adding to slides, 127
    advanced actions, 123, 153, 159–164
    basing on existing actions, 159, 164
    buttons, 130–131
    click boxes, 128
    conditional. *See* conditional actions
    creating, 164
    drag-and-drop interactions, 187
    executing, 165

hyperlinks, 127
object options, 113
opening projects and files, 123
project end, 233
quiz grading actions, 200
returning to quizzes, 175
reused effects, 110
saving and reusing, 124, 159, 164
setting up in properties, 122
shared actions, 164
text entry boxes, 132–133
types of, 113, 122–125
ActionScript, 203
adding. *See also* inserting
    advanced actions, 159
    conditions, 162
    new variables, 156
addition, 157, 160
administrator privileges, 8
Adobe Acrobat Reader, 247
Adobe AIR, 218, 219
Adobe Audition, 79
Adobe Captivate 7 App Packager, 242
Adobe Captivate Exchange, 213
Adobe Captivate Reviewer, 218–219, 220
Adobe Connect, 232, 234, 239
Adobe Dreamweaver, 204
Adobe eLearning Suite, 1, 60, 65
Adobe Flash
    adding animations, 64, 65
    effects from, 109
    exporting to, 1, 237
    including files in SCOs, 204
    .mp4 alternatives, 239
    widgets, 213
Adobe Flash Player, 237, 247
Adobe IDs, 219
Adobe Media Encoder, 88
Adobe Phone Gap, 242
Adobe Photoshop, 57, 60, 64
Adobe Presenter, 204
advanced actions, 110, 123, 153, 159–164, 255
Advanced Interactions panel, 166
.aggr files, 205
aggregator projects, 203–205
AICC publishing, 234, 235. *See also* learning management systems (LMS)
alert sounds, recording, 22
Align to Previous/Next Slide command, 140
alignment, 52, 102
Allow Mouse Click option, 128
alpha settings, 58, 65, 94, 97, 130

Alt text, 37, 93, 245, 246, 248. *See also* accessibility
anchors, drag-and-drop sources, 188
AND Logic, 162
Android, 242
animated GIFs, 247
Animation Properties pane, 65
Animation Trigger menu, 109
animations. *See also* effects; objects
  accessibility, 248
  adding, 4, 64–66
  exporting, 34
  flicker frequencies, 247
  hierarchical, 17
  library media, 210
  PowerPoint, 16
  published movies, 232
answers. *See also* feedback; questions
  answer options, 172
  drag-and-drop interactions, 189
  partial credit, 177
  points, 176
  progressive feedback, 174
  rating scale answers, 184
  shuffling, 178, 198
Appear After field, 111
Apple. *See* iOS, Mac
application regions, 21
application windows, 21
Apply action, 125
Apply Effect action, 109, 160
App Packager, 242
Arabic language text composition, 220
arrows, 94
aspect ratio (proportions), 16, 18, 59, 98
Assessment mode, 22, 25–26
assets. *See* Library
Assign action, 124, 157
asterisk indicators (*), 108
attempts
  captions for next, 173
  click boxes, 128
  designing questions, 28
  feedback, 147
  jumping to content from quizzes, 175
  limiting, 26, 128, 200
  progressive feedback, 174
  quiz results, 196
Audacity, 78
audio, 69–85. *See also* closed captions
  accessibility, 248
  action triggers, 124
  bitrates, 75
  breakpoints for slides, 79
  button alt text, 248
  calibrating, 76
  closed captions, 84

  compression, 75–76
  copying and pasting, 79
  deleting, 79, 82
  distributing over slides, 73–74
  drag-and-drop interactions, 188
  editing, 79–80, 82
  exporting, 81
  file size, 75–76
  importing, 71–73, 80
  input devices, 76
  keyboard tap sounds, 232
  Library, 79, 80, 81, 210–211
  microphones, 76
  mono or stereo, 232
  podcasts, 81
  PowerPoint, 16
  processing, 80
  properties, 38
  publishing settings, 231, 232
  quality, 75–76, 78, 231, 232
  recording, 22, 23, 76–79, 80
  settings, 23, 76
  silence, 80
  slide note transcripts, 39. *See also* slide notes
  system audio, 22
  text-to-speech, 39, 83
  tools, 4
  voiceovers, 75
  volume, 80
  waveforms, 73, 74, 79, 80
Audio Management dialog box, 81
Audio pane, 38
Audio Properties pane, 38, 82
Audition. *See* Adobe Audition
Auto-Adjust Rollover Area option, 119
Auto Calibrate button, 76
Auto Label feature, 93
Auto Play setup, 89, 233
Auto Rewind setup, 89
automatic recording, 22
Autorun for CD option, 237
.avi files, 86

**B**

back, sending objects to, 11, 103
Back button (quizzes), 198
background audio, 71, 82. *See also* audio
Background Audio button, 4
backgrounds
  animations on, 64
  color, 221
  editing, 144–145
  HTML pages, 227
  images in, 36, 37
  Library assets, 210
  master slides, 41

backing up projects, 220
backward movement through slides, 198
backwards compatibility, 9
.bak file format, 220
bitmaps (.bmp), 36
bitrates, 75
blank projects, 13, 15
blank slides, 33, 41
blurred shadows, 97
.bmp file format, 36
bookmarking (resume data), 235
borders. *See also* Fill & Stroke pane
    rollovers, 121
    shapes, 94
brackets (system results), 196
Branch Aware option, 175, 198
branching back into content, 175
branching quizzes, 175, 198
branching scenarios, 126, 130
brightness, 58, 94
Bring Forward/Front buttons, 4
bringing objects forward, 11, 103
browsers. *See* Web browsers
bullets, 52
business characters, 61
buttons. *See also* objects; playback controls/Playbar
    actions, 113
    adding, 4, 130–131
    alt text for, 248
    autosizing, 221
    custom questions in, 169
    Gallery, 130
    pausing slides, 111
    styles, 104
    submissions, 133, 148
    widgets, 212

**C**

cache, 220
calculations, 157, 160
calibrating audio, 76
callout types, 54–55
camera shutter sounds, 23
capitalization, 179, 180
captions. *See also* closed captions; objects; rollover
        captions
    adding, 4, 51–57
    autosizing, 221
    default styles, 26
    displaying variables in, 158
    drag-and-drop interactions, 187
    editing, 52–54
    exporting, 55
    Failure captions. *See* Failure captions
    formatting, 52–54

generating automatically, 23, 25
Hint captions. *See* Hint captions
importing, 55
incomplete questions, 173
inserting, 51
job aids, 240
languages, 23, 56
pointing towards objects, 54
styles, 26, 54–55, 104–107
Success captions. *See* Success captions
text effects, 53
Timeout captions, 173
tools, 4
transparent, 145
types of, 54–55
viewing while recording, 77
widgets, 54
Captions & Slide Notes button, 77
case sensitivity, 179, 180
casual characters, 61
CC. *See* closed captions
CDs, 237
center alignment, 52, 102
certificates, 155, 257, 258
certificate widgets, 118
changed slides, republishing, 237
Character pane, 52, 172
characters
    escape, 235
    maximum number of, 132, 148
    movies, 61
    special, 52
    text effects, 53
    upper or lower case, 132
chart widgets, 118
checkbox widgets, 117
Check Spelling feature, 208, 220
Chinese text composition, 220
Chrome, 238
circle matrix widgets, 117
circles. *See* shapes and Smart shapes
click boxes. *See also* objects
    actions, 113
    adding, 4, 128–129
    captions, 128
    custom questions in, 169
    practice slide ideas, 147
    quiz points, 129
    recording, 26
    successes and failures, 128
clip art, 61
cloning styles, 105
closed captions
    accessibility features, 245
    adding, 81, 84–85
    disabled, 84

editing audio and, 79
exporting, 55
multi-slide video method, 86
Section 508 requirements, 246
slide notes and, 39
timing audio and, 74
video, 86
video timing, 87
closing projects, 9
Collaborate button, 4
collaboration, 214–215, 216–219
collapsing
  Branching view, 126
  groups, 47
  panels, 10
  panes, 5
color-coded objects, 11
colors. *See also* fill colors
  backgrounds, 41
  captions, 52
  gradients, 95
  images, 58
  inverting, 59
  selecting and editing, 94–95
color video, 24
comments, 216, 218–219, 220
compacting slides, 35
compression, 75–76, 231
conditional actions. *See also* advanced actions
  adding, 161–163
  decisions, 163
  defined, 153
  multiple conditions, 162
  text boxes, 132
  variables, 155, 156, 258
conditional logic, 258
confirmation messages, 220
Connect. *See* Adobe Connect
constant bitrates, 75
constraining object or image proportions, 18, 59, 98
Contains operator, 162
Content Master Slide properties, 41
content master slides, 40, 41
Continue action, 122, 160
Continue button, 119
contrast, 58
converting video, 88
copying
  advanced actions, 159
  backgrounds, 144
  conditions, 162
  objects, 99
  slides, 45
correct answers. *See also* Success captions
  branching quizzes, 175
  captions, 173

configuring questions, 172
drag-and-drop interactions, 189
fill in the blank, 170
hot spots, 182
multiple, 172, 179
points, 176
reviewing, 199
sequence questions, 183
short answer questions, 180
counts, drag-and-drop limits, 187
.cpaa files, 164
.cp files, 123
.cps style files, 107
.cptx files, 123
.cptl files, 123, 206
.cptm files, 42
.cpvc files, 27, 123, 152
.crev review files, 218
cropping images, 18, 59, 225
Current Slide indicator, 4
Current Window option, 122
cursors. *See also* mouse movements
  hand icons, 129, 182, 189
  hiding, 141
Custom mode recording, 22
customizing interface, 5–7
custom types (drag-and-drop interaction groups), 187
cutting
  advanced actions, 159
  conditions, 162
  objects, 99

## D

dashed lines, 94
dates, 257
decisions (conditional actions), 163
Decrement action, 124, 157, 160
deducting points, 176
defaults
  button content, 200
  button styles, 200
  captions, 26
  feedback messages, 200
  highlight boxes, 26
  object styles, 105
  preview options, 12
  projects, 221
  quiz labels, 200
  quiz review text, 176
  styles, 26
  text entry boxes, 132
  variable values, 155
deleting
  advanced actions, 159, 166
  audio, 79, 82

conditions, 162
confirmation messages, 220
effects, 110
Library assets, 211
movies, 203
question pools, 194
questions, 194
slides, 44
stored materials in Library, 210
styles, 106, 107
variables, 155
video, 90
Demo mode, 20–22
demonstrations, 19–27. *See also* video demos
Disable action, 160
disabling actions, 124
Display For timing option, 111
displaying. *See* showing
distractors, 181
distributing
audio, 73–74, 79
objects, 102
video, 86, 87
division, 160
docking toolbars, 5
dotted lines, 94
double-click options, 129, 147
downloading interactive templates, 118
drag sources, 186, 187, 188, 189
Drag-and-Drop Interaction wizard, 186–190
drag-and-drop questions. *See* sequence questions
dragging actions, 28, 186–190
drawing. *See* shapes and Smart shapes
Dreamweaver, 204
drop shadows, 97
drop targets, 186, 187, 188, 189
dropdown list questions, 179, 183
dropdown list widgets, 117
duplicating. *See* cloning; copying
duration. *See* timing
Dynamics (volume), 80

**E**

editing
audio, 79–80, 82
backgrounds, 144–145
captions, 52
comments, 219
gradients, 95
interactive objects, 116
master slides, 40
points, 62
polygons, 62
PowerPoint slides, 34
question pools, 194

shapes, 62
software simulations, 137–152
styles, 104
typing actions, 138
video demos, 143, 149, 152
video timing, 90
effects
Apply Effect action, 160
asterisk indicators, 108
drag-and-drop interactions, 187
object effects, 108–110
pan and zoom video, 150
sound effects, 23, 71, 129, 232
text, 53
text animations, 66
transitions, 38
triggering with actions, 125
eLearning Suite. *See* Adobe eLearning Suite
Else conditional actions, 161, 163
e-mail, 123, 239
embedding PowerPoint files, 17, 35
.emf file format, 36
Enable action, 124, 160
end points, 149
end settings, 233
Equal To operator, 162
equations, 68, 210. *See also* calculations
escape characters, 235
escape versions, 235
evaluating answers, 132
event video, 86, 88
Execute Advanced Actions option, 123
Execute JavaScript action, 123, 160, 233
expanding
Branching view, 126
groups, 47
panes, 5
expiration dates, 233, 257
exporting
actions for other projects, 164
audio, 81
Branching views, 126
captions, 55
comments, 219
effects, 110
HTML, 204
HTML5, 12
Library assets, 211
placeholder object text, 55
Preferences, 221
Smart Shape text, 55
styles, 107
text, 55
XML, 222
Expression action, 160
expressions, 160, 162

eyeball icon, 11, 44, 101
eyedropper icon, 58, 94

**F**

.f4v files, 86, 88, 151
fading
    audio, 71, 82
    drag-and-drop objects, 188
    in on first slides, 233
    transitions, 98
Failure captions
    buttons, 130, 132
    click boxes, 129
    designing, 28
    disabling, 26
    feedback captions, 173
    practice slides, 147
    styles, 104
    text entry boxes, 148
    validating, 128, 133
feedback
    branching quizzes, 175
    buttons, 130, 132
    click boxes, 129
    default appearance, 26
    designing, 28
    multiple-choice specific, 175
    non-graded surveys, 180
    object styles, 104
    practice slides, 147
    progressive, 174
    question configuration, 172
    reviewing quizzes, 176
    text entry boxes, 26, 128, 133, 148
    types of, 173
    visual indicators, 199
file size
    audio, 75, 232
    Library assets, 211
    linking, 17
    maximum number of slides, 33
    necessary video only, 28
    slide image quality, 38
    SWF compression, 231
    video color, 24
Fill & Stroke pane, 63, 94, 182
fill colors, 63, 94
fill-in-the-blank questions, 132, 170, 179
fill textures, 96
Filmstrip, 3, 6, 8, 44, 45, 47
finding text or objects, 209
Fit to Stage option, 18, 59
.fla files. See Adobe Flash
Flash. See Adobe Flash
Flash Media Server, 86

Flash Video Streaming Service, 86
flashing frequency, 247
flicker frequency, 247
flipping images, 59
.flv files, 86, 88, 151
FMR. See recording; video demos
FMR Edit Options pane, 143
fonts, 52, 66, 85, 104
Force Re-Publish option, 237
Format pane, 52
formatting. See Properties panel; styles
frames per second (FPS), 64, 232
front, bringing objects to, 11, 103
FTP publishing, 239
full-motion recording. See recording; video demos
full screen browser windows, 204, 237
full screen recording, 20

**G**

Gallery, 64, 71, 130, 212
game widgets, 117, 118
General pane, 37, 54, 130
generating audio, 83
.gif files, 36, 60
.gift files, 194
glossary widgets, 118
Google Chrome, 238
Go To actions, 122, 160
graded quizzes, 167, 169, 170–171, 180
grades, 148, 175, 198, 200
gradients, 63, 95
graphics. See images; objects
gray scale images, 59
Greater Than operator, 162
grid, 4, 102, 220
grouped drag-and-drop interactions, 186, 187
grouping objects, 100
grouping slides, 47, 126
guides, 102

**H**

hand cursor, 129, 182, 189
handouts, 240
hexadecimal values, 94
hidden slides, 44
Hide action, 124, 160, 247
hiding
    grid, 102
    mouse cursors, 141
    objects, 93, 101
    Playbar in quizzes, 199
    slides, 44
    Smart Guides, 102
hierarchical animation, 17

high fidelity (PowerPoint imports), 17
highlight boxes. *See also* objects
  adding, 4, 25, 63
  fills and strokes, 94
  step-by-step job aids, 240
  styles, 26, 104
highlighted text, 52
Hint captions
  adding, 26, 187
  click boxes, 128
  designing, 28
  practice slides, 147
  styles, 26, 104
  text entry boxes, 148
hit area padding, 188
horizontal alignment, 52
hotspot areas
  cursors over, 129
  fills and strokes, 94
  rollovers, 113, 119
  styles, 104
hotspot questions, 171, 182
HSB color settings, 58, 94
HTML
  backgrounds, 227
  exporting, 12, 204
  JavaScript actions, 123
HTML5, 237, 238, 239, 242
HTML5 Tracker, 238
hue settings, 58, 94
hyperlinked text, 113

**I**

.ico files, 36, 204, 239
icons (EXE files), 204, 239
If/Then actions. *See* conditional actions
illustrated characters, 61
Image Edit pane, 58–59
Image pane, 58
image slideshows, 13, 18
images. *See also* rollover images
  adding, 4, 57–60
  buttons, 130
  characters, 61
  editing, 144
  Library assets, 210
  slide backgrounds, 18, 36
  on slides, 18, 36
  textures, 96
image zooming widgets, 117
importing. *See also* inserting
  actions from other projects, 164
  audio, 71–73, 80
  captions, 55
  comments, 219

effects, 110
External Library, 210
images, 18
Library assets, 211
Photoshop files, 60
placeholder object text, 55
PowerPoint slides, 16–17, 33–35
Preferences, 221
question pools, 194
questions, 194
Smart Shape text, 55
styles, 107
text, 55
XML, 222
Include in Quiz option, 169
incomplete answer captions, 173
incorrect answer captions, 173. *See also* Failure captions
Increment action, 124
Increment command, 157, 160
indentation, 52
initialization text, 235
inner shadows, 97
inserting. *See also* importing
  advanced actions, 159
  animations, 64–66
  buttons, 130
  captions, 51
  click boxes, 128
  conditions, 162
  equations, 68
  highlight boxes, 4, 25
  images, 57
  interactive objects, 115
  mouse movements, 141
  Object toolbar buttons, 4
  question pools, 194
  questions, 169, 194
  rollover captions, 4, 119
  rollover images, 120
  rollover slidelets, 121
  shapes, 62
  silence, 80
  slides
    animation slides, 64
    blank slides, 33, 36, 41
    image slides, 36
    master slides, 40, 41
    new slides, 36, 41
    placeholder slides, 206
    PowerPoint slides, 33
    question slides, 169, 195
    quiz results slides, 198
    recording slides, 146
    themed slides, 33
  smart shapes, 62

SWF files, 143
text animation, 66
text entry boxes, 132
variables, 158
video, 86–87, 89, 152
widgets, 54, 131, 213
zoom areas, 67
Insert Mouse command, 141
instructional design, 28
instructions, 28
Interaction IDs, 129, 177, 197
Interaction Wizard, 186
interactions, 4, 113–134, 186, 239, 248. See
    also questions
interactive diagrams, 113
interactive objects, 11, 113, 115–118, 248
interactive templates, 115–118
interface (Macintosh), 249–253, 254, 255
interface (Windows), 3–6, 254, 255
internal server LMS's, 234
internal servers, 218
Internet Explorer, 238
inverting colors, 59
iOS, 237, 238, 239, 242
iPads, 15, 237, 238, 239. See also iOS
iPhones, 15, 237, 238. See also iOS
item names, 93

**J**

JavaScript, 123, 204, 248. See also Execute JavaS-
    cript action
Jing (TechSmith), 145
job aids, 25, 55–56, 63, 240
.jpg files (JPEG), 36, 38, 231
Jump to Slide actions, 122, 160, 175
jumping to content from quizzes, 175

**K**

kbps (kilobits per second), 75
keyboard shortcuts
  allowing, 128
  conflicting, 248
  cut, copy and paste shortcuts, 45
  drawing shapes, 62
  grading, 148
  list of, 254
  Mac-based, 249
  On Click action, 121
  recording, 24
  replacing click actions, 147
  text entry boxes, 133
  Windows-based, 249
keyboard tap sounds, 23, 232
keystrokes, capturing, 23. See also typing

**L**

labels (slide names), 37
languages. See also translation
  consistency, 56
  exported captions, 55
  generated captions, 23
  non-Roman, 220
  spelling defaults, 208
Last Attempt action, 128
layer comps (Photoshop), 60
layering
  captions, 173
  objects, 11, 188
  Timeline objects, 103
layers (Photoshop), 60
learning management systems (LMS)
  Aggregator projects and, 204
  enabling reporting, 234–235
  Multi-SCORM Packager, 204
  reporting categories, 197
  reporting question results, 177
  reporting scores, 129
  submitting answers, 198
  verified LMS systems, 235
  ZIP files for, 237
left-to-right languages, 220
Less Than operator, 162
Library
  adding assets from, 210–211
  cropped images and, 59
  editing assets with Photoshop, 60
  editing audio, 79
  finding presentations, 34
  importing, 210
  importing audio, 80
  swapping animations, 65
  updating audio, 81
  updating video, 90
  video assets, 86
Likert questions, 171, 184
line spacing, 52
lines. See also borders; shapes and Smart shapes
  start and end types, 94
  styles, 94
links
  animation, 65
  Photoshop files, 60
  PowerPoint files, 17, 35
list items, 52
literal values, 160, 162
Live Preview button, 110
LMS. See learning management systems (LMS)
localization. See translation and localization
locking
  objects, 101
  slides, 46

looping
  accessibility and, 248
  animations, 65, 66
  audio, 71, 82
  movies, 233
lowercase characters, 132

## M

Mac, 204, 239, 249–251, 254
main master slides, 40
manual screen recording, 22
many-to-one relationships, 186
margins, 52. *See also* screen area
Mark Blank button, 179
master movies, 203
Master Slide panel, 40
master slides
  creating, 40–41
  editing, 40
  grouped slides, 47
  properties, 37
  quiz masters, 192
  templates and, 206
  themes and, 33, 42
  types of, 40
Matching questions, 171, 181
mathematics. *See* calculations; equations
MathMagic website, 68
maximum number of characters, 158
media
  Library assets, 210
  publishing formats, 239
Media Encoder, 88
medical characters, 61
menus (Macintosh), 249–252
menus (Windows), 4
merging
  images with backgrounds, 145
  Photoshop layers, 60
metadata, video, 257
microphones, 22, 76, 78, 80
Microsoft PowerPoint
  backgrounds and, 37
  creating projects from, 13, 16, 33–35
  high fidelity, 17
  Library assets, 210
  slide notes, 39
Microsoft Word, 25, 55, 240
minimum display time, 80
mobile devices. *See* Adobe Flash; HTML5; iOS; iPads; iPhones
modes, recording, 22, 25–26
modified objects, 106
Mono audio, 232
Moodle, 234

motion paths, 110
mouse clicks, 128, 139
mouse cursors, 248
mouse movements, 4, 24, 25, 139–142, 232
.mov files, 86, 151
Move Up and Move Down actions, 159
movies. *See* video
moving
  conditions, 162
  objects, 98
  slides, 45
.mp3 files, 69
.mp4 files, 86, 151
multiple answers to questions, 178
multiple-choice questions, 170, 175, 178
multiple conditions, 162
multiplication, 160
Multi-SCORM Packager, 204
multi-slide video, 86
music, 71. *See also* audio

## N

names
  grouped objects, 100
  Library assets, 211
  master slides, 41
  movies, 203
  objects, 93
  quizzes, 197
  slides, 37
narration. *See* audio
navigating projects, 8, 229, 248, 255
new projects
  Aggregator projects, 203
  blank projects, 13, 15
  image slideshows, 13, 18
  Multi-SCORM Packager, 204
  PowerPoint-based, 13, 16–17
  software simulations, 13, 19–27
  template-based, 207
new slides
  animation slides, 64
  blank slides, 33, 41
  image slides, 36
  master slides, 40, 41
  placeholder slides, 206
  PowerPoint slides, 33
  question slides, 169, 195
  recording slides, 146
  themes and, 33
new templates, 206
new windows, opening in, 122
Next Slide button, 4
No action, 125
non-Roman languages, 220

normalizing audio, 80
notes widgets, 117
numbered lists, 52
numbering answers, 177
numbering pages, 198
numbers in answers, 132

## O

Objective IDs, 197
objectives, 197
objects
  accessibility, 93
  actions, 113–134
  alt text, 246
  attaching audio, 72
  borders, 94
  color-coded, 11
  cutting, copying and pasting, 99
  deleting, 101
  drag-and-drop interactions, 186
  effects, 108–110
  fills and strokes, 94
  grouping and ungrouping, 100
  hiding, 93, 101
  interactive, 113–134. *See also* questions
  locking, 101
  master slide objects on top, 41
  modified styles, 106
  moving, 98, 101
  names, 93
  overlapping, 188
  placeholders, 40
  plus sign (+), 106
  properties, 91–112. *See also* Properties panel
  reflections, 97
  selecting, 11
  shadows, 97
  showing, 101
  styles, 104–107
  textures, 96
  themes, 42
  tiling, 96
  transforming, 98
  transitions, 98
Object Style Manager, 104–107
On Enter Action trigger, 38, 127
On Exit Action trigger, 38, 127
On Focus Lost Action trigger, 132
On Success Action trigger, 128, 133, 177
one-to-many relationships, 186
Open Another Project action, 123, 160
Open URL or File action, 122, 160, 247
opening projects, 8, 123, 160
option-specific feedback, 175
optional quizzes, 197

Options pane
  practice slides, 147
  quizzes, 173, 177
  text entry boxes, 133
OR logical operator, 162
outer shadows, 97
output
  Adobe Connect, 239
  Aggregator projects, 204
  alt text, 246
  e-mail, 239
  file size, 231, 232
  Flash (.swf) output, 204, 231, 237–238
  formats, 239
  FTP, 239
  HTML5, 237, 238, 239
  media options, 239
  Microsoft Word, 240
  options, 225
  preferences, 230
  print, 25, 240
  project information, 230
  publish settings, 232
  publishing, 236
  reporting and tracking, 234–235
  republishing only changes, 237
  saved project locations, 220
  skin borders, 227
  skin playback controls, 226
  start and end settings, 233
  YouTube, 239, 241
overlapping objects, 188
overridden styles, 106

## P

padding drop area targets, 188
padding gradients, 95
page numbers, 198
pan effects, 150
panels, 3, 5–6
panes, 3, 5. *See also* Properties panel
panning, 22
parent windows, 122
partial credit, 176
Pass/Fail messages, 198
Pass/Fail pretests, 191
Pass/Fail quizzes, 197, 200
pass-required quizzes, 197
passwords, 132, 233
pasting
  actions, 159
  backgrounds, 144
  conditions, 162
  objects, 99
  slides, 45

patterns (gradients), 95
Pause action, 125
pausing
  for drag-and-drop interactions, 190
  pause indicator, 147
  recording, 29
  recording for typo fixes, 28
  student pause or continue buttons, 119
  Timeline, 125
  waiting for clicks, 129
.pdf files, 204, 237
Phone Gap, 242
photographs. *See* images
Photoshop. *See* Adobe Photoshop
.pict files, 36
picture-in-picture effects, 151
PIP (picture-in-picture effects), 151
placeholders, 11, 40, 195, 206–207
Play Audio action, 124, 160
playback controls/Playbar
  accessibility, 245
  alt text, 248
  Closed Caption button, 84
  displaying for students, 226–227
  hiding in quizzes, 199
  video controls, 86, 89
playhead
  inserting silence, 80
  positioning, 74
playing slides, 12
playing video, 89
plus sign (+), 106
.png files, 36
podcasts, 81
points
  motion paths, 110
  points earned, 129, 153, 157, 176, 234
  polygons, 62
  sound files, 75
  variables for, 258
pools, question, 193–195
positioning objects, 98. *See also* moving
.pot files, 36
.potx files, 36
PowerPoint. *See* Microsoft PowerPoint
.pptx files, 17
practice simulations
  accessibility, 248
  Assessment mode, 22, 25–26
  capturing, 19–27
  characters, 61
  click boxes, 26, 128–129
  Custom mode, 22
  Demo mode, 22
  editing, 135–152
  text entry boxes, 26, 132–133

Training mode, 22, 25–26
pre-amplifier values, 76
preferences
  exporting, 221
  General settings, 220
  importing, 221
  Macintosh dialog box, 249
  preview settings, 12
  program-wide, 220–221
  project settings, 230–233
  quiz reporting, 234–235
  quizzes, 176, 197–199
  slide duration, 221
preloader, 233
presentations, 210. *See also* Microsoft PowerPoint
pretest questions, 169, 177
pretests
  questions, 169, 177
  settings, 191
Preview button, 4
previewing
  browser display, 123
  effects, 110
  JavaScript, 123
  Library assets, 210
  projects, 12, 203, 221
  slides, 12, 221
  styles, 26
Previous Slide button, 4
previous versions of Captivate, 9
Print Screen key, 22, 24, 29
printing, 240
process circle widgets, 117
progress indicators, 104, 198
progressive feedback, 174
project information, 228, 230, 248
project themes, 42–43
project types. *See* new projects
properties
  captions, 52–54
  images, 58–59
  master slides, 41–42
  objects, 93–99
  slide groups, 47
  slides, 37
  slide video, 87
  text animation, 66
  themes, 42
Properties panel
  Action pane, 38, 122–134, 147, 157, 173, 177
  Animation pane, 65
  Audio pane, 38, 82
  Character pane, 52, 172
  Content Master Slide pane, 41
  Fill & Stroke pane, 63, 94, 182
  FMR Edit Options pane, 143

Format pane, 52
General pane, 37, 54, 130
illustrated, 3
Image Edit pane, 58–59
Image pane, 58
Options pane, 133, 147, 173, 177
overview, 10
Reporting pane, 129, 169, 177
Shadow pane, 97
Slide pane, 37
Timing pane, 65, 111
Transform pane, 98, 102
Transition pane, 98
.psd files. *See* Adobe Photoshop
Publish button, 4
Publish to YouTube button, 4
publishing. *See* output
punctuation, 56, 177
puzzle widgets, 117
pyramid matrix widgets, 118
pyramid stack widgets, 117

**Q**

quality
    audio, 75–76, 78, 232
    images, 38
    .swf files, 231
QuestionMark Perception, 234
question master slides, 40
question pools, 193–195
questions. *See also* quizzes
    accessibility, 247
    branched quizzes, 175
    buttons, 130
    deleting, 194
    drag-and-drop interactions, 186–190
    feedback. *See* feedback
    fill-in-the-blank, 132, 170, 179
    graded vs. survey, 169, 170
    hot spot, 104, 171, 182
    inserting, 169, 194
    interactivity, 113
    matching, 171, 181
    multiple answers, 178
    multiple choice, 169, 175, 178
    partial credit, 176
    placeholders, 206–207
    points, 176
    pools, 193–195
    pretest, 169, 177, 191
    progressive feedback, 174
    properties, 172–175
    rating scale (Likert), 171, 184
    results, 196
    sequence, 171, 183

    short answer, 104, 170, 180
    shuffling answers, 178
    styles, 104, 199
    true/false, 170, 172, 178
    variables, 258
quiz master slides, 192
quiz results slides, 196, 198
quizzes. *See also* grades; points; questions
    branching, 175, 198
    click box questions, 129
    configuring, 172–175
    hiding Playbar, 199
    interactivity, 113
    optional, 197
    preferences, 176, 197–199
    pretests, 191
    progress indicators, 104
    quiz master slides, 192
    reporting and tracking, 234–235
    required or optional, 197
    results slides, 169, 196, 198, 199
    retaking, 200
    review area. *See* review area, quiz
    scores, 176
    variables, 258

**R**

radial gradients, 95
radio button widgets, 117
randomizing questions, 178, 193–195. *See also* shuffling answers
rating scale questions, 171, 184
.rd files, 123
.rdl files, 56
Record Additional Slides button, 4
Record Audio button, 4
recording
    additional slides, 146
    audio, 22, 76–79, 80
    defaults, 26
    keyboard shortcuts, 24, 254
    modes, 22, 25–26
    practice slide settings, 147
    screen size, 20, 21
    settings, 20–26
    shortcuts, 254
    slide placeholders and, 206–207
    smoothening movements, 23
    software simulations, 19–27
    system audio, 22
    themes, 42
    types of, 22
    video demos, 27–30, 146
rectangles, 62, 63
red recording frame (recording window), 19, 20, 23
Redo button, 4

redragging drag-and-drop objects, 189
reflecting gradients, 95
reflections, 97
refreshing. *See* updating
Reject captions, 187
rejecting comments, 219
relative progress, 198
remediation branching, 175
removing. *See* deleting
repeating gradients, 95
replacing
   finding and replacing, 209
   smart shapes, 62
   typos with text animation, 138
reporting, 129, 177, 197, 234–235
Reporting pane, 129, 169, 177
re-publishing only changes, 237
required quizzes, 197
resetting drag-and-drop sources, 190
resizing and rescaling
   drag-and-drop sources, 188
   HTML content, 237
   images, 58, 60
   imported slides, 220
   movies, 56
   objects, 98
   projects, 225–227
restarting courses, 235
results, quizzes, 196
resume data, 235
retaining text answers, 132
retaking quizzes, 200
Retry message, 173
returning to quizzes, 175
review area, quiz, 199
review messages, quiz, 199
reviewing
   projects, 216–219
   quizzes, 199
rewinding video, 89
RGB color values, 94
right-click actions, 129, 147
Right to Left composer, 220
RoboDemo, 123
rollover captions, 113
   adding, 4, 119
   converting tooltips to, 25
   fills and strokes, 94
   styles, 26, 104
   tool, 4
rollover images, 4, 94, 104, 113, 119, 120
rollover slidelets, 4, 94, 104, 113, 119, 121
rollover smart shapes, 119
rotating objects, 59, 98
Run as Administrator option, 8
runtime borders, 121

**S**

Safari, 238
saturation, 58, 94
Save Project button, 4
saving
   actions, 159, 164
   comments, 219
   projects, 4, 9
   templates, 207
   themes, 43
scaleable HTML content, 237
scaling. *See* resizing and rescaling
scenarios, 126, 130
scientific equations, 68
SCO (shareable courseware object), 204
scores
   points, 176
   pretests, 191
   quiz results slides, 196, 198
   reporting, 177, 234
   variables, 157
SCORM, 204, 234, 235, 236
screen area, 20, 21, 146, 237
screen captures. *See* software simulations
screen readers. *See* accessibility
screen size (video), 89
screencasts. *See* software simulations
Script window, 123. *See also* JavaScript
scrollbars, 133
scrolling actions, 28
scrolling text widgets, 118
seamless tabbing, 237
Section 508. *See* accessibility
security, 233
selecting objects, 11, 100
self-paced learning, 229
Send Backward/To Back buttons, 4
Send E-Mail To action, 123, 160
sending objects backward, 11, 103
sequence questions, 171, 183
servers, 218. *See also* web servers
session IDs, 235
Shadow pane, 97
shapes and Smart shapes
   drawing, 62
   fills and strokes, 94
   gradients, 96
   hiding backgrounds, 145
   hyperlinks, 127
   inserting, 4, 25
   replacing, 62
   rollovers, 119, 120
   styles, 104
   text effects, 53
   text in, 51
   variable values in, 158

shareable courseware objects (SCOs), 204
Shared action, 124, 159, 164
sharing projects, 216–219
sharpness, 58
Shockwave Flash. *See* .swf files
short answer questions, 104, 170, 180
shortcuts
    accessibility, 248
    cutting, copying and pasting, 45
    equation construction, 68
    grading, 148
    list of, 254
    Macintosh, 249
    recording, 24
    student clicking actions, 121, 128, 147
    text entry boxes, 133
    Windows, 249
Show action, 124, 160, 247
Show/Hide Grid button, 4
Show/Hide Themes panel, 4
showing
    grid, 102
    mouse movements, 141
    objects in work area, 101
    runtime borders, 121
    slides, 44
    variables, 158
shuffling answers, 178, 179, 198. *See also* randomizing questions
shuffling matching items, 181
silence, 79, 80
sizes
    files. *See* file size
    objects and screens. *See* resizing and rescaling
skins/Skin Editor, 42, 89, 226–229, 232
slide notes
    adding, 39
    closed captions and, 84, 85
    handout notetaking areas, 240
    importing, 37
    PowerPoint notes, 16
    spell checking, 208
    template setup, 206
    text-to-speech, 83
    viewing while recording, 77
Slide Properties panel, 37
slide types
    animation slides, 64
    blank slides, 33, 41
    image slides, 36
    master slides, 33, 37, 40, 41
    placeholder slides, 206
    PowerPoint slides, 33
    question slides, 169, 195
    quiz results slides, 196, 198
    recording slides, 146

slidelets. *See* rollover slidelets
slides
    actions, 113, 127
    adding, 33, 41
    audio, 73–74, 77, 79
    branching to, from quizzes, 175
    cutting, copying and pasting, 45
    grouping, 47, 126
    hiding, 44
    interactivity, 113
    locking, 46
    master slides, 33, 37, 41
    maximum, 33
    moving, 45
    multiple videos on, 86
    naming, 37
    number of views, 234
    previewing, 12, 221
    properties, 37–38, 246
    republishing changed, 237
    returning to, from quizzes, 175
    showing, 44
    tab order, 37
    templates, 207
    themes, 42–43, 207
    timing, 221
    types of, 31. *See also* slide types
    ungrouping, 47
    video demos, 152
slideshows, 13
Smart shapes. *See* shapes and Smart shapes
SmartArt, 17
Smart Guides, 102
Smart Interaction objects, 113, 115–118
smoothing movements, 23
Snagit, 24
Snap to Application Region feature, 21
Snap To Custom Size feature, 21
Snap To Grid feature, 4, 21, 102
Snap To Object button, 4
Snap to Playhead feature, 143
Snap to Window feature, 21, 146
social media, 214–215
software simulations. *See also* practice simulations
    accessibility, 248
    characters, 61
    creating, 19–27
    defaults, 26
    defined, 13
    editing, 135–152
    keyboard shortcuts, 24, 254
    recording modes, 25–26
    recording settings, 23
    screen recording size, 20, 21
    standard vs. video, 19
    styles, 26

types of, 22
Undo Marker, 29
sound. *See* audio
sound effects, 23, 71, 129, 188, 189, 232. *See also* audio
sources, drag-and-drop, 186, 187, 188, 189
spacing, 52
special characters, 52
Speech Agent (text-to-speech), 83
Speech Management dialog box, 83
spelling, 208, 220
splitting FMR files, 143
Stage color option, 37, 41
stage, fitting to, 59, 60
standard actions, 159–160. *See also* advanced actions
standard points, 176
Start and End settings, 233
Start Next Slide button, 79
start points, 149
starting Captivate, 8
static button widgets, 131
step-by-step instructions, 28
Stick Slidelet option, 121
Stop Triggered Audio action, 124, 160
storyboards, 240
streaming video, 89
Stretch TOC option, 229
stretching textures, 96
strokes, 94
styles
    applying, 104–107
    basing on objects, 106
    creating, 105, 106
    defaults, 26, 105
    deleting, 106
    editing, 104
    finding and replacing, 209
    labels, 200
    modified, 106
    overridden, 106
    project elements, 104
    text, 52
    themes, 42–43, 207
Submit All button, 198
Submit buttons, 133, 148
subtraction, 157, 160
Success captions
    adding, 26
    buttons, 130
    click boxes, 128
    designing, 28
    feedback captions, 173
    pausing for, 129
    practice slides, 147
    styles, 26, 104
    text entry boxes, 132, 148

text entry validation, 133
surveys, 167, 169, 184. *See also* quizzes
.swf files. *See also* Adobe Flash
    opening, 123
    publishing options, 237–238
    saving as external resources, 232
    size and quality, 231
symbols, 52
Sync to Playhead option, 108, 110
synchronized video, 86
system audio, 22
system information variables, 257
system variables, 155, 255–258

**T**

tab order, , 37
tab widgets, 118
tabbing, seamless, 237
table widgets, 118
tables, 246
tables of contents, 86, 90, 203, 205
tab order, 248
tapping sounds, 232
targets, drag-and-drop, 186, 187, 188, 189
Task icon, 23
tasks, 28
teaching points, 51
TechSmith Jing, 145
templates
    compared to themes, 207
    interactive objects, 115–118
    interactivity, 113
    opening, 123
    projects, 123, 206–207
    quizzes, 194
terminology, 56
tests. *See* quizzes
text. *See also* captions; text to speech
    editing, 138
    effects, 53
    exporting, 55, 222
    font formatting, 52
    highlights, 52
    hyperlinks, 113
    importing, 55, 222
    LMS initialization text, 235
    non-Roman languages, 220
    Right to Left composer, 220
    text animation, 4, 66, 138
    text entry boxes. *See* text entry boxes
    typing, 28
    typing sounds, 232
    typos, 28, 138
    variables, 158
text animation

accessibility, 248
adding, 4
effects, 66
properties, 66
replacing typos with, 138
Text buttons, 130
text entry boxes. *See also* objects
adding, 4, 132–133, 148
interactivity, 113
recording and, 26
styles, 26, 104
variables, 156
text-to-speech, 39, 83
textures, 96
themes
applying, 42–43
compared to templates, 207
new slides and, 33
quiz masters, 192
thresholds (sound), 80
thumbnails. *See* Branching View; Filmstrip
tiling, 96, 188
time limits, 173, 245, 247
time variables, 257
Timeline
actions and, 122, 125
audio cutoffs and, 72
audio objects on, 16
audio waveforms, 73
backgrounds in, 144
color-coding, 11
editing audio, 79
effects, 108
hiding objects, 101, 124
lengths of objects, 72
objects on, 11
playing video separately, 86
previewing slides, 12
selecting items, 11
slidelets, 121
timing objects, 111
video options, 86
zoom areas and, 67
timeline widgets, 117
Timeout captions, 173
timer widgets, 117, 118
timing. *See also* Timeline
accessibility, 246
animations, 65
audio, 72, 79
inserting silence, 80
objects, 11, 111
objects and audio together, 72
slides, 38, 221
videos, 86, 87
Timing pane, 65, 111

Tin Can standard, 234, 235
titles, 203
TOCs. *See* tables of contents
toolbars, 4, 5
tooltips, 25, 28, 227
Top Window browser display, 122
Total Slides indicator, 4
tracking. *See* reporting
Training mode, 22, 25–26
transcripts, 39
Transform pane, 98, 102
Transition pane, 98
transitions, 38, 98, 149. *See also* effects
translation, 23, 55, 208, 222. *See also* languages
transparency, 58, 130, 188
trimming video files, 143
true/false questions, 170, 172, 178
TTS. *See* text-to-speech
Twitter, 214–215
typing
correcting, 28
editing, 138
recording, 26
tab order, 37
tapping sounds, 232
text entry boxes, 132
typos, 28, 138

### U

Undo button, 4
Undo Marker, 29
ungrouping objects, 100
ungrouping slides, 47
unhiding. *See* showing
unlocking
objects, 101
slides, 46
updating
actions, 166
animation files, 65
audio, 81
Library assets, 211
Photoshop files, 60
PowerPoint slides, 35
video, 90
uppercase characters, 132
URLs, 122
usability, 28
User Input options, 132, 179
user variables, 155, 156

### V

validating user input, 132, 133
values (variables), 156
variable bitrates, 75

variables
  adding to projects, 155–158
  adjusting values, 124
  advanced actions, 159, 255
  captions, 53
  dates and times, 257
  defined, 153, 255–258
  Expression action, 160
  IF conditions, 162
  quiz results, 196
  quizzes, 258
  system information, 257
  video playback, 255–257
verified LMS systems, 235
versions (Captivate), 9
vertical alignment, 52
vertical spacing, 52
video
  accessibility, 247
  adding, 4, 86–90
  closed captions, 86, 87
  deleting, 90
  demos. See video demos
  distributing across slides, 86, 87
  editing, 149
  event video, 86, 88
  Flash formats, 86–87, 89
  importing, 86–87, 89
  Library assets, 210
  managing, 90
  metadata, 257
  multiple videos on slides, 86
  multi-slide, 86–87
  PIP (picture-in-picture effects), 151
  playback controls, 86
  playing separately from Timeline, 86
  Progressive Download Video, 86, 89
  screen size, 89
  splitting, 149
  streaming, 86, 89
  synchronized, 86
  tables of contents, 86, 90
  timing, 86, 87, 90
  transitions, 149
  trimming, 149
  type, 86, 89
  updating, 90
  variables for, 255–258
  web servers, 86
  YouTube, 86
video demos
  adding to projects, 13, 146, 152
  editing, 152
  managing, 149
  mouse motions, 24
  picture-in-picture, 151

  transitions, 149
  trimming or splitting, 149
views of slides, number, 234
visibility, 11, 44, 93, 101, 124
voiceovers. See audio
volume, 71, 80

W

.wav files, 69
waveforms, 74, 79, 80. See also audio
Wavepad, 78
web browsers, 122, 123, 128, 238
web object widgets, 118
web pages. See HTML; URLs; web browsers
web server video, 86, 88
Welcome screen
  creating projects, 15, 16
  creating slideshows, 18
  hiding, 220
  opening projects, 8
  recording projects, 20
widgets
  accessibility, 248
  adding, 212–213
  buttons, 131
  captions, 54
  Playbar, 226
  publishing, 232
  tab order, 248
  YouTube, 86
.wmf files, 36
Word. See Microsoft Word
workspaces, 7

X

XML files, 110, 222, 239

Y

YouTube, 4, 15, 86, 117, 239

Z

.zip files, 204, 234
Zoom area, 4, 67, 104
Zoom controls
  illustrated, 3, 4
  magnifying slides, 6
  Timeline, 11, 111
zoom effects, 150
zooming widgets, 117

**Visit the companion site at:**

## www.elearninguncovered.com

1. Download free resources.
2. Access practice files.
3. Sign up for our blog.
4. Ask about bulk purchases.
5. Explore the other books in the series.

E-Learning Uncovered
is brought to you by:

# ARTISAN<sup>SM</sup>
## E-LEARNING

Custom E-Learning Development

E-Learning Consulting

E-Learning Team Training

Specializing in:

Articulate, Captivate, Lectora,

and Other Rapid

Development Tools

www.artisanelearning.com

info@artisanelearning.com

(904) 254-2494

Made in the USA
San Bernardino, CA
14 August 2013